VICTORY UNDONE

VICTORY UNDONE

The Defeat of al-Qaeda in Iraq and Its Resurrection as ISIS

CARTER ANDRESS
WITH MALCOLM McCONNELL

REGNERY
PUBLISHING
A Salem Communications Company

Cataloging-in-Publication Data on file with the Library of Congress

ISBN 978-1-62157-280-0

Published in the United States by
Regnery Publishing
A Salem Communications Company
300 New Jersey Ave NW
Washington, DC 20001
www.Regnery.com

Distributed to the trade by
Perseus Distribution
250 West 57th Street
New York, NY 10107

Manufactured in the United States of America

10 9 8 7 6 5 4 3 2 1

956.7

Books are available in quantity for promotional or premium use. For
information on discounts and terms, please visit our website: www.Regnery.
com.

To my wife, Tanya, and my children, Callie and Henry—
the joy of my life

CONTENTS

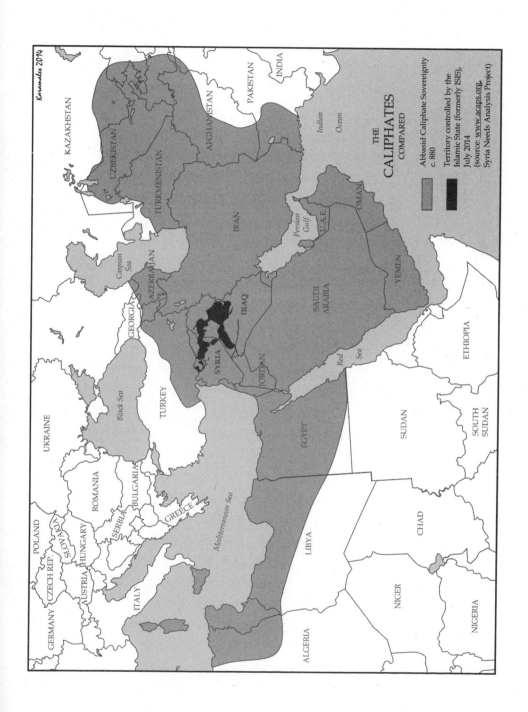

THE
CALIPHATES
COMPARED

Abbasid Caliphate Sovereignty
c. 880

Territory controlled by the
Islamic State (formerly ISIS),
July 2014
(source: www.acaps.org,
Syria Needs Analysis Project)

Kasander 2014

FOREWORD

WRITING THIS IN EARLY AUGUST, I have no idea how many of my Iraqi friends and brothers in arms lie fallen in battle against the invading jihadi hordes. Or they may be refugees in the humanitarian crisis involving the million Iraqis who have already fled—and the millions more who will flee if the Islamic State of Iraq and Syria[1] (ISIS, or simply "the Islamic State," the new name for al-Qaeda in Iraq)[2] is not stopped and thrown back into the desert hell whence it emerged. This is our mutual enemy. We must recognize the existential threat that these genocidal terrorists represent to the security of the United States. If ISIS succeeds in establishing a stronghold in the ungoverned space it has violently hacked out, first from Syria and now from Iraq, then Saudi Arabia and our other regional economic and political allies will come under attack, and Europe will be next. But America is the ultimate target. ISIS leader Abu Bakr al-Baghdadi, when he was released from U.S. custody at Camp Bucca in Iraq in 2009, threatened, "I'll see you in New York."[3] But for now, it's our Iraqi allies who are taking the brunt of this barbaric attack (from the sickening videos of Nazi-style massacres, it appears crimes against humanity are already being perpetrated by ISIS in large areas of northern Iraq).[4] And they're bearing that brunt without the support they need from us.

Since March 2004, my company, American-Iraqi Solutions Group, has employed over ten thousand Iraqis in AISG's operational activities. I am principal owner of the company and helped found it on the streets of Baghdad after I discovered that the firm I worked for was involved in war profiteering. As a consequence, I was briefly an unemployed whistleblower standing on a corner in the al-Harithia District of Baghdad attempting to persuade our Iraqi neighbors why we needed massive blast walls around our start-up's residential compound.

By the beginning of 2005, those same neighbors were requesting that we keep the checkpoints and walls up because they knew our security force would protect them from the death squads and jihadi suicide bombers rampant in Baghdad. Those threats would persist until the beginning of 2007, when the Kurds road-marched from Kirkuk to keep the peace. The U.S. Army then arrived in renewed force, and the Surge and the Sunni Arab Awakening, along with the rise of a constitutional democracy, defeated al-Qaeda in Iraq and its thousands of operatives and supporters from throughout the Islamic world and Western Europe. (These were mostly funneled through Syria—at Damascus's invitation—and crossed the border into Anbar and Ninewa Provinces.) By 2011, when we moved our headquarters to Basra, our local school board and the neighbors we had helped along the way were safe, but they still did not want us to leave. I know they mourn our departure now.

The current debate on Iraq has too often been about straw men. Supporters of military intervention in Iraq are called warmongers; they are supposed to have fallen prey to the man-with-a-hammer syndrome (if you only have a hammer, every problem looks like a nail). Opponents—including the president of the United States in his key constitutional role as commander-in-chief—are accused of cowardice in the face of the enemy. In reality, we are now in the gray area of judgment calls, but our deliberations must take into account two undeniable facts: The lack of substantive American military, intelligence, and security support for the Iraqis since troop withdrawal in December 2011 did not help the country to defend itself from invading jihadis who have now seized terrain all the way down to Tikrit and are holding the third largest city in the most ancient land in history, Mosul (site of nearby Nineveh in the Bible). And the Iraqi government has asked for renewed American military engagement, specifically airstrikes.

Where this goes no one but God—or Allah, if you will—knows. Some things, however, can be predicted with a degree of confidence: Baghdad will not fall, and the oil will continue to flow out of the south of Iraq, now the second largest source of crude in OPEC. President Obama can either make the move now to attack the jihadis or let the wound fester along the ancient fracture lines between Shia and Sunni, Kurd and Arab. One thing Mr. Obama can count on is that hardly anyone in Iraq wants to be ruled by the harsh, totalitarian jihadi version of sharia law. This has not changed, and the same thing is true in neighboring Syria.

(Just as in Iraq, Syria has a strong middle class and almost no indigenous Wahhabi-type fundamentalists. We could have supported the moderate resistance early on, and Assad would have toppled in a few months in mid-2011. All we would have needed to do was what the Obama administration did in Libya to overturn Gadhafi—before the U.S. abandoned that country to bloody chaos with no reconstruction efforts for those we supported. We failed to follow Colin Powell's "Pottery Barn Rule": you broke it, you own it. Then in a Mogadishu redux at Benghazi, our commander-in-chief and State Department head apparently missed the infamous 3:00 a.m. phone call. Barack Obama and Hillary Clinton took their eyes off American personnel in a combat zone. Lack of focus gets people killed, especially when the government has no ability to provide quick reaction forces.)

We all understand that Mr. Obama does not possess the predilection or inclination to pursue offensive war abroad. The American people elected him on a platform that included ending the wars in Iraq and Afghanistan—if not all war. This is why the nation and Congress rejected the president's tentative call for airstrikes after Assad used chemical weapons to kill more than a thousand of his fellow Syrians. If the chief executive is so ambivalent as to call on the legislature to make a decision on the use of force that resides, constitutionally, with the president, then the people's branch will certainly assert its will to the detriment of the executive. Nevertheless, the times call for action.

When American reconstruction efforts finished training almost a million Iraqi security men to be counterinsurgents—basically an up-armored version of local policing with SWAT tactics thrown in—no one envisioned that the United States would leave Iraq with no strategic protection from external invasion. But we left them bereft of air power (Apache ground-attack helicopters were delayed for months by Senator Robert Menendez, New Jersey Democrat and chairman of the Senate Foreign Relations committee).[5] Now evidently we pulled the CIA out in 2012 in a massive downgrade in mission size and, leading up to the invasion from Syria, have not shared intelligence with the Iraqis about jihadi communications and locations.[6] How could that be?

The Iraqi troops have courage. I've seen that time and time again during my four years on the ground during the Iraq War. But they do not have the tactical training or experience to stand and fight pitched infantry battles without air support in urban terrain, or open desert for that matter, against a hardened enemy. The ISIS jihadis have fought hand-to-hand for over two years against well-trained Syrian forces and battle-tested, fanatical Hezbollah, bolstered considerably by direct Iranian paramilitary support on the battlefield.[7]

Unfortunately, I fear that the corruption emanating from the top in Baghdad has overwhelmed the logistics chain and undermined leadership credibility through wide-scale theft. In addition, the Sunni Arab revanchist movement in Syria and Iraq—with critical financial support from the Gulf Arab states, particularly Qatar—made an alliance with the devil, the jihadis, to reclaim the Sunnis' former political dominance in Iraq. ISIS is out of their control now, but the harping on anti-Sunni prejudice has evidently created fissures in the leadership of the Sunni-inclusive security forces in Sunni-dominant north and west Iraq. Only time and future analysis will tell, but the flames fanned by Sunni revanchism surely did not help cohesion and may explain units disintegrating into mass flight after brief or no battle with the greatly outnumbered jihadi attackers. One can surmise readily that fifth columnists and lack of a sustained supply chain (possibly due to corruption) must have facilitated the Iraqi Army collapse.

The shock of the invasion and the Iraqi military's crumbling has allowed the jihadis to seize territory that their numbers will not allow them to hold effectively without local support. A political settlement in Baghdad is necessary to diffuse the distrust between Shia and Sunni and boost the morale of the units fighting ISIS. Calls for Nouri al-Maliki not to become prime minister for a third term might bear fruit, but the chaos of a change of leader would only embolden ISIS and cause delay in effectively grappling with the invasion. We can only hope that Maliki will soon mount another courageous "charge of the knights" as he did in Basra in 2008 to seize back the city from Sadrist Shiite militia forces. (The Iraqi PM went so far forward in the battle that he almost got surrounded.)

The best-case scenario is that this terrible recent turn in Iraq serves to catalyze a new sense of Iraqi national identity, thereby forcing reconciliation across sect and ethnic lines. The hardcore al-Qaeda in Iraq veterans will not be reconciled, and they need to be killed or driven out of Iraq and Syria. That will take a significant amount of time—potentially years, if undertaken by Baghdad alone, with political support from the Kurds, which will be costly in terms of their independence from central control; they have already seized the opportunity to gain control over Kirkuk, their Jerusalem (an appropriate metaphor, given the violently conflicting claims to the city). With U.S. air support, intelligence, and a Special Ops plus-up, however, the Iraqis could reclaim their nation and strike a blow against the jihadis—who are our enemies, too, looking to the next 9/11 with glee—from which they will never recover. Especially if, in parallel, America turns up the heat in Syria with in-country safe havens, no-fly zones, and extensive paramilitary support and training for the vetted moderate resistance struggling to continue the fight there. Bring in the Turks, Jordanians, and NATO. The fight to regain north Iraq will not be easy, even with American support, especially when we talk about going into Mosul and scraping the extremists out of every nook and cranny of the densely urbanized city. But it will and must be done—no civilized world can allow a nihilistic and genocidal extra-state group to sustain control over thousands of square miles of territory in the heartland of the Arab world, so near the doorstep of Europe.

Can the United States really turn its back on the Iraqis? Not for long, I would venture. We can attack now when it will be less painful, before ISIS has a chance to burrow in. Or we can wait and let the killing continue while our sworn enemy, directly tied to 9/11, lays the groundwork to bring terrorist jihad to American shores once again. Both American national interest and our moral responsibility dictate that we should respond to this threat. If we fail to do so, we will have abandoned a country we liberated from a genocidal, war-loving dictator and spent tens of billions of dollars to rebuild with thousands of Americans killed and wounded.

Our fecklessness in Syria, with "red lines" and premature predictions of Assad's demise but with little effort to ensure that end, is rightly perceived as weakness. We can see the results in the paradigm-shifting Russian annexation of Ukraine's Crimea—a land grab unprecedented in post-World War II Europe—with the parallel precipitous rise of Chinese irredentism in the western Pacific. Now we've allowed a power vacuum in Syria to metastasize into Iraq, severely setting back years of progress. Ever since Jimmy Carter, U.S. policy has been that America would use military force when necessary to defend its national interests in the region of the Persian Gulf, which includes Iraq. If the U.S. retreats from that policy now, with millions of Iraqis who allied with America at risk of massacre by vengeful al-Qaeda-in-Iraq jihadis, the chickens will come home to roost in a way that could be catastrophic for us and our allies in the Middle East.

I wrote this book to explicate how we defeated al-Qaeda in Iraq during the years 2003–08. And make no mistake, AQI (now relabeled as ISIS) was soundly defeated, before the U.S. pulled out of Iraq in 2011. We allied with the Sunni Arab tribes who rejected the moral nihilism of the totalitarian jihadis. We employed and trained thousands of Iraqis from all sects and ethnic groups in the construction and operation of dozens of Iraqi security services training facilities and bases throughout the Sunni Triangle including Fallujah, al Walid on the Syrian border, and Mosul. The vast majority of the Iraqi people sided with the U.S. in our mutual battle with al-Qaeda— just look at four United Nations–certified national elections in Iraq since the American occupation. We cannot abandon the Iraqis now, or the violent chaos unleashed by the jihadi invasion of Iraq will be that much closer, once again, to our own shores.

CHAPTER 1

THE BEGINNING OF THE END FOR AL-QAEDA IN IRAQ

"YOU'RE JUST A *CONTRACTOR!*" The Marine colonel's voice dripped contempt as he turned on his heel and walked away, abruptly ending our discussion. I had been trying to explain the need to get vetted Iraqi vendors listed on a Department of Defense (DOD) contractor database.

Our dispute had erupted in a windowless Crystal City hive in mid-2006, just one of the anonymous War on Terror bureaucratic neoplasms that had sprung up across northern Virginia since 9/11. I spent that summer crammed into small conference rooms surrounded by humming cubicles, taking part in long, heated discussions over a white paper for the Pentagon that I hoped would get me back to Iraq.

I *had* been a logistics and reconstruction contractor for eighteen months in 2004 and 2005, during the early years of the Iraq War. In fact, I had risen to senior vice president for operations of American-Iraqi Solutions Group (AISG), a start-up company that had been making real progress supporting the new Iraqi security forces—until disputes with the owner undercut our efforts and I was sent packing back to the States.

Now I had joined a consulting group, working for IBM as part of the DOD Warfighter Program. We had finally broken through the Department's barriers against any civilian at the Pentagon below the Secretary of Defense talking with a combatant commander in the field. We'd set up a video conference between Paul Brinkley, Deputy Under Secretary of Defense for Business Transformation, and Lieutenant General Peter Chiarelli, commander of Multi-National Corps–Iraq (in charge of day-to-day military operations nationwide), who was considered by many to be among the brightest general officers in the U.S. Army.

"How's it going out there in Iraq, General Chiarelli?" Brinkley asked. "Tell us how we can help."

"Well, Paul," Chiarelli answered, "you can stop these damn projects like the one we just completed in Sadr City. We sank tens of millions into a sewage treatment plant that is now the largest water fountain in the world. There are no pipes connected to it."[1]

Contacting the general directly had been a tiny victory against the inertia of a million-strong bureaucracy that seemed in the sweltering Washington summer of 2006 to be charging blindly ahead on cruise control, as if we were not fighting a shooting war with thousands of U.S. soldiers dead and wounded.

I just couldn't take it anymore, so I walked out and never returned. IBM fired me the next day.

✳   ✳   ✳

Just a few months later, in November 2006, I was driving west out of Baghdad at about a hundred miles an hour, my convoy headed into the great Syrian Desert. Once again I was representing AISG—this time as its owner and CEO on my first visit to Camp Habbaniya, where we supplied and operated the first Iraqi Army basic training facility in al Anbar province, homeland of the Sunni insurgency and safe haven for al-Qaeda in Iraq (AQI). With me in the armored Mercedes, Lebanese-American Tony Montana, my great friend—a former bodyguard for Rafik Hariri, prime minister of Lebanon, and before that a sapper with the U.S. 10th Mountain Division, and now director of security for AISG—cradled an Uzi submachine gun while commanding the convoy via radio from the front passenger seat. Ala Kadhim, a Shiite weightlifter and longtime AISG bodyguard, sat behind the wheel. To our front rode two of our up-armored suburban SUVs packed with heavily armed Iraqi security men; and two more followed us—with a scout car, one of the nondescript 1988 Chevy Caprices ubiquitous on Iraq's roads, leading the way more than a mile ahead. We were armed for bear, as this period was proving to be the most dangerous of the Iraq War—just two months later, in January 2007, attacks by insurgents would be hitting one contractor convoy in every five.[2] Now that's Russian roulette!

This was the reason I had come back to Iraq. After eleven Iraqi employees of AISG were killed in a bloody ambush near Lake Tharthar, their families virtually beat down the doors of "Fort Apache," our headquarters in central Baghdad, demanding the bodies, which were never found. AISG slipped to the edge of self-destruction and bankruptcy. In a last desperate effort to save the failing company, the owner, who had fired me at the end of June 2005, had brought me back to take over.

Now, as we sped along, leaving the high, yellowed concrete walls of Abu Ghraib prison and the last green sugarcane fields fading to nothing in the rearview mirror with Fallujah just before us, I told Tony, "We need to visit the Ramadi jail and talk to the informant who knows where the bodies are."

"We'll do it on the way back," Tony said.

"No, I want to do it now," I insisted as we rolled beneath a highway underpass. "Who knows how long it'll take at the project site. We certainly don't want to get caught coming back into Baghdad after dark, do we? The Iraqi checkpoints might open fire on us. Or, for that matter, the U.S.

military might. Remember when that Marine sniper wounded our guard when his convoy halted in front of Abu Ghraib to fix a flat?"

"Yeah," Tony said, "like it was yesterday...." He flinched, staring suddenly to the right shoulder of the road. "What the hell! Did you see that?" he shouted. Tony was a fiery leader who showed real passion in his work.

I had seen it. We had just blown by a highway robbery unfolding on the side of the road. One of the few long-range taxis still bold enough to make the five-hundred-mile drive across the Sunni badlands from Baghdad to Amman, Jordan, stood under the bridge with doors wide open, surrounded by masked men pointing "Iraqi stop signs"—AK-47s—at the passengers. The terrified expression on one middle-aged woman's face in particular would haunt me for months. Should we have turned back, gotten into a gun battle, and halted the robbery? We outnumbered the robbers on the scene by three to one, but who knows how many of their tribal brothers lurked in the surrounding desert? A part of me ached to kill some bad guys and test my mettle in a firefight. My service as an Armored Infantry officer had been back in the 1980s, before Operations Desert Storm and Iraqi Freedom.

In Iraq, the line between criminal activity and al-Qaeda was blurry—one reinforced the other. But we had a mission. We were neither the police nor the army, and to act as vigilantes would put at risk the day's plan and our legal status as defense-only military contractors. So on we hurtled toward Ramadi and Habbaniya. Decisions made in an instant, consequences known only in the future.

After a quick, superficial recovery from the shock of the open lawlessness, Tony and I picked up the thread of our conversation. "Let me talk to the men about heading to the jail now," he said.

Tony leaned over to Ala, a handsome, gorilla-like Shiite denizen of Sadr City (he would later make big money renting vehicles to AISG) and asked him in colloquial Iraqi Arabic what he thought about going into Ramadi: *"Jaahiz—nroih al sijn fi ar-Ramadi?"* Tony said. *"Itthlah, na'am?*

Shu wiya shabaab?" "Are you ready to go to the Ramadi jail? Let's head there now. What about the guys?"

As our driver straightened in his seat, I could see the hair on the back of his thick neck literally bristle. He took the radio handset from Tony and called out to the rest of the convoy, all Iraqis, mostly Shia and Kurd with a few Sunni, but none from Ramadi, the capital of al Anbar province. By design, this breakdown in our workforce reflected the ethno-sectarian ratio of Iraq's population: 60 percent Shia Arab, 20 percent Kurd, 18 percent Sunni Arab, with a sprinkling of various other groups, including Christians. The nervous twitter came across the frequency as Ala received their answers. I could tell no one wanted to appear afraid, especially not in front of the new boss and Tony, who had just returned a week earlier.

The ramp into Ramadi abutted a scarred cityscape of low apartment buildings scattered among densely packed walled houses of yellowed stucco and brick. We circled over and around the sluggish, gray Euphrates River, flowing by at near-full flood out of the Turkish highlands hundreds of miles to the north. The river was one of Iraq's principal agricultural arteries, the source of countless irrigation canals. If Turkey proceeded with plans to dam the Euphrates headwaters, much of the rural economy of al Anbar would be threatened.[3] The situation called for skilled and determined diplomacy on the part of Baghdad over the coming years—an effort that would be difficult in the middle of a nationwide insurgency.

Winding through a grimy residential area next to the highway, we passed children peeking out of the shadows and a couple raggedy checkpoints manned by a few grim armed men in civilian *dishdashas* who glared at our six-car convoy but made no effort to stop us. They were obviously not sure who we were and decided not to test us to find out. On the other hand, we were not quite sure who they were, either. We kept moving.

The al Jazeera police station, infamous for having been truck-bombed several months earlier—the building had been destroyed and dozens of newly recruited Iraqi officers had been killed[4]—was the only functioning police station serving Lake Tharthar and the desert between there and

Ramadi. This area was hundreds of square miles, empty but for a few scattered villages, and it constituted the safest area for the jihadists in all of Iraq ever since the destruction of the al-Qaeda-in-Iraq "emirate" in Fallujah in December 2004.

It was in al Anbar that AISG had lost a convoy to an ambush that killed eleven of our people in August 2006. A weekly supply party commanded by a Fijian security manager named Boney, who had previously worked as a UN peacekeeper in the border zone between the Lebanese and Israeli forces, had gotten impossibly lost. AISG management had hired almost thirty Fijians, primarily to protect the Americans while they slept at night, for fear of an insider attack from the company's then-disgruntled Iraqi guard force. After leaving Habbaniya too late in the afternoon, the convoy had tried to bypass an improvised explosive device (IED) that blocked the main highway back to Baghdad by heading into the desert and near midnight ended up thirty miles to the north on the shore of Lake Tharthar—a vast man-made reservoir situated truly in the middle of nowhere in the heart of al Anbar. The lost convoy passed through a small village, then hit a dead end at water's edge, turned around, and reentered the hamlet. Now alerted, the local Sunni tribesmen, closely allied with al-Qaeda, emerged out of the darkness and stopped the AISG vehicles. Eleven of our workers disappeared forever, but three escaped, including Boney and another Fijian along with an Iraqi, Ali, who killed the village sheikh and his son in the melee that erupted after our Iraqis heard the tribesmen talking about killing everyone in the convoy.

That ambush was the catalyst for my return to Iraq. The search for the bodies, so critical to peace of mind for any family wanting to see their loved ones laid to rest properly, had caused the relatives to basically camp out at Apache, raising hell with the old management—and now looking for fresh justice from Tony and me, the new managers. We had tightened up the AISG guard force procedures immediately upon our return. Earlier, the Iraqi guards had let in a family member with a pistol—a Kurd who had lost three brothers killed at Lake Tharthar, who then fired the weapon, fortunately only into the air, inside the company compound—a serious breakdown in security at Apache that clearly indicated greater management problems. Therefore the issue was still on my plate, and now I was trying to handle it.

Emerging from the congested residential area, we rolled across an open field to the makeshift jail, a former irrigation pumping station on the Euphrates River. The rebuilt al Jazeera police station stood about a hundred yards away to the right, surrounded by eight-foot HESCO barriers—circular, hollow, wire-meshed nylon cylinders that when filled with dirt provided quick and effective ballistic protection against both explosions and direct fire. Where we were headed was a simple concrete-block building painted in broad blue-and-white stripes, sitting on the edge of the river and with a guard tower that looked like a small lighthouse forming one side of the gate into the complex standing a few yards from the jail's entrance.

The jailers knew we were coming because Tony had called ahead to the Ramadi police captain, who had let us know earlier in the week that, serendipitously, the Ramadi police had recently detained one of the villagers who had been at the scene of the ambush, four months before.

We dismounted from the vehicles and walked through the gate of the al Jazeera police station. Operating with our standard low-profile tactics, we wore our body armor under oversized civilian shirts—mine was a short-sleeved, stylish knock-off Gap button-down that had a cross-striped pattern, which one of our Iraqis had purchased in a Baghdad *souk*. I left my AK behind in the car, but still had a smoothly functioning Model 1911 .45 Colt automatic strapped to my hip under the shirt. Tony carried his Uzi, an almost useless weapon in Iraq because it had no stopping power, being a 9 mm that could not penetrate car doors or windows—the primary battle conditions in our line of business involved automobiles—but one that he averred established his leadership status. (After weeks of harassing him about it, I finally convinced Tony to carry a 7.62 mm AK.)

Standing at the door to the jail, Tony greeted our friend, the captain, who was in full Iraqi police uniform: dark blue pants and light blue shirt with red and gold epaulets. I did a double take; this guy looked about twenty years old. The end of 2006 was a rough time to be a police officer in Ramadi. I guess his predecessors at the senior rank of captain, which usually denoted decades of experience, had either been killed or run off. On top of all that, the al Jazeera station may have been the only functioning police post in Ramadi at that time. The rest of the city was the scene of the last stages of an epic battle for control of the capital of al Anbar that was being fought between U.S. forces and al-Qaeda and its allies. Beginning in July, the American military had worked to eradicate this most critical Sunni insurgent safe haven. The ongoing campaign involved precision and coordinated use of force. Adhering to the counterinsurgency doctrine of living with the people, and forced into the role of police by the scarcity of functioning municipal law-enforcement, scattered Army and Marine outposts salted throughout the city conducted local-area policing. The operational and logistics challenges these small-unit tactics created in the heavily fortified and mined city were addressed by an integrative approach to urban warfare including the use of seventy-ton M-1 tanks by Army Colonel Sean MacFarland's armor-heavy Ramadi-occupation command. As we entered the jail, we could hear the nearby smack of explosions and thud of automatic-weapon fire.

It took a few moments to adjust to the interior gloom of the windowless pumping station after leaving the bright, autumnal Iraqi sun. We strode along a steel-mesh catwalk where about thirty feet below us in a dank, dungeon-like concrete pit were laid out dozens of steel cots with ratty mattresses holding prisoners chained to their beds. At the end of the catwalk, we entered an office. Tony and I sat down. On a table next to us, a plainclothes policeman set down two stiff wire cables, about a finger in thickness, three feet long, and wrapped in duct tape.

The precocious captain told us, "This man we are bringing up transported some of the wounded villagers in to the Ramadi hospital after the ambush. Your people had a pretty good shoot out at Tharthar. We discovered who he was from the hospital staff but he had already left, so we could not detain him. We picked him up in a sweep a few days ago. I think he will talk to you and tell you where the bodies are buried. All your people were killed. All eleven. And, we've determined that the sheikh and his son were killed by your people. The *erhabeen* [terrorists] are very angry about this."

Just as we began to respond, one of the jail guards threw the potential informant through the doorway, forcing the bedraggled Iraqi to his knees. He had a dark bag over his head and his hands were cuffed behind his back. The captain lunged as if to hit him in the face. The detainee cringed, and the Ramadi policeman said, "Ah, he can still see. Put another bag over his head!"

A nearby officer obeyed the command. Now double-hooded, the man from Tharthar bent his head toward the ground as if gravity was too strong for his neck. In a flash, the captain snatched one of the cables from the table and whacked the detainee across the back of his head with such force that I could feel it from my chair—and then raised his arm to administer another blow.

"*Wogaff!*" I shouted. "Stop!"

I looked at Tony who had shifted his Uzi to ready-fire as the captain hesitated. There was no way I was going to put up with this, no matter how much we wanted to know about the bodies. The captain stared at us as if we were aliens from another planet where this type of prisoner abuse was not simply the cost of doing business. He stopped and stepped back. Now I understood why this man had said he would tell us where the bodies were. He would say anything for a reprieve from this torture.

Shaken by the experience, I stepped out into the sunlight to look for the American advisors, who apparently were sleeping in the watchtower-lighthouse after being out patrolling the previous night. There were two Army sergeants and a lieutenant crammed into the tower. I talked with the lieutenant, and he committed to take the informant out to Tharthar to find the bodies and gave me his Hotmail address so that we could communicate. No matter how present on the battlefield and critical to the Coalition effort we contractors were, four years into the war we still had no way to communicate officially with the military except through our contracting officers' email and face-to-face contacts on the roads of Iraq.

The Coalition military refused to supply us with radios that functioned on their frequencies. This lack of trust evidenced a broader lack of understanding of our role: logistics and reconstructions contractors were essential to the renaissance of Iraq's security forces. In turn, this rebirth of forces loyal to the central government, along with the employment of the hundreds of thousands of Iraqis in DOD-funded projects, built the foundation of victory over both the al-Qaeda-led Sunni and the Iranian-spurred Shia insurgencies.

✳   ✳   ✳

I got an e-mail a few days later from the lieutenant reporting that he and his men had gone into the desert with the informant and traveled so far out that their Bradley fighting vehicle lost radio contact with the local U.S. military commands. Tharthar had become dead space at the intersection of three (two Army, one Marine) division commands—those located at Tikrit, Baghdad, and Fallujah—and therefore was ignored, with the consequence that the area had become a sanctuary for al-Qaeda.[5] As the team approached the village where the ambush had taken place, the detainee became increasingly vague about the location of the dead AISG men's graves. They had to turn back. No success.

✳   ✳   ✳

After finishing what we could at the jail, we now headed to our actual destination: Camp Habbaniya. A sense of relief coursed through the convoy, myself included, when we got back on the highway without further incident in highly "kinetic" (a U.S. military term for areas of active combat) Ramadi. The route into Habbaniya required us to drive beyond Fallujah, cut back across the desert in order to avoid that devastated and still-hostile city, and reach the back gate of Taqaddum ("Progress" in Arabic) base, now occupied by the Marines. Once clearing TQ, as everyone referred to it, we briefly re-entered the Red Zone on a bridge over Highway 10 and drove into the Iraqi base of Habbaniya, named after Lake Habbaniya, a high-end resort area during the Saddam era.

Camp Habbaniya originated as one of the two airbases left by treaty to the British after their forced withdrawal from League of Nations mandatory control of Iraq in 1932. Inside the post's perimeter were a poorly maintained British military cemetery and rundown, faded yellow, one-story brick buildings still standing from before the end of UK control in 1959, when a military coup finally enabled the Iraqis to completely expel their former imperial masters.[6] Now the base represented the brightest hope for the Government of Iraq to exert control over rebellious al Anbar province.

As we reached our offices, from which AISG ran the operations and maintenance along with the dining facilities for the base, some of the seven thousand Iraqi Army recruits marched by singing beautifully, in sync with the cadence of their steps.

I turned to Tony and said, "What are they singing about?"

The Arab American, who had served as a voice interceptor for all dialects of Arabic at the National Security Agency, stated, "Their love for Moqtada al Sadr."

That was the equivalent of singing the praises of Satan in the Vatican. Moqtada's fanatical Shiite Mahdi Army had fought vicious battles with American troops in Baghdad and the southern provinces earlier in the Coalition occupation. At this point he had fled the sprawling Sadr City slum in east Baghdad and was reportedly hiding in Iran.

Here we were, deep in the vast Sunni Triangle that runs from the borders of Jordan and Syria in the west of Anbar to Mosul in the north

and down to Abu Ghraib at the western suburbs of Baghdad, and all the
Iraqi government and the Coalition could come up with in the way of
recruits for the Iraqi Army were Shia imports who loved the rabid anti-
American agitator Sadr. I was not encouraged. Yet these men did possess
the courage to come into the heart of the homeland of the Sunni insurgency—knowing what would happen to them if they were captured by
al-Qaeda—in order to face the enemy that was sending suicide car bombers into their neighborhoods and massacring hundreds of their loved ones
on a near-daily basis. We would just have to continue to work at bringing
the local Sunni tribes to the table.

And this is what we did. Upon entering the gleaming industrial
kitchen set up to feed thousands, our workers—all Iraqis—crowded
around me and Tony, asking, as they always did when I showed up at a
site, for a raise or more vacation time. A great sense of joy in their work
animated these men; they were glad to have jobs in a time when the
unemployment rate in Iraq, by conservative estimate, hovered around
50 percent. (We estimated that for every Iraqi we employed, the salary
of that one worker fed and clothed at least ten people in his or her
extended family. If we were hiring outside Baghdad, the greater tribe
also benefited from each worker's salary. This fact aided our site and
logistics security.)

Unfortunately, at this time the demographics of our workforce in
Habbaniya mirrored that of the Iraqi army recruits—almost all our people were from Baghdad. The three Kurdish brothers killed in the Tharthar
ambush were subcontractors who had manned a bus that we used to
transport workers back and forth from the capital. As I emerged from the
crowd of AISG workers in the massive kitchen, two well-dressed Iraqis
stood off to the side near each other but obviously not together. These were
a couple of our suppliers.

Tony introduced me to the older of the two, whom I remembered
slightly from 2005, saying, "Abu Ahmed is looking for us to pay him in
advance at Fort Apache before his supplies arrive here."

I faced the grizzled Baghdadi, who was wearing a whitened, scruffy three-day beard, reached out and grasped his right hand, gave him the Iraqi-style cheek-to-stubbly-cheek, twice-on-each-side kiss, and asked him: *"Lesh?* Why?"

He smiled at the gesture and my Arabic—this was good because in their culture a smile is a sign of respect—turned to Tony, and said simply: *"Tareek muhzin."* The road was bad. This constituted a small understatement about the logistics route into this island of Iraqi government and Coalition control in a desert sea swimming with insurgents. Abu Ahmed did not want to have to travel with his supply trucks in order to be paid on delivery. He did not yet trust AISG to pay him after delivery on a monthly schedule, as we did with most of our vendors. After telling the businessman—one of the many Iraqi entrepreneurs our hundreds of millions of dollars in work for the U.S. Department of Defense had made successful—that I would think about it and get right back to him in Baghdad, we moved over to the next vendor, waiting patiently just out of earshot.

Tony, now speaking with evident excitement, said, "This is Mohammed from nearby Karmah. He has not yet supplied us with anything but is ready to help us here, and on credit."

That was an unexpected bit of good news.

The trip back to Baghdad, my new (and former) home, where I would live for the next two plus years, was fast and uneventful. We blew through the multiple heavily guarded Iraqi Army checkpoints leading from Anbar into the capital, with just a flash of my American smile and our DOD and Iraqi Ministry of Interior badges. Now I only had to get our company operations in good order. This meant cutting costs and finding new business because at that point we had a "run rate" that could put the company in the red and into bankruptcy within two months. But even more important, I needed to reconnect with the Iraqis in our workforce.

Apache looked like a junk yard—we had eight power generators on site, only one of which worked (the rest were surrounded by broken parts and pooled oil). We had four dubious Filipino mechanics practically living inside a broken generator set aside for main power; over the course of my first two weeks back, I watched them take it apart and then put it together again several times without result. Our employees, including some of our Americans, were actively stealing from the company and getting kickbacks from vendors. The Iraqis' attitude toward us, the invaders and occupiers, had been fostered by the trauma of the Saddam years with a kleptocracy for a government: if you let us steal from you, then it's your fault. I had to get our Iraqis, who numbered over 80 percent of the company's nearly thousand-strong workforce, to see the situation not as us-against-them, but as *us*, all of us at AISG, together in the ongoing war outside the walls of Apache, which threatened at the end of 2006 to tear the country apart, with a real potential for genocide.

✳   ✳   ✳

The Iraqi government, now sovereign for over two years, had begun to exert itself in the most mundane ways—extending bureaucratic control through demands for documentation, including of automobiles. AISG had almost fifty vehicles, many purchased in the chaos after the invasion, and few of them had the correct department of motor vehicles registration. I went down to the Baghdad DMV with Brahim, one of the original AISG employees from March 2004, trying to use my position as a DOD contractor to cut through the paperwork. Other than drawing a lot of curious stares— happily, none hostile—from the hundreds of Iraqi car-owners lined up waiting for inspection in a pattern any American would recognize from the local DMV, we got absolutely nowhere. My status meant nothing in the context of this most banal of modern tasks, in which the U.S. military never envisioned having any kind of role.

And yet a few days after my return from Habbaniya, the lack of documents caused three of our employees to disappear into the massive and growing Iraqi security structure. Apparently, on a supply run into the

Green Zone where we had a villa housing two business-development people (both of whom I later fired) who were ostensibly working with the U.S embassy for additional contracts, our three Iraqi employees—two drivers and an armed security guard—were stopped at an Iraqi Army checkpoint and seized because their vehicles did not have the proper registration. We could not find them. One week went by, and then a second. We searched everywhere and finally determined that the Iraqi Army had turned them over to the National Police. This struck fear throughout our workforce because the National Police were known to be closely allied with, if not the primary force behind, the Shia death squads rampant throughout the capital.[7] Over a hundred people a day, mostly Sunni, showed up dead on the streets of Baghdad, many with power-drill holes in their knees, genitals, and skulls evidencing savage torture before execution.

At that time we were deep into the Shiite backlash against the bombing of one of the greatest shrines of Shia Islam, the al Askari Mosque in Samarra north of Baghdad, in February 2006, which had been carried out by Sunni insurgents directed by AQI (al-Qaeda in Iraq). The Sunnis in large part continued to support the al-Qaeda-led insurgency, believing that the escalating violence against the majority Shia-led democratic Government of Iraq would somehow give them political leverage that would cancel out their impotence at the ballot box—on account of their minority status—and enable them to return to the absolute dominance their sect had held over Iraq since the Middle Ages. We struggled to balance this ethno-sectarian reality every day at AISG; many of our highly educated local employees, such as engineers and lawyers, were Sunni because of the former class structure in Iraq, while most of our workforce, including our security team, consisted primarily of Shiites.

Our supplier and subcontractor networks were fraught with real challenges, as almost all construction and manufacturing companies in Iraq had been Sunni-controlled, but most of their owners and managers had now fled Iraq because of the double threat of Shia death squads and AQI

attacks (retribution for working with the invaders). So we were left with
mostly Shia entrepreneurs who lacked the experience and capacity to
perform. We needed to train these people from scratch "on the job," while
executing technically and logistically challenging contracts with hard and
fast deadlines in a highly dangerous environment.

We sent relatives, lawyers, and anyone else who might help win the
release of our missing employees to the gate of the National Police headquarters—on Nusoor Square less than a kilometer from Apache—where
we believed the three to be held, including the Sunni driver who had been
present when a suicide car-bomber killed Namir al Mufti, my friend and
the early financier of AISG, in September 2004. When I found that out, it
brought back terrible memories of Namir's death. All our attempts at visiting the three failed, and we heard that they were being held at the police
HQ's notorious jail on terrorism charges, which meant under Iraqi law that
they could be detained for six months without habeas corpus. So we might
not get confirmation of their health and whereabouts for that long. In the
interim, we feared they would simply end up dead.

Meanwhile, I still needed to finalize the deal that had brought me the
ownership of AISG. The law firm in Atlanta that papered the transaction
was in the process of consolidating the corporate registration of the company and required my power of attorney. So I headed out to the U.S. consulate ensconced in the sprawling Green Zone to get the necessary
document notarized by a consular officer. I entered the basement of the
consulate, separated by about five hundred meters and multiple layers of
blast walls from the Republican Palace, which was still serving as the
American embassy until the contractor First Kuwaiti completed construction of the new chancellery. (Cost overruns and delays jacked up the price
of the embassy, the largest ever built, which exceeded estimates by over
$100 million to total up at $750 million.)[8] Walking through bulletproof
glass doors into the air-conditioned space with framed pictures of national
parks—most seemingly covered with snow—on the walls, it was easy to
forget you were in Iraq. The waiting area in front of the consular window,

which was also bullet-proof, was empty. I signed the power of attorney in front of a pleasant American female consul and then sat down while she processed the paperwork. In walked a U.S. Army major in camouflage and full body armor. He took off his helmet and I immediately recognized him.

We had gone through the Infantry Officer Basic Course together twenty years before. His name was Neil Anderson, and we had always stood in line near each other because the Army, evidently from a lack of imagination, did everything in alphabetical order by last name. At our graduation as young second lieutenants, he had played the bagpipes—a truly martial instrument that moved all of us in attendance with its mournful tones, evocative of British Empire battlefields. After reintroductions, I asked him what he was doing in Baghdad. Neil told me he was serving as a reserve officer. Back in the States he worked as a Celtic rocker and music producer, but his job in Iraq entailed advising the leadership of the National Police.

✳   ✳   ✳

Two days later, Neil, Tony Montana, and I entered the gate into the National Police HQ accompanied by an Iraqi American also working as a contractor for DOD, helping Neil and his fellow uniformed advisors work with the NP. We parked our armored BMW in a dirt lot surrounded by half-burnt-out buildings that no one had rebuilt since they were looted after the invasion in 2003. Then we entered the office of the Iraqi brigadier general in charge of the NP. At the door, the security men demanded that we clear our weapons. I removed the magazine from my .45 but, as always, kept my sidearm cocked and housed in a quick-draw holster. I did not clear the chambered round. The plainclothes policemen who escorted us into the general's office all appeared to be from the same family: short, squat dark-faced men with menacing, darting eyes. When I greeted the general in command of the NP, I could see that he was related to our escorts and cut from the same mold. Either that, or a tribe of evil trolls existed out there somewhere in the wilds of Iraq.

After some forced pleasantries, the general began: "It is great to see Major Anderson, as always, and to meet you both from AISG. We are holding your three men on terrorism charges and will decide what to do with them soon."

"This is unacceptable!" I lashed. Everyone in the room shifted uncomfortably at my sharp tone, and one of the little men standing next to the general pulled back his jacket to reveal he had a pistol—as if to menace me. I thought about the one round chambered in my .45 and continued. "These men are working for the security of Iraq. They have done nothing wrong. The reason they were arrested is because my company failed to provide them with vehicles that had proper registration. Therefore this is the company's fault, so put me in jail as a replacement for them!"

The general, seemingly not startled at all, said, "Now, you know we cannot do that, but I will promise that we will expedite the process. You can go and visit them now, if you want."

Tony and I crossed over the parking lot to a low-slung building missing all its windows and doors and with scorch marks on the walls and entered an office on the second floor. The man seated at the desk asked us for the names of our detained men. After a bit of haggling back and forth between him and Tony (the NP official appeared to be fishing for a bribe, but we stonewalled him), he directed us to where we could meet our Iraqis. Down we went to another building—this one had escaped the looting, keeping its windows and doors—and there our employees stood with hollowed eyes and gaunt expressions. The AISG security guard had black and blue marks on his face from being beaten. The worst thing for me was the look of shock on the face of Namir's driver, tinged with a sense of betrayal that we had let this happen to him. Nevertheless they were alive, and nothing was going to happen to them because of our visit with Neil, who'll always be my hero for making this happen.

When we got back to the car, Neil and an Iraqi-American named Mukhtar, who also advised the Iraq Minister of the Interior (MOI) for the U.S. government, stood waiting for us. Mukhtar immediately shouted at me, "Who do you think you are, George Bush, telling the general that what he is doing is unacceptable?! What, didn't you have your morning cocktail?"

I turned to Tony and said, "Now *this* guy is insulting me?"

"Look, bro," I added, "I'm going to do whatever it takes to protect our people. I appreciate you setting up this meeting." I shook his hand and got in the car, and we drove off.

The next day the National Police released the three. They all quit AISG that week. I don't blame them. But the rest of our Iraqis now knew that we would go anywhere for them, whether it be to a jail in Ramadi or into the maw of the notorious National Police headquarters.

Now I needed to get back to making sure that our work at Habbaniya kept rolling along, as that provided the main source of cash flow for the company. But before I could head out there again I had to fly to Amman, Jordan, where we did all our banking because Iraq still had no trustworthy banking system. At that point we were operating on a cash basis inside the country. As a result, we kept millions of American dollars sitting in a huge safe in the bathroom of my bedroom suite, protected behind steel doors, sandbags, and barred windows.

While visiting Amman for a few days, I met with some potential business partners from Anbar—heavyweight Sunnis now plumping up in Jordan on Iraqi-style grilled *masgouf* (river carp) dinners—whom the Coalition was talking with about undertaking large-scale logistics security contracts in the volatile province. The meetings went nowhere because I demanded bank guarantees before we would do anything. But interestingly enough they kept referring to me—and to AISG by extension—as being "with Abu Risha." I didn't understand what they were talking about, but I could pick up that they meant it derisively. I would find out on my next trip to Camp Habbaniya.

Abu Risha was the Sunni sheikh from al Anbar province who went on to found the *Sahwaat al-Iraq,* the Iraq Awakening, which would prove so effective in breaking the grip of al-Qaeda in Iraq.

CHAPTER 2

THE AWAKENING JOINS THE IRAQI SECURITY SERVICES

JUST AS I LAY MY HEAD DOWN on the pillow, well after midnight: *"Blam! Blam! Pop! Crash!"*

Mortars? I thought.

No, it sounded like a large pistol round smashing out one of our perimeter lights near the northwest gate of Apache catty-cornered to a Sunni mosque that serenaded us five times a day and even more on Friday with amplified calls to prayer.

Tired as hell—this was only my fourth week back in Iraq, but I was now almost acclimated, which usually took about thirty days in the war zone after an extended absence—I jumped back into my uniform: khaki pants, AISG polo shirt, low-cut desert boots with Vibram soles, along with my hip-holstered Colt .45 pistol and an extended magazine. I dashed out to the short hallway connecting my suite to the operations center in the largest of the eleven villas that comprised our compound in west central Baghdad from 2004 through 2011.

Rabih, our lean, hawk-beaked Lebanese security manager, turned to me after I clicked through the code and opened the ballistic steel door to enter the AISG network hub from which we watched the city and Apache's perimeter. The ops center maintained communications with and tracked all our vehicle movements throughout Iraq—and later Afghanistan—with satellite phones and a real-time encoded feed via the internet from a DOD-sanctioned satellite system called Tapestry.

"What's going on, *kabbadai* ["warrior" in Lebanese slang]?" I asked.

"Tony's gone out to tell them we're an American company, because it looks like U.S. Special Ops are taking down the mosque next door and the house between us and them," the *Beiruti* quickly told me.

Ops had networked CCTV cameras covering the entire perimeter of Apache, along with a rotating 100x lens on a forty-foot roof-mounted tower that could see out miles into Baghdad. I looked at the screen showing the now darkened corner closest to the wide street separating us from the Baghdad zoo and leading straight into the Green Zone's Iraqi VIP gate through the Ministry of the Interior's (MOI) Adnan palace. I immediately glimpsed Tony in the shadows of the Apache wall—arguing with the Spec Ops guys, swearing with his Lebanese accent that we were Americans. Somehow this did not appear to me as too convincing…so I grabbed my AK from my bedroom and hustled out to the gate.

As soon as I got there, I looked down at the camouflaged soldier facing us from just ten feet away yet submerged in shades of near-black gray. He was decked out in high-tech gear with no unit patch on the left shoulder of his nonstandard fatigues. The other similarly garbed U.S. Army troops were easily within earshot as they positioned themselves by an armored Humvee mounting a 7.62 mm mini-gun on the turret, another nonstandard configuration. I announced, "We're Americans! We're Americans!" Then, "Why did you shoot out our street light?" I knew the answer to that question: security in darkness. With night-vision goggles, the American military owned the night.

The man facing us answered back tersely, "Had to."

"What unit are you with?" I demanded from behind a section of twenty-ton "Alaska" blast-wall. Several of these wall sections formed our car-bomb-proof gate, which defended Apache against the fastest avenue of approach (only one city block long). This street offered the sole entry by car into the upscale, Sunni-dominated al Mansour district leading to the Green Zone that protected both the traditional political center of the national capital and the then most powerful American embassy in the world. A few days before, a car bomb had exploded not far from the gate. It had erupted in a nearby alley that ran back into our neighborhood, al Harithia, the home of some of the wealthiest people in Baghdad—doctors, lawyers, Baathists—and then hit straight up against the fourteen-foot "Texas" blast-walls at the western perimeter of the Green Zone. (That protected island straddled several miles of the west bank of the Tigris, which almost perfectly bifurcates the Iraqi capital.) Blackened and twisted pieces of a police-issue Isuzu trooper had landed inside the walls of Apache, making hail-like sounds on the villa roofs.

In many ways two peoples living starkly different existences divided Baghdad, a city of five to six million founded in the eighth century to be the capital of the Abbasid caliphate. Although the contemporary maps showed a large number of areas of central Baghdad "mixed—no majority,"[1] Baathist Sunnis or their associates dominated the best parts of the capital's upscale, palm-shaded western bank of the Tigris, built with decades of oil riches: Mansour, Karadayat Mariam (the Green Zone), and Harithia-Kindi, where we lived in Apache. Although the city probably had a significant Shia majority even before the American occupation, most of them—over two million—had lived crammed into the far east of the city slums called *al Thawra* (the Revolution) then, and now named *al madinaat al-Sadr*—after the Shia martyr executed by Saddam—and known to the world as Sadr City. Sewage ran through the pot-holed streets, many of which were only raw dirt tracks. The mostly poor Shia in Baghdad had migrated to the capital from the south in search of work in a pattern common throughout a progressively urbanized world. The Shia even had their own dialect of Iraqi Arabic: *jilfee*, which became a primary way for the Shia death squads to determine whether a person was one of them or a Sunni, depending on whether or not he or she could talk the Shia street language.

The city became more and more ethno-sectarian-cleansed, with significant areas nearly empty, as more than a million of its citizens sought refuge internally in Iraq or in Jordan (largely wealthy Sunnis) and Syria (where those who could not afford to go to Jordan ended up). By late 2006, the different groups consolidated even further, and the only Sunni-majority area east of the Tigris ended up being al Adhamiya, home to the world-famous Abu Hanifa mosque. The suburbs out west toward Abu Ghraib, and also al Rashid in the south toward the Triangle of Death, were still predominantly Sunni. The mixed area of al Dora, with a significant Christian population before the war, and home to the city's main power plant, became an al-Qaeda base of operations and an especially vicious sectarian battleground. Several parts of the city had become no-go areas for anyone but the sectarian warriors who controlled those neighborhoods.

✳   ✳   ✳

The closest soldier, wearing the egg-shell helmet that Delta Force favors, just glanced up at me standing about six feet higher on the wall and grunted in acknowledgement of my question about his unit.

As I looked across the darkened street, several American soldiers ran from the nearby mosque to the house next door. They dashed into a dark passage with a battering ram, and then "*boom, boom, boom!*" resounded as the Spec Ops guys took down this Baghdad city mansion in maybe forty seconds. The flash-bang grenades they tossed into each room, from the front door on up to the roof, echoed throughout the neighborhood. I had to look away from the glare of the bursts. They seized no one from the house, but they dragged away a couple of hooded guys from the Sunni mosque, leaving it with a blown-out front door.

The owner of the mansion, our neighbor, came out crying, "They took thousands of dollars from me!"

I scoffed at the thought that U.S. soldiers would do such a thing. But later, after reading the bestselling *American Sniper* and other raw war memoirs, I saw that some American troops had claimed the right of pillage when seizing positions in an unoccupied and raided property.[2] Why not among the elite Delta Force operators?

First light seeped through the Baghdad haze as I turned to head back into my room for a quick shower and then my regular executive staff breakfast meeting overseeing a thousand employees—not counting subcontractors—who were spread throughout Baghdad and the Sunni Triangle. We needed to supply the Iraqi Army with a stretch 747 cargo jet so packed with Hanes underwear that the loadmaster had even stuffed the familiar English-language cellophane packages into the cockpit around the pilots and navigator. The company had accepted the award for this job before I signed the ownership papers, another little time-bomb the old owner and his staff never mentioned in the minefield that Iraq—and AISG—had become at the end of 2006. Luckily our business development VP had charmed the female loan officer in Amman, Jordan, into lending us $750,000 on no assets other than a track record of running $100 million through their bank since 2005.

But four weeks after I became CEO, things were looking up for the company. The Sunni insurgency was about to be crushed in al Anbar province, just as we were to begin building the keystone of the Iraqi police infrastructure in that former al-Qaeda safe haven. General David Petraeus would extol development of the Anbari police—our project would be the crowning piece of their training facilities—before Congress in September 2007 during the most critical testimony of the Iraq War. Petraeus's highly credible and well-founded description of the Coalition's ongoing progress in defeating al-Qaeda virtually guaranteed that both the House of Representatives and the Senate would continue funding the Coalition at this important crossroads.

✫   ✫   ✫

On my next trip out to Camp Habbaniya, a few days after the Delta Force incident, we drove through Abu Ghraib (the Baghdad suburb where the infamous prison is located) and its surrounding irrigated sugarcane fields—evocative of Hawaii—passed Fallujah and Ramadi, and almost immediately came upon a roadblock framed with rocks and strips of cloth placed on the desert highway. Many of their faces masked by *shmags* (checkered cotton head-wraps traditional to all Arab tribes), the armed men stopping the sparse traffic looked like raggedy, unsuccessful bandits.

I glanced at Tony sitting in the front seat of our armored car as we slowed down without stopping. Taking note of my obvious concern, he waved affably at the men through the inch-thick, bulletproof window and said, "These are Abu Risha's people. They're working with the Coalition now as a sort of local home guard, searching vehicles for *erhabeen* [jihadi terrorists]." (This was the plural of the Arabic word *erhabi*, which was easy to remember from the name of an Egyptian movie called *al Erhab wal Kabab*—terrorism and grilled meat).

"Wow, great, maybe we could get them some better uniforms," I laughed in relief.

Prior to the arrival of Sheikh Abdul Sattar Abu Risha al Rishawi's men, there had been wide areas of vast emptiness and open season on contractor convoys for the jihadis. Now the local citizens, armed only with AK-47s, took up security posts far distant from the nearest U.S. military base, filling gaps that had served in the past as points of safe passage for al-Qaeda and staging grounds for their attacks. In addition, Abu Risha's men could immediately detect foreign, non-Iraqi Arabs from their accents (most of the suicide bombers and AQI leadership both came from outside Iraq), something that American troops found extremely difficult to do. These guards and their ramshackle checkpoints would soon become known to the world as the *Sahwa* (the Awakening) when the Sunni Arab tribes of Anbar turned en masse against al-Qaeda and began to support the Coalition and, most important, enter the security forces of the Government of Iraq.

This was the beginning of the end for the insurgency.

CHAPTER 3

THE ULTIMATE COUNTERINSURGENTS

DURING MY FORAYS INTO THE IMMENSE ANBARI DESERT west of Baghdad, the absolute emptiness of the terrain away from the cities and small towns always impressed me. This desert appeared endless, differentiated only by low ridges of monochromatic beige skewed helter-skelter to the horizon and beyond, seemingly devoid of life, untouched by modern civilization—except for the naked, geometrically straight concrete of the highways.

Only occasional sightings of sand-colored Sunni villages, half-hidden in the rippling curtains of heat mirages, revealed that people lived in this wasteland, their mud-brick houses clustered along irrigation canals or around the rusty wellheads that had replaced camel water caravans only in the mid-twentieth century.

Yet the Sunni tribal people who had scratched out an austere existence for centuries here—through a combination of market gardening and date farming, legitimate trading, smuggling, and outright banditry—were the

living heart of al Anbar. Out in the desert void, there was little terrain of
military value. The loyalty of the tribes was the ultimate target. In fact, I
came to realize, the Anbari Sunnis were the equivalent of the great nine-
teenth-century Prussian military theorist Carl von Clausewitz's "center of
gravity"—the physical and psychological focal point of enemy strength at
which dominance should be aimed to achieve victory.[1]

AISG and the other logistics and construction contractors were not
Prussian battalions, nor did we seek a military victory per se. But we were
an integral part of the struggle to shift the Anbari Sunni center of gravity
away from al-Qaeda and towards the Coalition. To achieve this we needed
to use all the tools of sound counterinsurgency doctrine.

As we attempted this difficult, complex task, I came to realize that
successful civilian contractors were in fact the latest iteration of the "revolution in the art of war" that had been studied in American military staff
colleges and honed on battlefields from northern Virginia in the Civil War
to Vietnam to Iraq for almost one hundred and fifty years.

Despite the narrow-minded opinion of that Marine colonel with
whom I had clashed in Washington, the military contractor in Iraq represented a revolution in warfare. By 2005, fully 30 percent of total American
forces in the conflict consisted of private non-government personnel—
some providing security for Coalition officials, others supporting the
training of Iraq's new security services, and still others helping rebuild the
country's infrastructure. Commercial entities effectively assumed Geneva
Convention–regulated defensive combat and logistical support assign-
ments, relieving the limited number of Coalition troops able to take the
battle directly to the enemy, and thereby greatly enhancing the critical
"tooth-to-tail" ratio on the battlefield.

To understand the importance of civilian contractors in Iraq—and
today in Afghanistan—we must examine the wars of the past one hundred
years, which provide the context. The major conflicts of the twentieth
century were fought between conscript forces composed of a relatively low
proportion of combat troops to a much wider base of service and support

units. One only has to think of the famous Red Ball Express of World War II, made up of African-American draftee truckers who hauled tens of thousands of tons of fuel, food, and munitions to Eisenhower's armies advancing toward Germany. In the Pacific, Navy Seabees (Construction Battalions) built hundreds of vital bases and airfields.

This ratio of combat to support troops lasted through the Cold War, as the conscript foundation slowly and steadily crumbled; it continued through the first Gulf War—even though by that point the great majority of the American-led Coalition militaries had come to rely on all-volunteer forces. (With the end of the Cold War, most Western armies were cut back to much leaner, less costly proportions.)

When the new American-led Coalition invaded Iraq in March 2003 and quickly toppled the Baathist dictatorship of Saddam Hussein, the broad insurgency that soon erupted caught it unprepared. Further, after demobilizing Iraq's genocide-linked Sunni-dominated army, the Pentagon failed to begin quickly rebuilding the security forces Iraq needed to combat both the guerrilla warfare waged by Sunni extremists in Baghdad and the western desert and Shia militants in the capital's sprawling eastern slums and the densely populated southern cities. This left the Coalition Provisional Authority (CPA) in Baghdad with the mandate of re-establishing the army and reforming the police, necessarily delaying and complicating the process[2] because of the CPA's ad-hoc nature and immensely challenging portfolio of political, security, economic, and social responsibilities.

By late 2004, the Coalition faced the impossible task of simultaneously fighting the swelling insurgency, reducing its own combat strength to meet domestic political pressure at home, and training and equipping a new Iraqi Army and police force planned eventually to total almost a million men. So DOD had to turn over most of the base construction and logistical support roles to private civilian contractors.

These contractors were required to operate across Iraq's "Red Zone," well beyond the sheltering blast walls of the large Coalition bases—often sending their truck convoys along hundreds of miles of empty highway, exposed to improvised explosive devices, vehicle-borne suicide bombs, and roadside ambushes. Coalition headquarters, therefore, permitted the contractors and their Iraqi employees to be openly armed—usually with the country's ubiquitous AK-47 assault rifles and Soviet bloc machine guns.

✳   ✳   ✳

In the process, we had become counterinsurgents. Contractors specially engaged for reconstruction work became—using renowned military strategist B. H. Liddell Hart's term—the most *indirect* forces, and therefore among the most effective in pacifying Iraq so that the U.S. military and other Coalition forces could go home and the Iraqi people could move forward. We were a counterbalance to the direct application of force—such as the 2003 Coalition invasion of Iraq to overthrow Saddam Hussein's regime and the urban battles of Fallujah (2004) and Sadr City in Baghdad (2008), which had been plagued with casualties and collateral damage. The approach appropriate to contracting in a counterinsurgency worked to undermine the necessary base of support for a potent insurgency: the people. As Liddell Hart observed in the preface to his *Strategy*, "In war, the aim is to weaken resistance before attempting to overcome it."[3]

In Iraq, contractors were able to probe for weaknesses in the insurgency's hold on the local population where we were hiring our workforce. Money and vocational training were strong lures to Iraqis struggling to find security for their families during a time when the jihadis and the Iran-allied Shiite militiamen were wreaking destruction for power and plunder. Once a tribe—for Iraq is a nation of tribes, whether in al Anbar or the Shiite South—had certain numbers employed by a Coalition contractor, then we had won over that tribe and achieved security in their geographic areas. We worked with sub-tribes of the Dulaimi confederation that dominated in Anbar and also with the al Jiburi and al Janabi, who ended up being the foundation of the Sahwa (Awakening). In and around Baghdad, AISG employed members of the Shammari tribe (possibly the largest tribe in the Arabian Peninsula that is Sunni in Saudi Arabia but Shia in Iraq). Brahim, one of the original Iraqi AISG employees, came from the Shia albu Mohammed tribe in the south, centered in Basra and likely the largest tribe in Iraq. That connection helped pave our way when we moved into south Iraq. In other words, the more Iraqis we employed, the more stability we brought to the locality. And until the end of the war hove within sight, almost every AISG project stood in an area of Iraq with a strong al-Qaeda presence. These violent jihadis presented the main existential threat after Saddam fell and his Baathist Iraqi Army collapsed.

"Maneuver warfare" (the U.S. military evolution of blitzkrieg) relies upon tactics similar to those of Soviet air-land battle theory of the Cold War, in which there are "gaps, surfaces, and sacks" along the FEBA, the Forward Edge of the Battle Area.[4] The key is to go into a "gap" on attack, not a fire "sack"—in other words, an ambush. In von Clausewitz's terms, you are looking for the *schwerpunkt* or center of gravity, at least on a local level: a focal or decisive point where you can unhinge the enemy's position. In a counterinsurgency campaign, the people are indeed this center of gravity—wherein lies victory, if their support can be wrested from the insurgents. The decision point against al-Qaeda came in al Anbar, AQI's safe haven in winter 2006–07. The characteristic totalitarian and genocidal nihilism of the jihadis, whose path to victory was strewn with chaos and death—while the Coalition, and then the Government of Iraq (GOI), offered security and material improvement in real, tangible terms—finally alienated the Anbari Sunnis.

✳　　　✳　　　✳

A reconstruction contractor such as AISG not only employs locals but also builds something permanent for the host-nation people, and in Iraq and Afghanistan this proved a force multiplier when it came to cementing trust with the indigenous populations. In counterinsurgency (COIN) contracting, you trace the "surfaces"—areas of enemy strength—and the "gaps"—the local, tactically decisive points—by letting out utilitarian projects that the prime contractor executes under U.S. government oversight and rigorous quality control. There are good business reasons for local hiring, which eventually drives down labor costs (imported workers are expensive to sustain). But beyond saving money, counterinsurgency (COIN) contracting, if properly applied, will result in a wide range of Western-standard skills training, tailored to local social and educational conditions, which will have value long after the war is over.

Given Coalition and international funding and the urgent need for infrastructure reconstruction, the conditions in Iraq were ideal for COIN contracting. The faster a project is completed, the faster there are revenue increases for local companies and labor sources—the rural tribes and their entrepreneurial urban cousins. Where you can effectively let out competitive contracts and build, operate, and maintain projects in an area formerly not under friendly control, you have pacified that region without having to kill and be killed—or, at the very least, with substantially fewer combat forces and casualties. The value of adequate funding and proper contracting of projects in support of the political-military strategic plan to gain political acceptance for the Coalition war aims—through security and subsequent material gains for initially hostile populations—cannot be overestimated in counterinsurgency warfare. Although COIN is often defined as a defensive strategic posture, contracts have value as offensive operations that serve grand strategy, beyond battlefield combat, to further economic, humanitarian, and political war policies.

By putting contracts out "on the street" in a war zone, we found "gaps" in the enemy's defenses: people who had the courage to step up in the face of death threats to undertake work with Coalition contractors. In Iraq, Afghanistan, and other "zones of conflict"[5] (to use British historian John Keegan's term) in much of the developing world, there are few independent individuals in the Western sense; almost everyone is a part of a collective such as a tribe or *qawm* (the word meaning clan both in Arabic and in Dari, the form of Persian spoken in Afghanistan). Those connections ensure that at a certain tipping point in the contracting process the local people come to identify with the Western contractor—because the contractor is training to international standards and interacting on a daily basis with motivated members of the local community, while providing substantial revenue to the tribe by allowing individuals to earn honest wages in a situation of high unemployment. The contracts put the local people well on the way forward to join the rest of the world in the global economy.

In Iraq, with its massive oil resources, the path to reintegration into the international market was clear. So we had a great deal to work with once the momentum in al Anbar and elsewhere went our way on the contracting front. The hold on the people exercised by al-Qaeda, the neo-Saddamists, and Iranian-allied Shia militias was loosened as leading segments of the population returned to work on construction projects and to serve in Iraq's new security services.

Then came the true force multiplier: developing the host-nation's military and, especially, its police. In COIN, local police forces are the final step in pacification. But in Iraq we undertook two discrete, though codependent, strategic actions simultaneously—stabilization operations and reconstruction.

The initial large-scale funding from the U.S. for the reconstruction of Iraq—approximately $18 billion for massive reconstruction projects that were to employ tens of thousands of Iraqis on power, water, sewage, and oil infrastructure—took almost a year to put together.[6] The enemy made good use of the delay as reconstruction funds slowly made their way through both Congress and the U.S-regulated contracting process before hitting the Iraqi war zone. The jihadis combined with former regime elements and, independently, the Iranian Quds-Force special groups nearly simultaneously got up to speed on attacking the Coalition and our Iraqi allies after the shock-and-awe destruction of the Baathist dictatorship. In retrospect this desolate and wasted interlude, lasting less than a year (2003–04), was as brief as the Mohamed Morsi government in Egypt. But in its wake, once the substantive contracting funds arrived, the combat units of the Coalition's Multinational Force-Iraq (MNF-I) needed to stabilize the security situation while the reconstruction was ongoing. This could not be done under the Coalition command structure and the level of contractor–military force integration then in place, hindrances that had negatively impacted the progress of U.S. war aims from the beginning.

As a result, some of the greatest names in international contracting— Parsons, Bechtel, Fluor-AMEC, Halliburton—even the Egyptians of Contrack International, which had more than $300 million in road-building projects—failed at all levels in Iraq during the days of the Coalition Provisional Authority. (The first major contractor in after the invasion, Bechtel pulled almost all of its two hundred employees out of Iraq by November 2006 after insurgents killed fifty-two people working on the construction giant's projects.)[7] And in 2005, DOD switched a good chunk of the money—over $4 billion—to reconstituting the security forces of Iraq. Water treatment infrastructure got the shortest shrift.[8] (Thus the unfinished and useless sewage system in Sadr City that General Chiarelli would call "the largest water fountain in the world.") Now, however, we had a contracting strategy that could function well. America got double return on its money for the work the U.S. Department of Defense competitively awarded AISG and a few other companies to build the police and army bases and academies across Iraq, along with undertaking the ongoing logistics and base operations for these facilities.

First, we were employing hundreds of people from the local populations and creating concentric supply chains that rippled through the entrepreneurial class. (The Iraqis have been recognized since ancient times for their trading skills.) Small business people were the leaders we sought and then bargained with to get the best prices AISG could offer DOD. With all our contracts firm fixed price—meaning if it cost more than our bid, we would have to eat the loss—and the vast majority of them competed for, we had to get the ground truth on costs, which required local knowledge and therefore geographical presence and, most critically, stable supply routes. (A succinct military aphorism of unknown origin: "Amateurs talk tactics, professionals talk logistics.") Every work site, whether in Abilene, Texas or Fallujah, al Anbar, was basically the same inside the fence. The challenge in the war zone was getting people, materials, and equipment delivered to spec and on time without losing any people, materials, or equipment along the way to insurgent violence or industrial accidents. (Absurdly, the U.S. Occupational Safety and Health Agency–enforced code of the Federal Acquisition Regulation governed war contracting in Iraq and Afghanistan.)

Second, and equally important, the new contracting guidance funded modern facilities in insurgent-contested areas for the Iraqi border patrol, army, special forces, local and national police, prosecutors, judges, and security bureaucrats necessary for Iraq to stand alone and for the Coalition forces to return home. By mid-February 2007, AISG had proven its ability to construct effectively in downtown Baghdad at the old Muthana airfield just as the Surge was getting going and the capital was still ground zero for the insurgency. Under a forty-five-day deadline, we took just thirty-nine days to build a housing base for a brigade of 2,500 *Peshmerga* ("those who face death"): Kurdish Iraqi Army soldiers. Unfortunately, the contracting officer in charge of the project, Commander Philip Murphy-Sweet, being the brave U.S. Navy officer that he was, took too many risks and got killed by an EFP (explosively formed projectile) anti-tank mine just as he was leaving the venomous Iraqi Ministry of the Interior, which was infiltrated by both Iranian-allied Shia militias and al-Qaeda affiliates. (There were often gun battles floor to floor inside ministry headquarters, on the edge of Sadr City. American military advisors—in no smaller than "Ranger buddy" two-man teams—wandered the hallways in full battle gear carrying M-4 assault rifles.)[9] We, and our mission, missed Commander Murphy-Sweet, a man who had shown real leadership and made the ultimate sacrifice for his country.

✴　　　✴　　　✴

In one rare event, Tony called me on the radio from his armored SUV. Usually "my shadow" (as the combat bodyguard referred to himself) rode with me when we were together on a convoy, but that day he wanted flexible physical movement control of our two echelons temporarily together in the desert. Tony was responding to one of our convoy's trucks breaking down several miles from where we had just exited the lonely back gate of the Marine base at TQ, the former British and once and future Iraqi airbase. (This demonstrated the downside of our low-profile tactics of operating in the shadows: old, beat-up vehicles were just that—beat up—and consequently more likely to break down).

"*Al Umbda, al Umbda,* this is *Abu Muna* [Tony's daughter's name was Muna and Abu is "father of" in Arabic], we're going to stay here until we get the brakes unlocked on the Scania. You should go back with your team now."

Al Umbda, which means the "mayor" in Egyptian *jilfee* colloquial Arabic, was the code name that Tony was trying out for me. One early afternoon—the hottest part of the day and a potentially sleepy time for *al-haras* (the guards)—when I was on my usual walkabout inside the kilometer-long compound perimeter at Fort Apache (our headquarters functioned like a city hall, with three hundred or so residents, staff, and visitors there every day except Friday, the Muslim day of prayer), Tony had started calling out on the Apache radio network in Arabic that "the mayor is coming." I quickly put the kibosh on that call sign after this trip. As a result—throughout hundreds of movements in the Red Zone—no one mentioned me by name or any moniker on the convoy radios again. Our security team only knew when I was there if they saw me get into my car or by the infrequent sound of my American voice over the radio.

My men and I tried to keep radio communications to the absolute minimum necessary for tactical movement control—in danger areas like overpasses, for example, and when we spotted unknown BOLO ("Be On

Look Out"), insurgent-type vehicles in a position to interdict our movement. All our armed security vehicles would flow up and down, weaving in and around other traffic, never leaving the same profile for long, under the radio orders of the convoy commander and other sub-leaders during the multi-car movements of cargo or personnel. (We also tried to keep the two separate. There was too much risk to personnel traveling with slow moving, and high-profile-target, tractor-trailers). In addition, we tried to keep our broadcasts to Iraqi-dialect and accented voices, as much as possible; you never knew if the bad guys were monitoring. But on this occasion, I responded to Tony's transmission.

"*Ehna suwa min bidaya lin nihaya!*"—"We're together from the beginning to the end," which was something I reiterated to our Iraqis in their own dialect—quite different dialect from Modern Standard Arabic—every day I worked in their country.

"Hoo-ah!" Tony, a former sapper with the U.S. 10th Mountain Division, answered me in American-G.I. jargon over the radio on our Government of Iraq–assigned proprietary frequency.

"*Abtall!* [heroes]," I rejoined, in my universal greeting and affirmation to our Iraqi and Lebanese convoy security and close protection (bodyguard) team. I hoped they always received it as reflecting the deep respect I had for our people taking the risks they did on behalf of my company and the mission we served. My former greeting, which I had called out all the time when I first arrived in Iraq, had been, "*Ikhwan!*" This means brotherhood or simply brothers in Quranic Arabic. But to the Iraqis, it evoked the Islam-wide Sunni Muslim Brotherhood and also the early twentieth-century *ghazis* (shock troops) of the jihadi Wahhabis who had raided Iraq out of the Arabian Desert. As a result, the term was almost never heard in Iraq, especially among the Shia majority, until I blundered into using it with our hundreds of Iraqis at Apache and throughout the country. I quickly ceased using the term once I understood its nuances.

That afternoon in 2006 I was returning from my second visit to Habbaniya since I had become CEO of AISG; it was December, the nicest time of the year in Iraq. At this time we were the only American-owned entity bidding against five Iraqi- and Middle Eastern–owned companies for the contract to build the training academy for the newly recruited Anbari police. The construction site was now part of "Camp Habbaniya," which stood adjacent to the former fighter base of that name.

We stopped our convoy and got out of our vehicles to wait for the brake problem to be resolved. We were standing on the edge of the Western Desert along the randomly U.S.-patrolled two-lane sand Seabee-quality graded main supply route (MSR). To the east and west lay unfriendly territory, but this route was secured by the Marine command at Camp Fallujah, which was located in the desert ten miles from where we were waiting for the brake problem to be resolved—on the far side of its namesake (and devastated) city.

Things were looking bad for the damaged truck. Tony, who was also a master mechanic with an embarked crew of ingenious fixers, called me back.

"You should go. It looks like we may be here into the night. Business awaits back in Apache...."

"Fired up!" I said into the mike, after a moment's reflection on *what am I doing here* versus *what do I need to be doing?*

My four-car convoy peeled off from the security SUVs with their PKC machine guns echeloned among the empty cargo trucks. (We had made a delivery as part of our visit to the Iraqi Army basic training post, where we continued to improve the quality of the food that we supplied and served in the chow hall, among other operation and maintenance (O&M) tasks: power, water, garbage collection, laundry, and sewage.) Our heavy vehicles kicked up plumes of fine desert sand as we sped toward the Baghdad highway and home. Just as we gained momentum on the European-standard, six-lane east-west highway, with its paved shoulders randomly pocked by the occasional recent and still-unrepaired IED-blasted pothole, we hit a massive traffic jam. It extended across the highway; visibility was limited by a growing horizon of dust. Tony radioed to say they had freed up the truck but were moving very slowly—about twenty-five miles an hour in a creeping line of cars and trucks. My team had easily cruised along at highway-plus speeds until we were suddenly looking out over a solid wall of Iraqi cars threading in and out of the desert in chaotic patterns, seeking to somehow bypass the blockage.

In the middle of a cleared center strip of the 150-meter-wide highway (counting the broad, deep ditches on the shoulders), several Marine armored Humvees were circled up. We knew that no one was allowed to come within five hundred feet of the troops inside what we called a "coil" in the U.S. Infantry—a circle of vehicles with guns and hoods pointing outward to all points on the compass. Otherwise the troops would fire warning shots or flares near the perimeter offender, to be followed (Iraqi drivers knew this well after years of experience with the U.S. military) by automatic fire if they did not back off immediately. So this platoon of motorized Marines presented a blockade on a main highway into Baghdad. By the time we arrived, they had stopped the movement of over a thousand vehicles. No air power or other friendly forces were to be seen—just this flower-shaped, heavily armed khaki pod in the middle of what looked like a wind-swept *Revelations* wasteland because of the huge 360-degree absolutely empty zone enforced by the visibly nervous American troops.

Iraq was on the move again, as we could see from the motley array of cars and trucks blocked from getting to the capital from out west and kicking up a sand storm hazing the bright mid-afternoon Mesopotamian sun of a formerly crystal-blue winter day. The traffic jam was more evidence of progress to complement the radical new development I had just observed at the Habbaniya army-recruit base: the entire training cohort was now Sunni. Heretofore these young Bedouin men had served as an al-Qaeda-only labor pool for the infrastructure and support operations of suicide car bomb and IED factories. (The Iraqis themselves did not often join the jihadi cause as *intehareen,* or suicide bombers; a substantial majority of those consisted of non-Iraqi Arabs including Yemenis, Libyans, Saudi Arabians, Syrians, and Sudanese.)[10] Earlier that day, on our way to inspect the chow hall, we had driven by a crowd of young desert warriors who had instilled a bit of fear in me—the first time I had felt that way about Iraqi recruits. Until recently, these tall, fit men had been our enemies....

We'd won the al Anbar contract partly because of our price. The other companies—especially our main competitor, Almco, owned by a Shia Arab from southern Iraq—had added too much for security to their bids, out of fear. But we ran the roads nearly daily, had lost over fifty employees due to enemy action, and had worked tens of thousands of man-hours involving over $30 million in local expenditures and wages in Anbar. Our combined technical proposal, past performance, and lower cost to the government easily won the bid. AISG had, as they say, shed blood and treasure in the sands of western Iraq. As a result, we had real "ground truth" on security and prices, which were now stabilizing in an area that the Marine Anbar command had recently declared a "failed cause" in intelligence reports back to the Pentagon, which were quickly leaked to the media.

USMC Colonel Peter Devlin, the chief military intelligence officer for the Marine command in charge of western Iraq, had written in late summer 2006,

> The social and political situation has deteriorated to a point that MNF [Multi-National Forces] and ISF [Iraqi Security Forces] are no longer capable of militarily defeating the insurgency.... Barring the deployment of an additional MNF division [twenty-thousand-plus American troops] and the injections of billions of dollars in reconstruction money and investment into the Province, there is nothing MNF can do to influence the al-Anbar Sunni to wage an insurgency.[11]

✻   ✻   ✻

Now, waiting on the highway near the fringes of Abu Ghraib, I studied the northern side of the main route from the west into Baghdad. The small

Marine unit had hunkered down in a khaki Humvee blossom near what appeared to be an apartment complex above the wadi-like roadside ditch. We immediately drove down toward the low ground in my Mercedes and escort sedans. Just as we entered the ditch, our isolated little caravan emerged out of the sprawling dust-clogged mass of vehicles held up by the stand-off zone to the west of the American obstacle that was keeping thousands from heading home in the approaching dusk over dicey IED- and jihadi-plagued territory. On the east side of the road block, it looked like the stalled traffic was probably backed up all the way to the Marines' Forward Operating Base (FOB) encompassing Abu Ghraib Prison.

"What the hell was *that?*" I shouted, startled by a green flash bursting by my rear window. Of course, someone had fired a flare at us from the Marine coil in order to halt our movement down the wadi and onward to Apache.

I immediately ordered Ala, our top driver, "*Wogaff!*"—stopping our group's forward movement.

Maron, Lebanese AISG security manager, fluent in English, who was riding shotgun in the front seat quickly advised, "We need to wait here.... Next will be live rounds."

I opened the door, and the Lebanese shoved the U.S. military-style Kevlar helmet I never wore but always carried into my hand and motioned for me to put it on. I did so as I stepped out of the car and began to walk toward the Marines in the highway to request permission to pass. As soon as I got a few paces outside my armored vehicle, I saw an olive-green-gloved hand raise up to rapidly wave me forward, indicating I should run. So I did, sprinting about eighty meters onto the highway as masses of stalled Iraqis watched.

The Marines stared—some hostile, some surprised at my American appearance, Iraqi-style convoy, and beard—as I cautiously crossed between two Humvee hoods and into the interior of their 360-degree position. (You never knew with the Marines; they had been known to throw American contractors in the stockade with insurgent detainees.)

The platoon commander growled, "Who the hell are *you?*"

In the moment I saw this man standing in the midst of bloody bandages and pooled blood staining the Iraqi highway—blood from one of his Marines, for whom he was morally and physically responsible—I deeply felt his pain. I showed the officer a pre-deployment Annapolis, Maryland–issued DOD badge displaying a photo of my pale then-forty-three-year-old face in the right-hand corner and a readable computer chip mounted below the Pentagon seal in the middle.

"About twenty minutes ago, we got hit by a sniper from that apartment complex you just ran by," the young officer informed me. "I just medevaced our WIA [Wounded in Action] man ten minutes ago."

"Sorry to hear that, lieutenant," I said, looking back at my little convoy, seemingly very distant over the open ground in front of the apartment complex. It appeared to be of the better-quality construction that marked residential areas for the military and the security services under Saddam. Some of those guys could shoot straight, evidently. If the sniper had not already left the scene, he had probably chosen not to shoot me because he knew that a dead contractor didn't generate anywhere near the kind of media coverage that a dead Marine did. "I need to get home to Baghdad. Can I drive by you with my little convoy? You can see them just over there waiting for me to come back."

He shrugged and waved for us to pass.

✳   ✳   ✳

The stage was set for the final act of al-Qaeda's takeover of the Western Desert. At an early site survey for our al Anbar Police Academy contract, Saib, our best Iraqi project engineer, a man with the presence of a sheikh, got splattered with sand from 7.62 mm near-misses showering his feet. The sniper (or there may have been more than one) was firing from close by— just one hundred meters across a leaning and decrepit wire fence. On the other side of the tangled wire squatted a collection of shabby three-story apartment buildings, which for some reason had been nicknamed the "French Village." Ostensibly, this working class housing area stood inside the base perimeter. But it was controlled by the nascent Iraqi military, not by the U.S. Marines next door in TQ. Applying the brightest shine to a wormy apple, you might say the Iraqis took a more building-by-building than whole-perimeter-protection security approach.

Yet during three nights spread out over a week AISG trucked all the buildings required for academy operations from a factory east of Baghdad—in Hibhib, near the house where Abu Musab al Zarqawi, the notoriously murderous leader of AQI, had been killed by an American laser-guided bomb after being tracked by a Predator drone. The U.S. military finally eliminated him as the last step of a long Joint Special Operations Command (JSOC) operation to target Zarqawi led by then–Lieutenant General Stanley McChrystal. The Jordanian-born ally of bin Laden had been killed just over nine months earlier, very close to our caravan pickup-point in what was then a jihadi-controlled area of much-contested Diyala province.

We built the police academy project on time and to spec. Consequently the Coalition awarded us the Operations and Maintenance (O&M) contract. The Marines trained and DOD-certified our primarily Iraqi guards, and we took over static security for the high-profile facility that was now training the Iraqi policemen who would put AQI out of the insurgency business and on the run from their safe havens in al Anbar. The predominantly Sunni population of Anbar Province was made up whole cloth from Arab Bedouin tribes who recognized no frontier. They had lived off smuggling for millennia. They were also the group in Iraq closest to the *Salafi* version of Islam, with which the jihadis' tortured and totalitarian vision of *sharia* law has great affinity; thus AQI saw the Anbari Sunnis as offering the best opportunities for them to gain succor and metastasize further.

But in 2007 the Sunnis' ultimate rejection of al-Qaeda was like a host expelling a parasite. The sea of popular, ideological support had dried up for bin Laden and his ilk in Anbar and—as thunder follows lightning—throughout Iraq.

CHAPTER 4

BACK TO FALLUJAH: CONTRACTORS TAKE THE LEAD

"*WEN AL BAJJ?*" I YELLED directly into the muzzle of a machine gun. "Where is the badge?"

The weapon was pointing straight at me through the narrow firing slit of the sandbagged bunker guarding a key intersection in the center of Fallujah, Anbar Province. The local police fired their AKs into the air and over our heads as I stood in the middle of the street, shouting. I was demanding the return of the United States Department of Defense identification that my all-Arab security team had used to flow through military checkpoints on the battlefields of Iraq. As the president and CEO of AISG, one of a limited number of civilian construction and logistics contractors in Iraq, I needed freedom of movement to get to our project sites in the country. And I was acutely aware that the Joint Contracting Command in the Baghdad Green Zone had little use for a security services contractor who couldn't travel around the Red Zone, which meant all of the country outside the safety of Coalition bases and the Kurdistan Regional Government areas of control.

Omar, one of our Sunni-Arab Iraqi bodyguards, had handed the AISG badges to the Iraqi police in the bunker as proof of who we were and why we were the only people who were driving civilian cars through a restricted military zone. We were legitimate contractors supporting the expanding Iraqi government military and police. But now the police weren't handing them back. And without the badges, we would have serious problems even getting back home to Fort Apache in Baghdad.

We were at the center of what had been the greatest battle site of the Iraq War. I had scrambled out of my black armored Mercedes sedan—formerly owned by Saddam's eldest son, the homicidal Uday—as Omar argued unsuccessfully with the traffic police, dressed in crisp white shirts, who had stopped us: *"Ehna min al wizaraat ad defaa al Amriki!"*—"We are from the American DOD. You cannot stop us. It is our right to pass!"

George, my Lebanese-American security manager, had told me, "Do not get out of the car, sir! I will handle this." Yet he did not make a move as we stood rooted in the middle of a traffic circle surrounded by decapitated minarets of mosques and abandoned buildings with gaping, blown-out holes of tank rounds and bombs. So I had opened the door and stepped out into the baking sun, squinting through the dust bellowing over the heavily potholed main avenue. The scene—Fallujah, which had never been reconstructed since the epic battles of 2004, was still looking devastated in the summer of 2007—rocked me. And the effect on the rest of my team was readily apparent.

At that moment, as streams of sweat were already coursing under my body armor in the heat, a twenty-man detachment of Fallujah police arrived in U.S.-provided F-350 extended-cab Ford pickups, dismounted, and formed a defensive perimeter. Then the shooting began: *"Thud, Smack, Crack,"* as they fired AK-47 rounds randomly. Several bullets passed close over our heads, landing who knows where in the shattered neighborhoods beyond. The intimidation was real. I could see it on the faces of my Iraqis and feel it in my bones. A U.S. Marine patrol of armored Humvees drove by at speed without stopping. We were very much alone. Startled by the gunfire, a flock of crows took flight over the blasted stub of a minaret that cast a jagged, mid-morning shadow in the traffic circle.

The July sun scorched the asphalt and gritty dust swirled around me as I stood in front of the machine gun, thinking I was going to have to crawl through the bunker's firing slit to get my badge. *Why am I even here?* I thought. Fallujah, although still dangerous, had ceased to be the capital, or even the focus, of the al-Qaeda–led Sunni insurgency in Iraq. By this point in mid-2007, almost twenty thousand al-Qaeda jihadis and supporters drawn to the killing fields of Iraq had met their deaths or would soon do so at the hands of the U.S. military and newly trained Iraqi security forces across the country.

The American Army's 2003 conquest of Baghdad, one of the great centers of Islam, had inspired the radical jihadi followers of Osama bin Laden to attack from throughout the global *ummah* (the Muslim community of believers). And attack they did. But this time the extremists confronted the American military and its allies ready for a fight—not unsuspecting men, women, and children going about their daily lives, as on 9/11. A different scenario resulted in a different outcome for al-Qaeda.

Now, after months of analysis and debate, the Bush administration had finally opted for a "surge" of new forces: nearly forty thousand fresh troops comprising five Army brigades for Baghdad and four thousand Marines out here in al Anbar province west of the capital.[1] There had been an initial spike in American casualties, but the enemy insurgents—both al-Qaeda–led Sunnis and Shiites in the Mahdi Army of the fanatical cleric Moqtada al-Sadr—had suffered ten times more dead, wounded, and captured.[2]

Bin Laden's failure to force the United States out of the Arab heartland of Iraq, combined with his quick eviction from Afghanistan, certainly looked then to have broken al-Qaeda's back as a force with any real pretense to lead a jihad to destroy Israel, eject the West from the lands of Islam, and establish a global fundamentalist Islamic Caliphate.

At the battles for Fallujah in April and November–December 2004 and
for Ramadi from July to December 2006, the American military destroyed
the most critical Sunni insurgent safe havens—both located less than sixty
miles west of Baghdad. After weeks of warning the local population to flee
the self-declared jihadi emirate, Marine-led forces took a sledgehammer
approach in depopulated Fallujah, smashing mosques with tank and artillery rounds and laser-guided bombs, and blowing holes in practically every
house with infantry-planted explosives. Following the battle and for years
to come, the Sunni city—formerly best known for its hundreds of minarets—reminded me of Dresden, circa *Slaughterhouse-Five*.

The Bedouin tribes of western Iraq had then turned on al-Qaeda, as
the terrorist group became more extreme; their kidnappings for ransom
and their assassinations were especially hateful to tribal members. After
their combat defeats at the hands of American troops and elite Iraqi Army
and police commandos, al-Qaeda became more vulnerable in the "hearts
and minds" of the Anbar Sunnis. During the final throes of the battle for
Ramadi, the Sahwa or Awakening rose up in what had been the ultimate
safe haven in Iraq for the radical jihadis: the austere Sunni desert cities and
villages of al Anbar.

As I've discussed, the Sunni tribes revolted against the primarily foreign suicide bombers and the leadership of al-Qaeda in Iraq after the
extremists killed several non-cooperating sheikhs, forced marriages on
young Anbari women, and committed other atrocities reflecting their
Taliban-like totalitarian brutality.[3] The tribes began denying them a safe
haven, signaling the beginning of the end for the al-Qaeda–led insurrection
in Iraq. Yet still they came—mainly across the desert "rat lines" from
Syria.[4]

As chief executive of AISG—which now provided food, water, and
other vital supplies along with construction services to the growing number of Iraqi military bases located nationwide—I had to ensure the logistics
for the biggest army and police training camp in the hard-won and still
unstable al Anbar province. The major base in Habbaniya stood between

Fallujah to the east and Ramadi to the west. The main supply route into the city, however, went around those two larger Euphrates river towns through the desert to the west of Ramadi—where I had been briefly stuck with that disabled truck several months earlier—and across a bridge over a canal linking two wide, man-made lakes. We had been sending our supply convoys on that route for two years, until the remaining AQI-allied Sunni insurgents blew up the bridge as a part of an effective campaign to complicate logistics for the Coalition in Baghdad and Iraqi forces in al Anbar Province.

Often using truck bombs, the insurgents destroyed key spans among the hundreds of bridges in Iraq—highly effective tactics in a nation known as *Bilad al Rafidain* or Mesopotamia, "the land between the rivers." The attacks cut three of Baghdad's major bridges over the Tigris, severely disrupting traffic in the capital. However, though we didn't know it at the time, this campaign served as the last gasp of militarily effective operations for the Sunni insurgency. Fortunately al-Qaeda and its neo-Saddamist Sunni allies suffered collapse during their "bridges" campaign—under simultaneous assault from the Sahwa (Awakening) paramilitary, U.S surge troops and JSOC's Special Operations Forces, and a more effective local security presence brought about by extensive American training efforts, supported by DOD contractors.

Besides the now-collapsed bridge, the only other route the U.S. military allowed us to use went straight through Fallujah. So we were there on a route reconnaissance to check whether AISG convoys could drive through the post-apocalyptic and still hostile city—when we confronted the local security services blocking our movement and seizing our badges.

The Iraqi soldier inside the bunker finally handed out our DOD cards, and we turned the little convoy around and headed back the way we had come. Reaching the entry control point into the city, I sought out the Marine sergeant in charge of the gate. The Marines had completely cordoned off Fallujah. The city had formerly been home to three hundred thousand, but a much smaller number now inhabited the battle-scarred concrete houses and low-rise apartment buildings crammed along a mean-der of the Euphrates River. The local citizens could not drive their cars into the city; they could either catch a bus or walk from one of two gates on the city's east side where the Marines allowed local entry.

That was why we had stood out in Fallujah, contrary to our standard low-profile approach of melding into traffic. We were driving the only civilian cars on the streets. AISG had had a contract running the east Fal-lujah Iraqi Army and police camp in early 2005, but after it was completed, our company had no reason to operate in the city. So when forced by the bridge closing to use a route directly through the city, we went to our extensive network of Iraqis—by this time we had employed over eight thousand locals—for information and connections, but we could find none. (Fallujah was unique in Iraq, having a pure Sunni population with a substantial presence of Osama bin Laden's extremist Saudi-based Wah-habi sect of Islam. That was why it had provided a natural home for AQI. Even under Saddam, other Iraqis feared the Fallujans; they purportedly provided the fiercest torturers serving the Baathist dictatorship.)[5] So we went into the city blind, with only a few days to determine whether we could run convoys safely through Fallujah; if we couldn't get the new route established, the seven thousand Iraqi trainees we supplied—one of the first complete cohorts of local Sahwa recruits—could potentially run out of drinking water and food.

On our way in, the Marine sergeant, a friendly African-American who didn't see too many civilian fellow countrymen roll up to his post, had welcomed the opportunity to chat and bragged to me about his martial arts skills. Now, surprised by our early return, he asked, "What happened?"

"The first Iraqi traffic checkpoint turned us back. Can you get me a Marine escort?" I asked.

He radioed his headquarters in Camp Fallujah, and the answer came back: "No, too busy."

While I pondered returning to try again and noted the fear on my security team's faces, a couple blue-and-white Toyota pickup trucks carrying Fallujan police rode up. The Marine sergeant, Barry, and I talked with the local cops who explained, "The word in the city now is that you are Israeli Mossad."

Great! That's all I needed.

Barry and I agreed that that was probably not the best calling card in Fallujah. I studied my map and discovered another bridge not marked on the official military supply routes. So we drove off into the desert through shimmering heat and dust devils to check it out. After a flurry of emails and cell phone calls to Camp Fallujah, the Marines finally acquiesced to our using the alternative bridge.

The mission continued.

✻   ✻   ✻

For the Coalition war effort and mission, we clearly served one combat-service-support function—in military terminology: logistics. According to the *New York Times*–bestselling (a first) Army-Marine Corps field manual on counterinsurgency authored in 2007 chiefly by General "King David" Petraeus, who at the time was a rising rock star–like figure in the media, counter-insurgency best practices break down into logical lines of operations (LLO). "Information operations," to give the new, Orwellian name for what used to be called propaganda campaigns—embrace, drive, and are part of the end goal for all five of the LLOs: combat and security operations, local security forces, essential services, governance, and economic development. Reading the well-received Field Manual (FM 3-24), I saw that one critical element was missing: a greater understanding of the role of contractors in the combat zone during a counterinsurgency conflict. Contracting plays a greater or lesser role in all the LLOs.

Another unaddressed issue was what to do when "the people" *are* the enemy. That was the problem that General Ray Odierno faced when commanding the U.S. Army's 4th Infantry Division in the *Tikriti* homeland of Saddam right after the early-2003 invasion ended and the occupation began. It's tough to separate the people from the insurgency—the end goal of COIN, according to the Petraeus manual—when the people are the insurgency. In this case, a tribal confederation that used to control a nation could not accept their diminished role in a democracy—or come to terms with the fact that their tribal leadership would be held accountable for past crimes against humanity.

In Iraq, as throughout the Arab world, the surname of an individual oftentimes comes from the place of his birth. In al-Qaeda the *noms-de-guerre* of key figures included al Zarqawi (from Zarqa, Jordan), al Kuwaiti, al Masri (from Egypt), and so forth. When Saddam seized full power in Iraq in 1979 after removing the by-then nominal president, Hassan al Bakr, he slaughtered other potential rivals in the Baath Party by forcing fellow members of the ruling council to execute each other in front of a video camera.[6] After that, so many members of his tribal grouping rose to positions of power in Iraq that Saddam forbade the use of "al-Tikriti" as a last name. Henceforth he would be called simply "Hussein"—normally a first name in Arabic.

Unfortunately, some people are irreconcilable and need to be imprisoned or killed. Given the jihadi "holy warrior" enemy we faced in Iraq and continue to struggle against in Afghanistan and elsewhere in the world, this is often the case. Even in COIN, sometimes and in some places you have to kill your way to a solution. The situation in Tikrit was a metaphor for the entire Iraq War, for until they spilt enough "blood in the sand"— meaning dead and wounded neo-Saddamists and their al-Qaeda allies— the Sunni Arabs could never accept a Shia government after having ruled Iraq for almost 1400 years.

Yet the suicide soldiers were the extreme faction. In the right environment the universal drive toward entrepreneurship could quickly wean the general population from active or even tacit support of the oppressive *al muqawama* (the jihadi self-proclaimed "resistance"). We discovered in al Anbar and elsewhere in Iraq that reconstruction contracting gave real support to COIN's strategic and tactical efforts in at least three ways. By providing a better material environment in targeted areas for local employees and vendors and their extended families, contracting activities diminish resentment and hostility. Through the construction and maintenance of the local security services infrastructure, contractors establish and sustain the required operational facilities for the police and army in insurgent-contested areas. And lastly, the Iraqi or Afghan business network (for example) developed by the contractor becomes a source of intelligence for security and political purposes.

One of the few Americans who spent as much time in country and traveled as widely in Iraq as I did during the war was General Stanley McChrystal, head of the Joint Special Operations Command for almost four years (2005–08). His autobiography, *My Share of the Task*, illuminated many previously secret aspects of the helicopter-borne U.S. commando activities in Iraq. These air-assault missions, heading west to jihadi country from the Green Zone, buzzed low over Apache so often every night during the latter stages of the war that they became part of the background noise to my sleep patterns.

McChrystal's number-one target upon arrival in Iraq as the new overall commander of the jihadi-hunters was al Zarqawi, head of AQI. McChrystal, a near-legendary Delta Force officer, recounts in his book how his Joint Special Operations Command (JSOC) finally got a firm lead on Zarqawi's spiritual advisor through technological methods such as drone-camera tracking. It took weeks of work by his intel center, and an American Spec Ops team in *mufti* (as disguises are known) exposing themselves on a busy Baghdad street in a civilian car to eyeball the target, to confirm that—even though the man lived in a Shia area called Shula—he was Zarqawi's sheikh.[7] We could have helped. AISG had several trusted employees and their families living in and around Shula; so all we would have had to do to obtain confirmation was to inquire of them discreetly about who resided in the house where the tracking drones took JSOC after the potential Zarqawi connection surfaced. But no one ever asked us, even though we had been a source of actionable intelligence for JSOC in the past.

Our local employees, "sourced" mostly from the five-million or so Baghdadis, knew the impact of Zarqawi's forces up close. Suicide bombers had slaughtered thousands of people in the capital's markets. By this time, in early 2007, our majority-Shia workforce—reflecting the ethno-religious makeup of Iraq—had lost dozens of relatives to the al-Qaeda suicide car bombs that targeted crowds shopping and participating in religious processions. Ali, the AISG employee who had, by chance, shot and killed the local village sheikh and his son in the melee during the ambush of our lost convoy at Tharthar, lived near Shula. When the assailants were tying his hands in the dark, no one noticed that he had pistol in his belt. So he grabbed the handgun, fired several shots in their direction, and fled into the desert. A couple months after I had returned as CEO, al-Qaeda *umara* (elite jihadi assassins called "princes") tracked him down. They retaliated for the deaths of the sheikh and his son by dragging Ali out of his car and assassinating him in front of his children right next to his home on the edge of Baghdad's Sadr City.

So we knew Shula. We knew Baghdad as few Americans did because our employees and subcontractors were locally hired. And the Iraqis who worked for and with us were invested in the success of the American mission because they wanted to prosper in business in order to protect their families and their future. If AISG did well, so did our local partners and employees. With the new skills and business training we provided, our Iraqi employees, partners, vendors, and subcontractors were prepared to compete—and did so—in the marketplace long after the U.S. military left the streets of their hometowns. Thus our contracting activities fed a virtuous cycle. We served as agents of long-term stability. Counterinsurgency and Security and Stability Operations (COIN and SASO in U.S. Army jargon) are synonymous—at least in that they should be approached in the same way, by first and foremost protecting the local civilian population.

Military-contractor operations also had real material impact in the construction and maintenance of security and other strategically focused infrastructures, which were force-multiplied, in turn, by the employment

and skills training of the local populace. This is the one true weakness in
Petraeus's COIN manual. It only deals with contractors in a tangential
manner. His writing team does brush up against the contribution contractors can make to the counterinsurgency endgame in the summary of the
final chapter: "COIN logistic objectives should include encouraging and
promoting HN [host nation, meaning Iraqi or Afghan, for example] pro-
viders [contractors].... If there is a final paradox in counterinsurgency, it
is that logistic postures and practices are a major part of the effort and
may well determine the operation's success."[8]

There is no paradox here—when local nationals undertake logistics
and all other aspects of security operations, then success has arrived for
COIN. The confusion reflected in the conclusion drawn by Field Manual
3-24 arises from a lack of understanding of the critical role played by
contracting in stabilization operations. The focus on military and civil
operations (by government and Non-Governmental Organizations, or
NGOs) and the lack of business knowledge and experience in the war-
fighting leadership of the U.S. military make it difficult for that leadership
to recognize the substantial contribution of the contracting effort to our
victory in the Iraq War and interfere with the institutionalization of the
contractors' role for the future.

At a rather random event in America—a wedding of mutual friends—
I met now–Brigadier General Sean MacFarland, the brigade commander
and hero of the Battle of Ramadi, which proved so critical in establishing
security in al Anbar through practices explicated in the COIN manual.
We chatted about the infamous al Jazeera jail—he was surprised to meet
a civilian in suburban Maryland who had been there—and I asked: "How
did you manage contractors on the Ramadi battlefield?"

He answered without hesitation and with finality: "I had someone
else handle that." End of discussion. Apparently, this was just a transac-
tional relationship, buying goods and services, and his S-4 (logistics
officer) who handled supply for the brigade would probably be the one to
grapple with contractors.

That's understandable, of course; as a commander of over five thousand troops in combat, MacFarland had many operational and security
issues to attend to. Yet it is also symbolic of the lack of strategic, operational, and tactical vision of combatant commanders into the role of
contracting in winning the battle against insurgents who draw sustenance
and safe haven from the surrounding civilian population. There are two
sides of contracting on the battlefield. There is the business relationship,
which is all about money and delivery—you have to have performance, as
giving money away to buy peace doesn't work; that only creates inflation
by jacking up local prices, and the deal collapses as soon as the bribes stop.
The other side of contracting, more important from the perspective of
fighting an insurgency, concerns creating security and stability for the
people, whose "hearts and minds" the COIN battle is being fought over.

(Despite his dismissal of contractor relations as something "someone
else" handled, MacFarland did write that, with his brigade's support, "local
contractors ... [began] reconstruction in cleared parts of Ramadi before
the fighting was over elsewhere. Maintaining the initiative in this way was
the single most important thing we did throughout the campaign." He
made that assessment in the "The Anbar Awakening: The Tipping Point"
in the March–April 2008 *Military Review*, published five months after my
similarly titled article for National Review Online.)

CHAPTER 5

THE SURGE

AFTER THREE-PLUS YEARS of nightly gun battles and explosions, Baghdad finally grew quiet six months prior to the arrival of the full complement of U.S. Surge troops. The Kurdish brigade from Kirkuk that occupied the base we built had "road-marched" in vehicles down to the capital as a part of a quid-pro-quo deal negotiated between Iraqi Prime Minister Nouri al-Maliki and President Bush for an additional forty thousand American troops. As reporter Bob Woodward and many who actually took part in the negotiations attest, the president actively participated in war strategy, and there were frequent video conferences between him and the Iraqi prime minister.[1] Maliki had no other available forces, yet he had committed the Iraqi government, so here were Kurdish troops from ethnically cleansed Kirkuk (the "Jerusalem" of the Kurdish people). Saddam supporters, who had so recently controlled the capital city and its wealthy neighborhoods, could not help but fear retaliation for past genocide against the Kurds. Once the Kurdish Peshmerga began to patrol downtown Baghdad,

the city itself ceased to be an active combat zone with the exception of
Shiite Sadr City, home turf to Moqtada al-Sadr, the limited Sunni areas of
Adhamiya, and the southeastern districts of al Dora and al Rasheed.

Noting the suddenly quiet nights around Apache, John Olvey, who had
been with me at Custer Battles, LLC, the security contractor for whom I
worked when I first arrived in Baghdad in January 2004 and was now newly
with AISG, morbidly yet astutely joked that "the Sunnis must be afraid that
the Kurds will bring their bulldozers with them." He meant that the Sunni
Arabs were afraid that the Kurds would do to the Arabs of Baghdad what
Saddam did to the Kurds when they Arabized Kirkuk—level their houses.

Sadly, several years later John killed himself by jumping off a water tower
on Christmas Eve. He had never recovered psychologically from his Gulf
War experience. In February of 1991 he was serving as the commanding
officer of an Army artillery battery that Major General Barry McCaffrey
directly ordered via radio to fire on a column of elite Republican guards
retreating from Kuwait after the official ceasefire of the hundred-hour
ground war. This was the infamous "Highway of Death" incident. John's 155
mm self-propelled howitzer battery, shooting DPICM (dual-purpose
improved conventional munitions), which scattered anti-armor bomblets,
wiped out an entire Iraqi tank battalion. But situated in the middle of the
column was a school bus full of children. John told me, "Afterwards I saw a
video of the strike from a chopper gun-camera. The children are in the
bus—I can see them through the windows—and then, there's nothing but
debris and dust...."

The arrival of the Peshmerga brought the first tangible results of the
Surge. Before the Kurdish troops arrived, the Sunni Arabs of Baghdad—the
core of the Saddamist ruling class—had at least tacitly backed al-Qaeda,
seeing the insurgency as gaining them leverage to achieve more political
power than their minority status would afford them in democratic elections.
But with the Shia death-squads rampant, and now with the arrival of justi-
fiably vengeful Kurds, no one from the al-Qaeda–led insurgency moved to
protect the Sunni Arab population of the capital. The jihadis were more

interested in terrorizing civilians than in getting chewed up in a civil war where they would have to stand and fight on the wrong side of the U.S. military's killing machine. Thus the remaining Baghdadi Sunni Arabs, those that had not already fled to Jordan or Syria, ceased to provide willing safe haven and support for AQI and their allies. These critical political elites began to turn irrevocably to the U.S. and the ever-strengthening Iraqi security services for protection.

We built the Peshmerga base in record time. Key U.S.-funded construction in Iraq tended to be of "temporary" facilities. Congress ruled over "permanent" military construction money, and so it was divvied up according to political pull. DOD could spend temporary money more freely. As a result, we mostly installed caravans, like you'd see in any park of doublewide family trailers. These massive aluminum boxes, painted white with windows and doors cut into them, rolled out of the factories around Iraq or across the border in Saudi Arabia and Kuwait. (No one dared bring them from Jordan or Syria across vast Anbar.)

The trailers were as recognizable in Iraq as in Middle America, including to the insurgents, who knew they had to be Coalition-bound. Trucks bearing trailers were like ducks in a shooting gallery. We beat this issue by assembling and welding the caravans onsite, not in the Baghdad factories, which were continually put out of business by rockets, or in foreign factories, which required delivery from across the frontier via the IED-filled highways. Thus what had taken twelve highly exposed vehicles in a convoy now required only two tarp-covered flatbed trailers loaded with steel girders alongside sheets of aluminum and glass, pulled by beat-up trucks that could have been hauling anything, including supplies for the bad guys. That last possibility kept the insurgency from reflexively attacking our trucks, camouflaged to blend in to local conditions, en route to our job sites. The extremist groups and their operations required logistics also, and by design they had no idea what the other hands in their secretive, compartmentalized organizations were doing. Therefore we had achieved both speed and surprise—key aspects of warfare.

As is the wont of any bureaucracy, immediate lessons were not learned immediately in Iraq. We tried to fight it, but in our next project—building the al Anbar police academy, where we would get to see the Awakening's best join the Iraqi uniformed police who would eventually secure every city, town, and village in the Sunni Triangle—the contract mandated that we deliver wholly assembled trailers to the job site in Habbaniya via Abu Ghraib, past Fallujah, and in front of Ramadi. We did this at night in the dark of the clear desert sky, avoiding long lines of halted military convoys by crisscrossing the median ditch (of the 120 tractor-trailers we transported down the Baghdad-Amman highway to place on the site, we managed to roll only one truck over on its side). The Army and Marines controlled the night on the highway because of various electronic vision technologies—including unmanned aerial vehicle drones (UAVs); thus they undertook tactical operations most effectively in the dark. This was the reverse of the American experience in earlier counterinsurgencies, such as the Vietnam War. It also eased the wear and tear on people and machines for the Coalition military to fight and to drive almost all supply trucks at night, especially during the summer in Iraq, when the daytime temperature shot above 120 degrees.

*   *   *

The war had grown more violent in the latter half of 2006. Every month Sunni suicide bombers and Shia death squads slaughtered thousands of Iraqi civilians. The fatality rate for U.S. troops fluctuated from seventy to over a hundred per month, with their sacrifice appearing to have little impact on the raging insurgency. This situation sparked George Bush to order a politically risky escalation of American combat power in 2007—the so-called "Surge" of troops. Democrats had taken control of the U.S. Congress in the November 2006 election, campaigning on an anti–Iraq War platform reinforced with claims of deception by the Republican administration after it was reported that no weapons of mass destruction were found in Iraq—a major pre-war, Bush-administration justification for the invasion. Democrat Harry Reid, the Senate majority leader, would soon declare the war "lost."[2] The American people suffered from war fatigue after four years of conflict with no conclusion in sight, compounded by the pre-war rhetoric of officials in the Republican administration who had forecast a relatively easy pacification of Iraq and quick extraction of U.S. forces after the invasion. Many, including the then–Iraq commander, Army General George Casey, advised President Bush that the U.S. needed to continue to draw down American forces and turn the battle over to the Iraqi security services, ready or not.[3] Instead, 40,000 additional U.S. troops entered the battle, pushing up the total American troops committed to the war to 170,000 by July 2007, with the vast majority going to Baghdad.

The new Iraq commander leading the surge, General David Petraeus, now got the opportunity to practice what he had preached in the COIN manual. He had already proven himself a successful practitioner of a population-centric counterinsurgency strategy in Mosul during his command of the 101st Division (Air Assault) in 2003 and as head of the U.S. mission to train the Iraqi Army in 2004–05.

The Surge troops spread throughout the capital, setting up small-unit combat outposts and vastly expanding the use of anti-blast walls to protect and control the city's five million citizens. The signals intelligence–driven raids that had been honed in the al Anbar campaign—and were now also fed with information from a Baghdadi population exhausted by the extreme violence of the radical jihadis—took on strategic importance. General Stanley McChrystal's JSOC Delta Force with support from other elite counter-terrorism units, the British SAS and Polish "GROM" special-forces[4] (and U.S. Army Rangers), rolled up cell after cell of al-Qaeda terrorists throughout the city. These highly targeted operations, run at a pace of several per night until early 2008, finally denied the Sunni insurgency an operational safe haven in the capital—the main objective in the battle for Iraq.[5]

(Before the Surge, AISG had responsibility for protecting hundreds of cell towers for the Iraqna mobile phone service, many in al Anbar (2005–06). Large numbers of the towers basically had no security, just a rented space on top of or next to people's homes in such places as Ramadi and Fallujah. At first we wondered if the towers would survive, but we came to realize that the insurgents wanted to be able to jabber to their comrades— and U.S. intelligence services wanted to listen!)

Initial Surge troops rushing into the breach created by limited U.S. forces in Baghdad included rapid-deployment units from the 82nd Airborne Division, "the All-Americans" of D-Day fame. The problem was they had no place to live, so the Army went to KBR (Kellogg Brown and Root), which had the LOGCAP (Logistics Civil Augmentation Program) contract that fed and housed all U.S. military forces located on Forward Operating Bases (FOBs) in Iraq. These mega-bases housed thousands of troops in near-U.S. conditions with Burger Kings, Subways, and convenience stores. Well, KBR couldn't get the job done in the timeframe allowed with their existing fifty-thousand-person workforce of Americans and imported labor.[6] So they turned to us to do the job, having heard about our quick work for the Kurdish brigade.

When they awarded us the contract to convert the looted remnants of aluminum-sided warehouses at the Taji army base, just north of Baghdad, into air-conditioned barracks for four hundred paratroopers, the Joint Contracting Command (Iraq) gave us seventeen days, start to finish…. And, when we asked how much time we had to mobilize, the contracting officer told us: "Tomorrow."

No one can do that, I thought, *but we'll give it a try.* There's an old saying in the Army: "It's easier to ask forgiveness than to get permission." So if it took longer and we were showing real progress, we could count on receiving an extension (forgiveness), especially given the battles going on in and around Baghdad during this period—the road north out of the capital past Taji and onto Samarra and Mosul on our main supply route into the project from our logistics hub at Apache passed through an active combat zone, where IEDs and ambushes were too common.

The main problem we had, however, was that there was no American site manager "on the bench" and available to us in country for the mobilization timeframe of "tomorrow." Our methodology entailed putting an American onsite wherever we operated: Fallujah, Mosul, and Habbaniya. Yet we couldn't just put any American out in the mix with a primarily Iraqi crew. These site managers had to have three capabilities: prior military experience (to deal with the security situation in a war zone), technical competence (to deal with construction), and, most importantly, the patience to work with and train the Iraqi workforce. So initially we put our top Filipino, a highly skilled architect, on the job. This did not work out too well, as the Iraqis would not listen to him.

So after a week of flailing around (almost half the time allotted for project completion), I sent to the job the only American available—our vice president for business development, who had won the crazy job for us in the first place. He got it done in a nearly miraculous seventeen days, and not because of his competence in construction. The Iraqis wanted to work for him and therefore delivered, and our logistics got all the necessary materials to the site on time and to spec. When I went back for the opening of the barracks on the eighteenth day and saw hundreds of joking G.I.s under drop ceilings with bunks, mattresses, plugged-in computers, and chill air-conditioning, I remembered the trashed, ramshackle shell of less than three weeks before and could only laugh.

As I returned to Apache from Taji, this success reminded me of something I had read. In the most successful counterinsurgency operation by U.S. forces in the Vietnam War, we infiltrated and wiped out the Viet Cong political cadres in their former safe havens after the annihilation of their protective military force when the VC made the mistake of coming out of hiding and openly attacking the American military during the 1968 Tet Offensive. In *Silence Was a Weapon: The Vietnam War in the Villages,* U.S. Army advisor Stuart Herrington quotes a South Vietnamese officer after a successful operation against the North Vietnamese army late in the war (1972): "Our sacrifices have been difficult to endure but . . . Every time we see the tall American in jungle fatigues, we are reminded of your country's stake in our success."[7]

I could understand that only in a theoretical way until I heard Tony Montana castigating our Iraqi guard force for some serious deficiency while waving his U.S. passport over his head: "*Indi jawaz safar azraq wa mumkin aroih ala kaifak, laakin intu laazim tbaqoon fi hatha jahanim!*" ("I've got a blue [U.S.] passport and can leave any time, but you must remain here in this hell!") Not very diplomatic of Tony, but quite effective. The Iraqis knew we could go back to America—where many of them and seemingly half the world wanted to immigrate—and that we did not need to be in Iraq, so our commitment meant something to them. The risk we voluntarily shared with them created the necessary credibility to lead them effectively.

It is a hotly debated question whether the Surge or the Sahwa (Awakening) was the principal reason for the success in defeating al-Qaeda in Iraq, which allowed U.S. combat forces to leave behind an Iraq capable of defending itself on its own, given a continued American alliance. I believe that you cannot separate one from the other. They were mutually supporting and accelerating. The commitment President Bush made to the Surge against the advice of his top military commanders in Iraq and at the Pentagon, his secretary of Defense, and the Democrat-controlled Congress, which had come to power after the elections of November 2006 riding the tailwind of anti–Iraq War sentiment in much of the country, served to inspire all of us on the ground, including the Iraqis, to continue the fight against the terrorist insurgency.

The presence of additional American forces in and around Baghdad and al Anbar enabled the Iraqi security forces to develop under a protective shield while they were beginning to be fed by the Sahwa recruits who took the fight directly to their co-religionists—the Sunni insurgency. The real battle was concentrated on Baghdad, where the political elites and the international media resided, but you could not control the capital without securing the area around the city—the so-called "belts." And Anbar served as the key staging ground for the insurgency's strategic weapon—car bombs—which actively threatened Baghdad. So as Anbar goes, so goes Baghdad.

The AQI-led insurgency was based in the minority Sunni population, much like the Chinese guerrilla movement in ethnic Malay-majority Malaya that the British fought in the 1950s and unlike the Viet Cong in Vietnam. Al-Qaeda's narrow support base and the opposition of the majority of the population (Shia Arabs and Kurds) to it enabled the success of a less resource-intensive counterinsurgency. The real challenge for U.S. and Government of Iraq forces was ensuring that the Shia majority remained, at the least, neutral in the fight. The minute we lost the Shia, as the British had done in the 1920s—a loss that eventually forced the imperialists out in 1932[8]—we would lose the war.

Iran's allies, the Sadrist militia, never reflected the will of the Shia majority. But Iranian military aid—especially armor-killing explosively formed penetrators (EFPs)—meant a virtual proxy war between Iran and the United States. In effect the Coalition fought a long and bloody conflict with Iranian infiltrators who were well enough equipped to destroy our best tanks and armored personnel carriers.

If any overarching strategic success for the American military can be claimed prior to, during, and consequent to the Surge, it was in never allowing Sadr to take up the mantle of all Iraqi Shia. As a result, we were able to concentrate the bulk of our efforts on defeating the AQI-led Sunni insurgency, which Iraq's ethno-sectarian makeup limited to less than half the country and which was operating out of potential safe havens provided by only 20 percent of the population, about six million Sunni Arabs. Ever since U.S. Army General Eric Shinseki, chief of staff of the Army, stated in pre-invasion Congressional testimony that the occupation of Iraq would require "several hundred thousand troops,"[9] critics have questioned how the limited U.S. troops available could defend the people *and* take the battle to the guerrillas. They failed to count host-nation forces in the ranks of the counterinsurgents. Yet we had to help recruit, train, and deploy those forces for them to make up the difference. In the end, this was the exit strategy: build up the Iraqi military and police to the point where American and other Coalition troops could go home, leaving behind a stable Iraq.

All of us who'd been on the ground in Iraq for a year or more realized that the quality and fighting spirit of the new Government of Iraq security forces would probably take a very long time to match that of the Coalition troops. But we also had faith that, with continued American support, the army and police the Coalition had trained and equipped could eventually defeat any regional threat or internal insurgency.

That was why General Petraeus, in his strategic, momentum-changing testimony reporting the progress of the Surge before Congress on September 10, 2007, made special note of the rapid development of the Anbari police—with the establishment of the AISG-built and -operated al Anbar Police Academy being a crowning piece of that success story. His testimony included an accounting of the total Iraqis on the "payroll" of their nation's security services: 445,000.[10] Petraeus's testimony carried strategic weight because there existed two battlefields for the U.S. mission in Iraq, just as there were in the Vietnam War and in fact every conflict since World War II: first, the actual combat zone and second, the American body politic.

A couple of months earlier, the commanding general's partner before Congress, U.S. Ambassador to Iraq Ryan Crocker, had spoken to the media in what I considered defeatist terms. So I had responded from Iraq in an op-ed in the *Wall Street Journal* that ran less than two weeks before their Capitol Hill testimony:

> This Isn't Civil War
> By Carter Andress
> August 28, 2007
> Baghdad
>   We are winning this war. I write those words from my desk in the Red Zone in downtown Baghdad as hundreds of Iraqis working with my company—Shia and Sunni, Arab and Kurd—

execute security, construction and logistics missions through-out the capital and Sunni Triangle. We have been here now over three years.

American-Iraqi Solutions Group, which I helped co-found in March 2004, has been intimately involved with creating the new Iraqi security services. Our principal business as a U.S. Department of Defense contractor is to build bases for the Iraqi Army and police and then supply them with water, food, fuel and maintenance services. We are on the cutting edge of the exit strategy for the U.S. military: Stand up an effective Iraqi security structure and then we can bring our troops home.

We are not out of the Iraqi desert yet. But the primary problems we now face on the ground are controllable, given a strong American military presence through 2008. These prob-lems include the involvement of Iran in fueling Shia militancy, the British failure to uphold their security obligations in the south and the tumultuous nature of a new democracy.

Ambassador Ryan C. Crocker recently said the one word he would choose to describe the feelings of the Iraqi people was "fear." A bad choice, from my observation.

That's not the prevailing state of mind, except maybe for those sheltered souls in the Green Zone who are getting hit on a regular basis for the first time in more than a year by primar-ily Iranian-supplied rockets and mortars. What I see on the faces of the thousands of Iraqis working with us, including our subcontractors and suppliers as well as on the faces of the Iraqi Army and police, patrolling and manning the checkpoints and assisting U.S. soldiers in searching for the insurgents, is grim determination to get the job done.

I also see exhaustion—exhaustion with the insurgency, whether it be al Qaeda, neo-Saddamist, or Jaish al Mahdi (JAM), or the Shia militia of Moqtada al-Sadr. The exhaustion is real, and the evidence of the falling support among the Iraqi people for the insurgency in its various guises is inescapable—unless you are deliberately looking the other way.

A large proportion of our thousand-man work force—of which 90% are Iraqi citizens—comes from Sadr City, the Shia slum in east Baghdad. Many carry weapons. These Shia warriors have emphasized in the past several months that they and their neighbors are tired of conflict and only want to feed their families.

You only have to note the lack of U.S. casualties in the ongoing surge to clear JAM out of the highly dangerous urban terrain of Sadr City to realize that the people there do not want to fight us. They are sick of fighting.

As for Sunni resistance, I recently visited the boot camp we operate for the Iraqi Army at Habbaniya in al Anbar, former heartland of the insurgency. For the first time we are seeing entire Sunni Arab recruiting cohorts at the camp, where before we only saw Shia from outside the province.

The Sunnis of al Anbar—finally tired of al Qaeda assassinating their sheikhs when they disagreed with the terrorists—have committed their children to the security services of a government dominated by the majority Shias, and paid for and run by the Americans. With such a development, you have real progress in integrating the diverse elements in Iraq.

Slowly but surely, Iraqi security services are building up. You only have to travel outside the Green Zone to see them undertaking heroic risks as they work to control the streets in growing numbers and with growing professionalism. In the past couple of months, the Ministry of the Interior established an operations center for all of Baghdad that effectively coordinates nonmilitary logistics movements throughout the capital—a function previously only undertaken by a coalition contractor. From chaos has come order and in turn, step by step, the Iraqi military is becoming a truly national, not sectarian, force.

I see no civil war between the Shias and Sunnis as I travel practically every day on the roads of Iraq with my Arab and Kurdish security team. The potential for renewed internecine warfare faded earlier this year, when al Qaeda failed to reignite the waning sectarian struggle the second time around with another attack on the Golden Mosque in Samarra.

The perfect storm at the beginning of 2007 created the necessity of reconciliation. The Sunni Arabs who had used al Qaeda as leverage in the political struggle to re-establish their minority rule faced genocide in Baghdad from the Shia death squads. With pressure from the new Democratic majority in Congress, the Shia government of Nouri al-Maliki realized that time was running out for a dominant American presence in Iraq and finally allowed the U.S. military to clean up Sadr City, thus alleviating the death-squad activities.

Both the Sunni and Shia Arab sides of the Iraqi political equation (the Kurds have sided with us from the beginning) now see that there is no alternative to American protection. As a result, Sadr's people and the Sunnis have both returned to parliament. As always, democracy is messy, but it is working. We have to be patient, particularly because this nascent reconciliation has left al Qaeda as the odd man out.

Just as the rockets landing in the Green Zone are from a foreign source—Iran—the Jihadis who destroy themselves in explosions aimed primarily at mass killings of Shia civilians are almost all foreigners. This is al Qaeda, not Iraq.

Even more to the point: The Iraqis basically ignore the al Qaeda car bombs, mourn the dead and then go to work, to school, join and continue to serve in the military and police—and life goes on. There is no terror if no one is terrorized.

Let us, the American people, not be terrorized into retreating before our enemy—al Qaeda—just when they have begun
to stand alone, stripped of allies, in a country beginning to
enjoy the fruits of a democracy we have sacrificed much blood
to help create.[11]

★   ★   ★

By this point, the erosion of popular support for continued U.S.
involvement in Iraq had swept up the entire leadership of the congressionally ascendant Democratic Party, along with the mainstream media.
Senator Hillary Clinton, the presumed standard-bearer for Democrats in
the upcoming 2008 presidential elections, claimed (quoting Coleridge)
that to trust General Petraeus's upcoming testimony would require: "a
willing suspension of disbelief."[12] The *New York Times*, an established
thought leader for the American media, violated its own internal code of
conduct, which forbids personally abusive advertising, by publishing, the
day prior to the testimony, a full-page ad referring to a man who had
dutifully served his country for over thirty years in uniform as "General
Betray-us."[13] Truly had few war speeches in American history been so
critical.

In 1975, Congress cut off all funding for military operations including
aerial bombing in support of South Vietnam, in direct violation of the Paris
Treaty negotiated and signed by Secretary of State Henry Kissinger (for
which he shared the Nobel Peace Prize) that included a requirement for
the U.S. to intervene in the defense of South Vietnam. The North Vietnamese then invaded and conquered the American-allied South Vietnamese government, not by means of a popular uprising but through a
blitzkrieg-style conventional-force attack down coastal Route 1 and into
Saigon. The U.S. Air Force could have annihilated this mass of Soviet-
supplied tanks and vehicles but for congressional sanction. We had been
there before, and we were near there again in Iraq when Petraeus stopped

the defeatist trend with a straightforward report of the measurable, actual progress resulting from the Surge.

The commander had gained us time in the Iraq War's second battlefield for the American body politic, but we had to win the war on the actual battlefield back in Iraq. Petraeus's focus on the Anbari police reflected an acute awareness of the real end game beyond the Surge. For police to operate they must live among the people. Therefore there must be a level of security already present. The police cannot function in an active combat zone because they do not have the necessary armor or heavy weapons and do not operate in large enough units to protect themselves in that environment. The police investigate and prevent crime; so before you can have the cop on the beat patrol, the insurgency must have de facto become a criminal-level threat, something the police can manage, in the sense that there is no direct, existential threat to the government nationally or at the local level generally.

The questions all of us on the Coalition side faced were tough: How do we roll together all these elements of success in the Surge? Aside from the additional Baghdad- and Anbar-focused combat forces and the diplomatic-political efforts to enact a democratic constitution through democratic means, the success of the U.S. mission in Iraq had to mean ending the war with the Iraqi security forces able to operate effectively on their own.

This complicated and fraught process began to take off with the establishment of facilities where recruits could train, and only contractors had the ability to stand up these facilities on the scale required—given the Total Force concept that included contractors, as envisioned in U.S. military doctrine beginning with DOD's Quadrennial Defense Review (2006).[14] As a result of the all-volunteer force structure of the American military and the troop limits established by Congress, our uniformed forces were only so large, and the new doctrine envisioned that contractors would fill the gaps.

The role of the military contractor inspired many and varied reactions from the military in the field. We were free actors, able to travel where the work required, whereas the military were bound by order and unit bound-aries. I could go anywhere in Iraq at any time. One time we loaded up my Iraqi security team, machine guns and all, got on a chartered cargo plane, and flew to Basra from Baghdad. We landed, picked up a local security team with vehicles, and off we went without a single approval from the U.S. military, other than what we already possessed contractually. The key, of course, was that we had to have the money to sustain ourselves in the war zone, a very expensive proposition—all costs were pushed higher by security requirements. There was no credit source in Iraq and everything was in cash—stacks of crisp U.S. one-hundred-dollar bills. And the mili-tary was loath to give us any support, as they had hired us to support them, not the other way around! Therefore contractors could only survive if they continued to win contracts. And with few exceptions, by 2007 the U.S. government had moved to a competitive process for contracting. The whole world could seek out contracts in Iraq—all they had to do was surf the internet and go after the projects listed on Fedbizops.gov, the website for all U.S government open contracting valued at over $25,000.

Yet at the end of the day, of the tens if not hundreds of companies that tried to enter what we will euphemistically call the Iraqi warzone "market," I can only count one other American-owned reconstruction contractor not named KBR or DynCorp that had a real presence on the ground nationwide. That company was Sallyport, owned by a West Pointer who had launched off of Custer Battles, LLC, in a more tangential way than AISG. They had been vendors and visitors to CB's offices in Baghdad, whereas the founders of AISG, including me, had started as CB employees and turned federal whistleblowers after discovering fraudulent activity by the company. Sallyport really made their way in Iraq as a security company first for the construction giant Louis Berger and then for USAID. They did almost all, if not all, of their construction and other work on U.S. military bases, employing mostly expatriates, meaning Westerners, and so-called TCNs—non-Western third country nationals, people not from Iraq. There was a helluva winnowing process in the competition, but the market produced the necessary vendors to get done what the U.S. mission required as our competition arose from Iraqi, Jordanian, Turkish, and Saudi-owned companies.

Initially, we had the edge over the non-American companies that were not led by former soldiers, like me, who were willing to take the risk for the mission. So we were left pretty much alone in being price competitive in bad places like Fallujah and Abu Ghraib, where we had built part of U.S. FOB India in 2005. In addition, the DOD contracting officers were dealing in English, they expected Western-standard responses to requests for proposals, and everything had to be in compliance with the two-thousand-page Federal Acquisition Regulation! But by 2007 these non-U.S. companies had caught up, so competition had boiled down to price and delivery.

✳   ✳   ✳

To discuss the security contractor Blackwater killings in Nusoor Square on September 16, 2007, less than a week after the Petraeus testimony, Elizabeth Palmer of CBS News interviewed me in Baghdad. As I started to talk about the role of DOD contractors in the mission, she immediately interjected, "You're here to make money!"

Sitting in the glare of the TV klieg lights and fresh off the Iraqi street, I tried to slow my pulse and responded, "The reason I came here is for the mission.... I have been a successful businessman here and made some money and I'm thankful for that. But it takes a different kind of motivation when your competition is not just trying to kill off your business but kill you also.... That's where we stand as a community."[15]

About this time, a reporter from NewsMax reached out to me first via phone and then in an email exchange. In the last email he sought my response to a quote from Ralph Peters, a retired U.S. Army lieutenant colonel and bestselling author of several futuristic military novels, one of which I had read and thought was good entertainment: *God's Children*, about a mechanized infantry company battling Soviet invaders in West Germany. According to the reporter, however, Peters had opined that military contractors were "bottom feeders." (I have since seen some quite aggressive statements from Peters about contractors in Iraq.)[16] Not happy with that accusation as I sat near ground zero of the Surge's "Battle of Baghdad" while both the journalist and the novelist enjoyed the good life in the U.S., I too quickly snapped back. My reply surmised that Peters' antagonism toward contractors came "out of jealousy because he did not have the necessary skills to succeed over here."

In Iraq, there was now no turning back from contractors in the U.S. combat force. Contractors had taken on mission-critical roles that revolutionized U.S. military logistics on the battlefield by substantially reducing the need for the limited number of available uniformed troops to undertake roles that contractors could fill. Military scholar John J. McGrath, in "The Other End of the Spear: Tooth-to-Tail Ratio," his authoritative paper for the U.S. Army's Combat Studies Institute Press, estimated that in 2005 contractors amounted to 58,000 personnel directly supporting a military force of 133,000 in Iraq. Thus, in McGrath's estimation, civilians provided an unprecedented 30 percent of the total U.S. force deployed inside Iraq.[17] Tooth-to-tail ratio traditionally means the number of combat-arms soldiers proportionate to combat-support and combat-service-support troops. In the Iraq War, the relatively large number of contractors had redefined the term "combat" while allowing a significant shift of the ratio in the direction of combat-arms soldiers.

McGrath missed, however, the real count of contractors serving the military mission in the counterinsurgency that the Iraq War became for America after the collapse of Saddam Hussein's Baathist regime in 2003. At any one time during the Iraq War, starting in 2004, there were actually approximately 160,000 contractors employed by the U.S. government. Therefore only during the peak of the Surge, when there were more than 170,000 American troops in country, did uniformed soldiers outnumber DOD and Department of State contractors. Without the stabilizing activities of the contractor reconstruction mission employing Iraqis and building and maintaining infrastructure for the nation—an effort in which hundreds of people died and untold numbers were wounded—the COIN mission would have failed in Iraq.

When effective, U.S. government warzone contractors combined two of the most esteemed elements of American culture: the entrepreneurial and warrior spirits. But if you understand Joseph Schumpeter, one of the most eminent economists of the twentieth century—he coined the term "creative destruction"—you will see why capitalism is progressive to the human condition. In Schumpeter's assessment, the free market allows those who in feudal, pre-capitalist times expressed their "atavistic" aggressions in the fight to seize what their neighbors possessed in combat, which is a zero-sum game, to channel those same impulses and ambitions into business—where both buyer and seller win.[18] The hard-charging entrepreneur of modern times has evolved from the conquering warrior of pre-modern times. That same evolution from warrior to entrepreneur is speeded up in warzone contracting; in Iraq we saw crucial segments of the population realize that there was a better way than violence to achieve a safe and prosperous future for themselves and their families. The twenty-first-century American warrior still fights—not to acquire an empire of conquered peoples and lands, but to serve a nation that seeks to spread democracy, human rights, and free markets. The contractor combatant not only serves the same cause but through reconstruction and employment transforms an insurgent safe haven into a marketplace.

CHAPTER 6

BLACKWATER

LEAVING BAGHDAD always had its plusses and minuses. One of the minuses was the grimy international airport, basically the only efficient way in and out of the city (the drive to Kuwait or Jordan took all day, either way). So the airport was the single place where you got to see all the contractors of every variety, along with Iraqi officials, businessmen, and their families. The metal latticework façade of the terminal lured you into believing you were exiting the harshness of Iraq to enter a nice space, but once you went through the body search and had your luggage sniffed by the bomb dogs, you knew better. The steel-framed glass entranceway took you into the puke-yellow-carpeted building, itself an artifact of the "Scandinavian modern" style popular in the 1970s, when Iraq was still connected to the world. For a brief time chaos seemed ruled by order as you crossed into a cattle chute manned by uniformed Iraqi border patrol to get your tickets checked and your bags scanned once more. Then, after making it through passport control and having your carry-on bag scanned yet again,

79

you and the rest of the herd of fellow escapees from the combat zone emerged into a waiting area of low-slung, artificial-leather couches sagging with age. And wait you did, because the flights hardly ever left on time ...

As you were stuck there, you had a chance to observe the other passengers while sipping on gritty Turkish coffee from one of the sketchy shops bordering the waiting area. The KBR guys, and some gals, provided the largest contingent of passengers, lining up conspicuously for their special charter flights out of country or to one of the super Forward Operating Bases (FOBs) scattered around Iraq. These people were the salt of the earth—American-style—with calloused hands from working at hard physical labor all their lives. Country boys and girls, now leaning toward middle age with leathery skin and spreading girth from too much trans-fat in their French fries, but you just knew they could make any piece of machinery known to man run properly, and if it was broken, they could fix it. That's why these civilians were here: to operate, maintain, and supply the greatest military in history actively degrading in one of the largest deserts on earth. And these enterprising folks with their oil-stained Redman and Caterpillar baseball hats, who seemed like fish out of water in the Middle East, did exactly that. Even Pratap Chatterjee, the author of *Halliburton's Army* and one of KBR's harshest critics, did not challenge the company's "estimation" that by early 2008 its "50,000 workers in Central Asia and the Middle East [primarily Iraq and Kuwait] had cooked more than 720 million meals, driven more than 400 million miles in various convoy missions, while providing 12 billion gallons of potable water and more than 267 million tons of ice" in support of the U.S. military.[1] The KBR employees might remind you of *Mayberry R.F.D.*, but they had come for the mission. Their pay was not high—$6,000–7,000 per month, usually—considering the risks they were running; the company had suffered more than a thousand casualties, with over a hundred employees killed during the Iraq War.[2]

Next in size of representation at the airport were the security contractors. Muscular men with mostly short military haircuts—arms and necks thick with tattoos of various snakes, crusader crosses, and dragons—strutted about, seemingly always ready for a fight even in the highly secure terminal. (During the entire U.S military presence in Iraq, Baghdad International Airport or "BIAP" never experienced a terrorist incident on the ground. Plenty of indirect fire, mortars and such, landed at the airport; and insurgents shot at planes from outside the wire, but no man-carried bombs or other weapons were used inside the airport's perimeter.) Pumped up from running the IED-filled roads on a daily basis—most of the security work in Iraq revolved around moving from safe place to safe place—the security contractors laughed loudly and spoke with mostly British or South African accents.

The UK had cornered the high-end market in private security. Aegis, for example, owned by Tim Spicer of "blood diamonds" notoriety—his former company had helped defeat an insurgency in Sierra Leone—protected all the U.S. senior military officers not directly involved in combat operations as they moved around Iraq in high-profile armored cars. This $200-million-a year-contract really highlighted the necessary focus of the limited available U.S. combat forces—killing or capturing the enemy and protecting the Iraqi population from the insurgency. Anything other than that, including even bodyguard services for military officers around the Green Zone or between FOBs, contractors could accomplish. Spicer's crew did a good job of it.

The South Africans—whose estimated ten-thousand-plus personnel in country made them the third-largest armed foreign contingent (after the U.S. and UK), even though their government did not participate in the Coalition—dominated the top end of the third-country-national security presence. I always wondered about these guys, almost exclusively white. They were true mercenaries without any dog in the hunt, as we would say down South. South Africa, however, had a long tradition of providing mercenaries, going back to the newly independent Congo in the early 1960s.

The one group you did not see much of at BIAP was the biggest, baddest of the U.S. private security firms—Blackwater. They kept a low profile, flying in and out of the country either from non-civilian terminals or as individuals. You knew them primarily by their reputation for aggressive competence and from seeing their convoys of shiny black ballistic-proof GMC SUVs shuttling diplomats around Baghdad. That was all about to change.

*   *   *

"Sir! Sir!" George, our Lebanese-American security manager, had come rushing into my office. "There were burning cars and bodies everywhere! The U.S. Army had just arrived," he exclaimed breathlessly.

"Where?" I immediately asked.

"At the traffic circle on the way to airport road, right in front of the National Police headquarters. It looks like Blackwater got into a firefight there in mid-morning traffic and a lot of dead people. We had to turn around our convoy to BIAP and come home. The Iraqi police and the U.S. Army are in a stand-off with a couple of Blackwater's suburbans in the middle. American choppers are overhead."

Thus began the Blackwater-Nusoor Square saga, from my perspective. We didn't really even use the official Iraqi name Nusoor ("Eagles") Square, but now it would be burnt into our consciousness. The traffic circle, called a square in Arabic, although it was really a British-style roundabout with a dry concrete fountain in the middle, sat approximately one kilometer by car and less as the crow flies from Fort Apache. I had been around it countless times because it served as our primary route to the airport. Nusoor was on Damascus Street, the main boulevard from the west into the heart of Baghdad, and it had a massive Iraqi police presence as it bordered both the National Police headquarters and an access road to the Green Zone.

Thinking after George had left my office, I couldn't imagine the insurgents going Viet Cong and staging a firefight there. That would require the deaths of too many of their limited number of trained soldiers. AQI would have just put a car bomb at the circle and be done with it. A large-scale shooting didn't make sense other than for one reason—which I truly hoped was not the case.

By the next day, I received a series of emails all requesting interviews about what had happened at Nusoor Square. The requests came from CBS, ABC, and CNN. My book *Contractor Combatants* (August 2007) about my first couple of years in Iraq (2004–05) had just been published. One of the reasons I had written the book was that, because no one involved but journalists had published anything outside military journals during the Vietnam War, almost everything we knew about the war emerged from the actual participants after we had already lost the conflict. I had wanted to put the ground truth I had witnessed out into the ongoing debate in the second front of the Iraq War—the battle for the American body politic. Now I sensed all contractors would be under fire because of the Blackwater shootings, which had killed seventeen Iraqi civilians, as the investigations later determined. In our notoriously camera-shy industry, someone had to step up and tell the positive side of our story. Apparently I set out alone on this task because, for a brief couple days, I dominated the airwaves about the number-one story coming out of the then-number-one topic of international news: the war in Iraq.

Hala Gorani from CNN was first up to bat. George had organized a small convoy and we jumped into our body armor, grabbed our AKs and raced across Baghdad after dark. Not something we did very often, as the Iraqi security services and the U.S. military tended to be antsy at night—not to speak of the risk of getting caught in the wrong place by insurgents operating under cover of darkness. We entered a fortified neighborhood, constructed while I was living there when working for Custer Battles in early 2004, right next to Checkpoint 2 leading into the Green Zone from the north. Almost all the Western media had their living quarters, offices, and ad hoc studios behind "Bremer" blast walls in this upscale neighborhood of Baghdad mansions directly across from the Iraqi Foreign Ministry.

Quickly dropping my body armor, I stepped in front of the camera, live and beaming out to CNN worldwide. I couldn't see Hala, as she was broadcasting from the Atlanta studio, but I could hear the journalists' voices out of an earpiece some assistant had slid on my head as I walked

up on the roof of the mansion with a stunning backdrop of the blue-domed
Mansour mosque, familiar to anyone watching American TV broadcasts
from Iraq over the years.

Michael Holmes, the anchor for CNN's *Your World Today*, introduced
the story: "Blackwater in hot water. Iraq's government moves to boot out
the U.S. security firm after a fatal gun battle." As he went on to point out,
"after a firefight that left eight Iraqis dead, 14 others wounded, Baghdad
revoked Blackwater's license to operate in Iraq." And Hala Gorani chimed
in, "Security contractors like Blackwater have been accused of killing
innocent Iraqi citizens, but no one has ever been charged."

As Holmes explained, viewers would likely remember Blackwater from
the horrific events in Fallujah in 2004, when "four of its security personnel
were burned and mutilated," triggering the famous battle there. Barbara
Starr, CNN's Pentagon correspondent, explained the Nusoor Square incident in Baghdad—apparently a car bomb had led to a firefight involving
a Blackwater convoy, eight Iraqis had been killed and fourteen more
wounded, and the Iraqi government had "yanked the license of Blackwater
to operate." She also pointed out that the role of contractors in Iraq was
"controversial." On the one hand, "Things simply cannot be done in Iraq
at this point without these private security contractors." On the other hand,
when contractors get into firefights and civilians are killed, there are bound
to be questions about jurisdiction and accountability.

At this point, Hala Gorani turned to me for "some interesting perspective on that Blackwater controversy from a private security contractor in
Baghdad. Carter Andress is CEO of a security company and author of the
book *Contractor Combatants*. He joins us now live from Baghdad." She
asked me to tell her what our team had seen on the spot, and I filled her
in:

> Well, we travel through that square every day. Nusoor Square
> is on our way to the Checkpoint 12 going into the Green Zone
> and also going to the airport. So, one of our routine movements

passed by the scene of the incident several minutes afterwards....

This is the entrance way to the national police headquarters. It's also a very busy circle. This was late morning rush
hour...the circle is packed with cars during this time. People
trying to get around, go about their business in Baghdad. Our
people saw a couple cars destroyed. People—dead bodies,
wounded people being evacuated.

The U.S. military had moved in and secured the area. So,
it was not a good scene.

I also had the chance to explain the role of contractors in Iraq:

Well, primarily we're a U.S. Department of Defense contractor.
We operate under the Federal Acquisition Regulation, which is
our governing body according to the contracts that we're under
in Iraq. And in turn, what has been represented, because we are
a relatively new phenomenon to war, is what I referred to in my
book as "contractor combatants."

So we fall into a bit of a gray area. So in reality there is no
law that you can prosecute. No effective body of law that you
can prosecute anyone that's found guilty of any kind of crime
in....

When Hala suggested that that meant there was "no accountability," that
it was "really the wild, wild west there, isn't it, in Iraq for people like you
who have these security companies," I begged to differ:

Well, I wouldn't say that there's no accountability. But there's
not a criminal accountability. There's not an accountability
under law in a criminal sense. But Blackwater could be fined.
Blackwater could lose its contract with the Department of State.

These people could be—that were involved could become *persona non grata* in Iraq, forced out of the country, lose their livelihoods. But we're talking about the fog of war here. And this incident is regrettable. But you know, it's something that has happened.

Next, Hala asked me to play the critic and propose what "should be changed with regard to these security firms operating in Iraq," and I pointed to the advantages that flowed from our majority-Iraqi workforce:

Well, my company, American-Iraqi Solutions Group, our security division is Salaamat al Iraq, Iraq Safety [in English]. And we're the first foreign company to receive a security license from the Ministry of Interior in Iraq for a foreign company. And we, though, are 90 percent Iraqi.

We pride ourselves on working closely with the Iraqis. And as a result, these high-profile operators like Blackwater seem to operate in an aggressive and arrogant manner that alienates the exact population that we need to win over as the mission here in Iraq.[3]

✶   ✶   ✶

Not my best outing, but I had stood in front of the camera and taken the hits and kept on rolling. The report and interview included several mistakes, such as always occur in initial reports due to the fog of war. First of all, I was mistaken in that there was in fact criminal accountability under law—but the U.S. government had not by this time ever prosecuted military contractors. The reporters were responsible for other errors in the segment. For example, it turned out that there were seventeen Iraqis killed, not eight. There were legal protections for the guards, as the company worked for the U.S. State Department under the international laws of diplomatic immunity. And Blackwater did not have its license revoked by the Iraqi government—because they had no security license. Only U.S. Department of Defense contractors and Iraqi private security companies possessed Ministry of Interior licenses. At this time, there were over a hundred of those, with the mix about even between foreign contractors and Iraqi companies.

Next up that same evening—just over fifteen minutes later—came CBS. George and I walked down the street in the barricaded media neighborhood and entered another mansion. This was truly a great house with a sweeping white-marble staircase in a high-ceiling front entranceway that would have almost fit in the antebellum South. And coming down the gilt-edged steps as we entered strode the queen of warzone reporting: the vivacious Lara Logan. She didn't do the live interview though, someone else did. I basically repeated what I had said for CNN, but in shorter form. The preface to the story, quoting the U.S. embassy in Baghdad, stated that "a car bomb went off and a firefight broke out," with graphics showing a bomb exploding next to one of the Blackwater suburbans.[4] This had not happened, and I already knew it.

Off we went to ABC, basically across the dusty street, where we had the same backdrop of the blue dome as on CNN. I guess I was getting smoother—not sure, but it seemed to be getting easier to give the sound bites. Immediately after ABC I got the call back from CNN, asking for the kind of long-form interview for which the cable news network is famous. Then I really got going ...

All these questions on the fly set me thinking about the incident. There was no way so many Iraqi civilians could have died in a legitimate, two-way firefight. Especially without any dead or captured bad guys or explosions nearby. These civilians died from bullets and at least one 40 mm explosive-round from a U.S. military- and Blackwater-standard M203 (basically an M-16 assault rifle with a tube hung under the barrel for launching grenades). As his team drove by, George had seen the bloody impact of a grenade on the windshield of a small sedan that—as news reports from the beginning stated—contained a family heading out on an

errand. I could see what must have happened in my mind as I walked back
to the second CNN interview of the evening: the Blackwater convoy had
entered the packed traffic circle evidently without a client (in other words,
with only the security team itself in their vehicles); then they must have
made the impossible demand for the stand-off buffer of 500 feet allowed
by the official rules on the use of force; then when the family did not
immediately comply, one of the Blackwater shooters must have fired the
grenade into their windshield; and reacting to the consequent explosion,
other guards would have opened fire into the dense crowd of Iraqi cars,
killing seventeen people who were just trying to lead their lives in the
capital city.

After discussing all the details of the Nusoor Square incident—only
in more depth than with the initial CNN interviewer—it all finally came
together, and I said, "These guys [the Blackwater guards] are continuing
their lives as soldiers. And as a soldier, your job in this mission we have
here is to put your life at risk before you put the Iraqi civilians' lives at risk,
and your clients' lives at risk, too. And…I get the feeling here that that
standard wasn't met."[5]

That played over and over throughout the day on CNN. I was just
waiting for the Blackwater guys to come after me. But when, several weeks
later at a meeting of the Private Security Companies Association of Iraq,
one finally did confront me, I offered him a copy of my book. He quickly
cooled down. We all knew who the real enemy was, and it was definitely
not us. Some of his guys had made serious mistakes, and we all knew it.
Someone needed to be held accountable.

The Blackwater guards were only human—despite their bulging
biceps. We all were. I knew all too well the dry-mouthed fear that gripped
you when the possibility of an IED or gunfire ambush was a near-constant
danger. That was why I worked so hard to maintain discipline among the
AISG security.

I had already done a little research but now wanted to get the final
word on where we stood in terms of legal liability. I studied up on the

Military Extraterritorial Jurisdiction Act, which allowed federal prosecution in the United States of Defense Department contractors who committed crimes abroad that could result in a felony conviction and incarceration of not less than one year. At the time of the Nusoor massacre, however, this law had never been used. In my writings and on the several additional TV and radio interviews I did, including one with Elizabeth Palmer of CBS, I began to call for the law to be enforced. We needed this as an industry, otherwise there would be no level playing field because there would be no transparency, no accountability. We would all be tarred with the same brush—as war profiteers and war criminals. The bad contractors would not get weeded out, we would all collapse from their corruption, and without us the Coalition mission would fail in Iraq.

The story continued on July 31, 2008, with a feature by CNN in which the network and Arwa Damon, the Arabic-speaking daughter of Brent Sadler of CNN Gulf War reporting fame, juxtaposed Blackwater and Nusoor Square with AISG and our almost purely Iraqi security force.[6] In May 2009—long after the news reports incorrectly projected the company's expulsion from Iraq—I finally got to meet Erik Prince, the founder and owner of Blackwater. I proposed a solution to their ongoing problem with the Iraqis and the State Department, which was about to decide on renewing their security contract worth hundreds of millions. Our Iraqis would be the outriders on the State convoys, and the Blackwater guards would be in the interior vehicles with the clients. In traffic jams, our Iraqis easily interacted with their fellow citizens, thus facilitating movement—no one got across Baghdad in rush hour faster than our convoys. (Our Iraqis even brought a new English phrase into their everyday slang on the company radio network—"wrong way!"—because the Iraqi police allowed us to go counter-directional on the roads when that would expedite our travel in the city.) We knew the Iraqi police and the army at the numerous checkpoints, and they knew us from our years of operating in the city. We always gave them bottles of cool water and a kind word or two. Erik seemed fired up about the concept, asking several questions about the approach. But the next day, the State Department announced Blackwater's termination from the Worldwide Personnel Protective Services contract.

CHAPTER 7

THE TIPPING POINT

ON SEPTEMBER 11, 2007, I wrote an op-ed from Baghdad for National Review Online titled, "The Connection: Six years in, Iraq is center stage for the international jihadist movement":

> From the vantage point of downtown Baghdad at the end of a long, hot summer six years later, September 11, 2001, continues to be the battle call for all Americans fighting in Iraq.
>
> Whether one approves of the U.S.-led invasion of Iraq in 2003 or not, the reality we face on the ground here is that al-Qaeda is present in force and in all its nihilistic evil. Just look to the suicide car bombs and can you not hear the clear, ringing echoes of the Towers crashing down and the people—normal men and women who left home that morning just to go to work to feed their families, now leaping to their sure deaths just to avoid the inferno within? An inferno wrought by jihadis...just

the type the people of Iraq now confront when they, in turn, try to go about their daily lives and feed their families. Suicide car-bombers are not Iraqi; this is al-Qaeda.

As a direct result of the 9/11 attacks, the al Qaeda trap we have created in Iraq is part of what I call the *Field of Dreams* strategy: Build it and they will come. First we knocked off Saddam's tyrannical rule, and then we drew every Jihadi worth his salt to fight us in Iraq. From shadowy figures hiding and plotting against us in the dark alleys of the Middle East, they have become fodder in the kill zone of the U.S. military.

In the radical Islamist theory of war, there is the "near enemy" and the "far enemy." Bin Laden had decided to concentrate on the far enemy—America—thinking he could knock off a super power, as the mujahideen did with the USSR in Afghanistan, and thereby give rise to a world-embracing Islamic caliphate. The near enemy was the non-Jihadi Arab governments, such as those of Egypt, Jordan, and Lebanon. The far enemy became the near enemy, however, the moment the American army invaded Iraq. How could al-Qaeda think of attacking America when the U.S. Army was occupying one of the inner lands of Islam? Yet the difference now is that the jihadis are not facing Americans going about their everyday business, but soldiers and others ready for a fight. This is the primary reason we have not seen an al-Qaeda terrorist attack in the U.S. in the six years since 9/11.

After the al-Qaeda attacks on the U.S., we were no longer *Festung Amerika*, protected by wide oceans from the violent chaos and suicidal fanaticism rampant in the Middle East. America was now target number one. Once the Taliban ceased to rule Afghanistan in late 2001, the leaders of al-Qaeda fled to other safe havens. Many ended up in the lawless Northwest

Frontier of Pakistan, others in Iran. Both locations, however, restricted their operational movement.

One leader, however, went to Iraq, where Saddam was gloating publicly over the success of al-Qaeda in New York City and Northern Virginia. This leader's *nom de guerre* was Abu Musab al Zarqawi. There is clear evidence that Osama bin Laden had funded, at least in part, Zarqawi's operations in the Taliban's Afghanistan. Zarqawi then came here to Baghdad—a city so well controlled at the time by Saddam's secret police that not one single effective U.S. spy operated in the city. Almost no accurate information leaked out to Western intelligence services after UNSCOM departed in 1998, and this dearth of intelligence was not for lack of trying or financial resources.

Zarqawi made his way to the far southeastern corner of Kurdistan, occupied at the time by the terrorist organization Ansar al-Islam, another known al-Qaeda affiliate. In 2004, Zarqawi publicly declared his fidelity to bin Laden and changed the name of his group to "al Qaeda in Iraq." Connect the dots.

The *casus belli*—the cause for the war—is intimately tied up with September 11, 2001. We entered this war to engage decisively the aggressive, genocidal actions of a totalitarian dictator who used weapons of mass destruction on his own people and that of a neighboring country, then celebrated the 9/11 attacks while allowing a known al-Qaeda-affiliated leader to pass through his capital and seek sanctuary within his country's borders. This is why the United States is and must be in Iraq.

At this point in the struggle against al-Qaeda—four-plus years into the Iraq war and more than three years since I first came, employing hundreds of Iraqi citizens as a U.S. Department of Defense contractor—we are seeing great progress against our largest enemy: the international Jihadi. The Iraqi people are exhausted with the nihilistic violence of al-Qaeda. As a result, they have turned against the foreign Jihadi terrorists that are the suicide car-bombers. This you can see in the growing security of the city where I now live and in the end of sanctuary for al-Qaeda in Anbar province, its former base of operations.

All Americans should take pride in the willingness of our nation to sacrifice much in the cause against the perpetrators of 9/11 and in support of the Iraqi people's natural desire to be free of our mutual enemy—al Qaeda.[1]

*   *   *

In early fall 2007, the shift in strategic momentum in the war became evident to us on the ground in Iraq. The roads out in al Anbar opened up for our convoys. The Awakening Sunnis had forced the jihadis out of their former safe haven in the desert west of Baghdad. After the construction and ongoing supply by AISG of over fifteen training facilities and bases on the Syrian border and in al Anbar, Abu Ghraib, Baghdad, Najaf, Baquba, and elsewhere, the Iraqi security services began effectively to take control of the fight from U.S. and Coalition forces.

The change came incrementally, but it was undeniably real. Leadership and commitment mean everything in war. The will to stay the course, and the intelligence to adapt without losing focus on the end goal, when most are in doubt and ready to cut and run, are the decisive factors. Think of the forty-five years of the Cold War. In Iraq, the necessary change arrived with U.S. Army General David Petraeus and his media-savvy counterinsurgency strategy. Having written his Princeton doctoral thesis on our military failure in Indochina, Petraeus was a man who had internalized the lessons of Vietnam. He knew that journalistic attitudes were a key to the battle for the American body politic—the second battlefield whenever the U.S. has embarked on war-making in modern times. The "protecting the people" aspect of COIN sounded almost like charity work. But in parallel—and this aspect was much less publicized—Petraeus amped up McChrystal's killing and capture of al-Qaeda operatives and took U.S. combat troops into pitched battles against the Mahdi army in heretofore sacrosanct and densely populated Shiite Sadr City. He would have to kill his way to a solution; there could be no other option given the irreconcilables in AQI and in the Iranian-supported Shiite special groups. But there wasn't going to be a lot of discussion of that angle of the plan in the press.

Military historian Victor Davis Hanson argues that Petraeus is one of the few military leaders in all history to have earned the moniker that served as the title of Hanson's book *The Savior Generals: How Five Great Commanders Saved Wars That Were Lost*. According to Hanson, "Before Petraeus quieted Iraq, 'counterinsurgency' was an abstraction to most of the American people; afterward, the public believed their sons and daughters could defeat far-off insurgents on American terms."[2]

That's high praise but not far from the mark. When I returned to Iraq at the end of 2006, defeat permeated the air. Chatter among civilians in the Green Zone centered on a "Saigon exit." There were conversations about how to keep people from hanging onto the wheels of the Blackhawks (they have wheels, unlike the skids of Vietnam-era Hueys) taking the last Americans out of Baghdad—in other words, whether or not to shoot them off. The U.S. embassy had not issued us a "White Christmas" code—the broadcast of the Bing Crosby song on April 29, 1975, alerted all Americans and those South Vietnamese in the know to go immediately to pre-designated evacuation points[3]—but you almost felt like it was not far off. The Private Security Companies Association of Iraq, of which we were a charter member along with Blackwater, Aegis, DynCorp, Control Risks, and Triple Canopy, had even written such a scenario into its by-laws dealing with closing down the association's offices in Iraq. But when I met General Petraeus in early fall 2007, the cloud of fear had already begun to lift with the impact of the Surge in nearby Baghdad and the rise of the Awakening.

John Olvey, son of a brigadier general who had chaired West Point's social sciences department when Petraeus served on the faculty there, as detailed in *The Fourth Star*,[4] arranged for me to hand deliver a copy of my book to the commander of Multinational Forces–Iraq. After driving down the now secure but formerly infamous Airport Road, we entered massive Camp Victory, housing more than twenty thousand soldiers, adjacent to BIAP. George parked the SUV and we walked across a causeway to an island in the middle of a shallow artificial lake where Saddam supposedly used to fish. We then stepped into al Fao palace, named in commemoration of the titanic battle and turning point in the 1980s Iran-Iraq War—a battle finally won when Baghdad deployed mustard gas on the Iranian troops, forcing them from Iraq's al Fao peninsula just below Basra and back across the Shatt al Arab River into Iran.

The hulking yellow stucco and concrete structure served as head-quarters for U.S. and Coalition forces in Iraq, so it was the nexus of all combat power in the country. The door and foyer, guarded by muscular, sharp-looking Polynesian troops from Tonga—the tiny Pacific island nation's contribution to Bush's "Coalition of the Willing"—immediately debouched into a fifty-foot-high domed chamber with an ornate tiled ceiling dangling expansive gold-plated chandeliers. Typically over the top, the Saddam-style gauche décor, found in all his palaces from Bagh-dad to Babel, seemed to me like a clash of Stalinist wedding-cake gothic gigantism with faux Versailles gilt—with Islamic peaked arches and scribe-work thrown in for good measure. Sweeping staircases flanked the chamber. Out of one of the several doors to the far side of the white marble floor emerged the hyper-fit David Petraeus in camouflaged fatigues with four black inch-wide stars stitched vertically on the chest of his uniform. I spotted his deputy off to the left coming down the stairs—U.S. Army Lieutenant General Ray Odierno, completely bald and six foot six inches tall in his combat boots. This man had led the troops who harshly pacified Saddam's tribal homeland of Tikrit in 2004 in a sort of "gene-pool cleansing."[5]

U.S. Army Colonel Mike Meese, who was on leave from the West Point social sciences department to serve in the Petraeus "brain trust" and whom I had met during my days on the IBM warfighter contract prior to returning to Iraq, introduced me to the general. I handed him a copy of my book. He took a brief look at my photo on the cover standing on the roof of one of our villas overlooking downtown Baghdad cradling my Russian-made Kalashnikov assault rifle. Petraeus then glanced toward Colonel Meese and said with a bit of a mocking bite, drawing out the syllables with his New York accent, "Look, Mike, he's got an *Aaa-Kay!*"

I quickly responded, "Sir, I've got about eight hundred of them. At one point in time, we had over fifteen hundred Iraqis under arms. Now we've just a got a couple hundred security men in our almost one thousand Iraqi workforce."

The tone of the conversation shifted immediately. Several days later, I received a letter from Petraeus on his four-star command letterhead via the military postal service (we picked up the mail regularly in the Green Zone), which to this day I keep framed and hanging on my office wall. He wrote, "Our nation is indebted to the services provided by contractors, and I appreciate your efforts in helping the Coalition bring safety and stability to Iraq."

I would've gone to hell and back for General David Petraeus.

I should have felt the same about Mike Meese at the time. Shortly after the meeting with the Coalition head honcho, we won an award to build the first new Iraqi Army base in Basra. Prior to this intervention by the U.S., the south of Iraq had been primarily a British responsibility. We had to get involved after the situation spun out of control when London reined in the UK army's ability to carry out operations amid fear of casualties. The war was hugely unpopular back in Great Britain, where the media referred to Prime Minister Tony Blair as "Bush's poodle" for supporting the U.S. in taking out Saddam's aggressive dictatorship.[6] The failure of the British to protect the Iraqi people from the predations of the Iranian-allied militias was ironic in light of the arrogance displayed by the Brits earlier in the war. They had continually remarked that we, the Americans, didn't know how to do COIN, whereas they possessed the expertise after Northern Ireland. That was their explanation for why the insurgency roared in the north and not in *their* south of Iraq. The real story was that the south had no al-Qaeda because it contained no Sunni population to harbor them. But once the Iranians understood that the UK had assumed a passive posture, they increased their support for the anti-Coalition, anti-GOI Shia militias in south Iraq.

The next step, therefore, in the progression per the Coalition plan, was standing up in Basra the new Iraqi Army that had begun—on its own merits—to take the fight to the enemy in central and northern Iraq. As AISG hadn't operated in Basra since mid-2006, when we ran the Iraqna cellphone-service office in the city, the company had no readily available network of sources for security, labor, materials, and equipment to set up the site. So we had to mobilize a major convoy with food, water, fuel, cranes, generators, housing materials, workers, and enough security personnel to man the perimeter at the new base. Once down there, we were confident that suppliers of all necessary goods, services, and materials would appear, drawn from the city of Basra, the second largest in Iraq, and from the country's primary seaport, Umm Qasr. And then everything would be cheaper.

The movement convoy set out from Baghdad on the three-hundred-plus mile route from the capital to the job site. Below the central Wasit province, we entered a chaotic void. The road had now crossed into the original UK occupation zone, formerly controlled by the British-commanded Multi-National Division–Southeast (MND-SE), based at Basra airport. The Sadrists had gained control over Maysan province south of Wasit and bordering Iran when the British prematurely turned over political control to the Iraqis in 2006. At one of the checkpoints near Amarah, the provincial capital, Shiite militia–allied police seized the convoy and held all of our Iraqis, a couple Lebanese, and our American site manager, Jim Bob. The convoy pushed the "panic button"—a part of the Tapestry satellite tracking system—that alerted the U.S. Army Corps of Engineers Logistics Movement

Control Center (LMCC) in Baghdad. The LMCC in turn alerted the contractor regional operations center (ROC) run by Aegis nationwide and in the south co-located with the British military command in Basra. In U.S. military-controlled areas, the alarm brought an American quick reaction force (QRF) within thirty minutes, usually less. In Amarah, still a UK area of security responsibility, it brought no response.

Meanwhile, the policemen holding Jim Bob pistol-whipped him. Fortunately the Sadrists knew (or more accurately, believed) that keeping an American hostage would bring the roof down on their heads very quickly when the U.S. military arrived. So the Shiite radicals relented and released the convoy and Jim Bob, missing a front tooth but otherwise physically sound. After just a couple days as unwilling "guests," they continued down the road to Shaiba, about ten miles west of Basra city. The militias, however, now knew our convoy was coming. Because of our low-profile tactics (we looked like locals) we usually did not get hit by IEDs. This was the exception. A roadside explosion damaged our primary generator for the site, but luckily did not wound anyone. So until Jim Bob repaired it—like practically all our American site managers, he could fix anything—he and his guys were without power.

Now came the real problem—our convoy security team had to get back up to Baghdad. We needed them for other missions. Off they went, and this time no American rode along to provide the aura of protection. But the real flaw in their security, though we didn't realize at the time, resided with the British command in Basra. We decided to send the team back up Route 8 on the western side of Iraq nearer to Saudi Arabia. The thought was that route would provide safer passage than the highway along the Iranian border we'd used earlier in the mobilization movement. The return convoy made it only about a hundred miles up the road when a rogue police checkpoint in Samawa, like the earlier one in Amarah, seized the vehicles. Our men pushed the panic button and no one came.

A few days went by with no results through either the Baghdad-based LMCC or the Basra ROC, so I called Colonel Mike Meese. He immediately

directed me to the senior officer in Coalition headquarters for liaison to
MND-SE, who in turn connected me with the MND-SE chief of staff, a
British army colonel named Ryder. I sent email after email, figuring that
it's amazing how much traction you can get when copying someone (Mike
Meese) with the MNF-I command address. The recipient would never
know if Petraeus wasn't watching.... Still, nothing tangible emerged. Our
men sat rotting away in some hell-hole of a jail in south Iraq. Unlike the
first time, with the Sadrists, these rogue police seemed to be just criminals
looking for ransom money we were not going to pay. Getting angrier and
angrier that the British would do nothing for us, I stalked the halls of
Apache raging against perfidious Albion.

So after almost two weeks of intense frustration had passed, I decided
it was time to go to Basra. We chartered a Sky Link flight at BIAP and
loaded our arms and ammo as cargo on an open-bay transport plane. My
ten-man security team and I walked through the metal detectors in the
passenger terminal, then boarded the plane on the tarmac through the
back ramp and sat down next to our weapons.

After landing at Basra international airport on the commercial side
tarmac, I had to make it to the military side, where I had an appointment
with Colonel Ryder. Two Tommies appeared forthwith. Here were two fine
examples of the renowned British soldiers who had fought for and won an
empire that circa World War II encompassed over a quarter of the world's
landmass and a third of its population.

The corporal in charge of my escort asked me what I had in the
rucksack slung over my shoulder. I told them, "Just a couple of .45 pistols—I left the long gun with my security team."

They laughed and the corporal said in a cockney accent, "Don't
mention that to the Iraqis when we go through passenger security." We
did another nonsensical turn through the terminal. And when I didn't
place my bag on the scanner belt and the metal detector went off like a
fire alarm, the soldiers in unison told the Iraqi border police: "He's with
us—not to worry!" Back on the tarmac again, we got in a desert

camouflage Land Rover and drove across the runway to MND-SE headquarters.

The air-conditioning felt good as I sat next to an Aegis representative from the Basra ROC on a leather couch in the chief of staff's office. Basra in September was still quite hot—and miserably humid. Colonel Ryder, a sandy-haired Sandhurst grad who looked like he would be more comfortable on a polo pony, asked, "Ah, so, Mr. Andress, what can we do for you here?"

"Well, you can send a QRF [Quick Reaction Force] up to Samawa and get my people freed," I responded, cutting right to the chase.

The Aegis guy interrupted, "We understand that these are just Iraqis."

The colonel then stated, "Yes, they need to get their own government to intervene, not us."

Feeling the blood rush to my face, I gritted my teeth and said, "These men are serving the Coalition mission, Iraqi or not. Our project in Shaiba is a MNSTC-I contract, and these men are part of that. You as the Coalition authority over Samawa are responsible by contract to respond in support of our activities, especially when under direct threat as is the case here. If we cannot count on your QRF and you abandon my Iraqis, then how can we get the Iraqi Army base built at Shaiba, so urgently required by the mission? More importantly, we will now have a failure of trust with the people we must support and protect and we will all fail as a result."

Colonel Ryder, whom I knew to be under considerable stress from a multitude of demands, given his position, paused, looked at me kindly and thoughtfully, and quietly responded, "You're quite right, let me see what we can do...."

I left elated. I got into a locally provided movement team with my Baghdad bodyguards and went to the job site, which was actually popping along very nicely. The *Basrawi* merchants—famous, pre-Saddam, throughout the Persian Gulf for their trading skills—were practically beating down our doors at Shaiba to sell us whatever we needed. This was going to be easy compared to the Sunni Triangle! Three days later, the Australian "battle group" based at Tallil airfield, home to the four-thousand-year-old Ur Ziggurat and Abraham's traditional birthplace, undertook a "leadership engagement" via cellphone with the commander of the al Khidr police station just south of Samawa. Our people went free after seventeen days in captivity.

✳   ✳   ✳

On October 4, 2007, I wrote another opinion piece for National Review Online, for a column they were calling "The View from the Red Zone." The article was titled "Tipping Point: Where and how to go on in Iraq":

> The recent Blackwater incident in Nusoor Square, not far from our Baghdad headquarters, gives cause to reflect upon the Iraq war in general. As a result of my recently published book—*Contractor Combatants*—the TV networks called for my take on the incident that killed a reported eleven Iraqis, and wounded several more, in late morning rush-hour traffic in downtown Baghdad. Why, how, when, where—the questions came fast and furious live on TV, in a couple cases with CNN and CBS. The latest interview on Fox News brought to light my observation that we're at a tipping point in the war. The threat level is falling off rapidly so those of us involved in security here need to change tactics accordingly.
>
> Gone are the roving suicide car-bombers who, in the dozens, sought out targets in Baghdad, like the State Department convoy that Blackwater was protecting in Eagles Square (the name in English for the traffic rotary where these security contractors got into a firefight with hundreds of civilians caught in the crossfire). I can remember in late 2004, when a logistics convoy I was leading into the second battle of Fallujah crested a highway bridge not far from Nusoor Square, only to

be blocked by the wreckage of two SUVs carrying now-dead USAID workers, framed by a 30-meter-wide scorched circle, centered on the remnants of a massive bomb packed into a Chevrolet Caprice. In the 24 hours that followed that incident, there would be more than ten such car-bomb attacks in the Iraqi capital. This al Qaeda-directed killing would continue on a regular basis for more than two years. With the eradication of the car-bomb factories in al Anbar and the western Sunni suburbs of Baghdad, a process which began to take root in early 2007, those days are now behind us.

The tipping point has arrived, I believe, because the Iraqi Sunnis have turned en masse against al-Qaeda. With al-Qaeda retaliatory bombings of Abu Risha in al Anbar, and with a reconciliation meeting between Shias and Sunnis in Baquba, the capital of Diyala Province—a mixed region where al-Qaeda has fled after being forced out of the Sunni west—there is no turning back. Al-Qaeda is now at war with the very people that must provide the support necessary for the foreign-dominated radical jihadi movement to survive in Iraq. There can be no political victory for al-Qaeda in Iraq now. We just have to keep the pressure on and they will continue to implode.

The war in Iraq is winding down for over two-thirds of the population. There are fewer than 15 insurgent-related incidents a day in Mosul (down from five times that amount a year ago and many of the current incidents are roadside bombs being found before detonation due to information from the local populace). The attacks in Basra are even fewer, especially now that Iran has backed off, realizing that the B-52s are a presidential phone call away. Even though it is the main insurgent target, Baghdad has seen attacks drop by half—and death-squad killings reduced by 75 percent—as the new Iraqi security services take on a more aggressive and present role. The city where I have lived now for a total of almost three years has never been quieter. We will continue to see the occasional spectacular car bomb, but this will have no lasting effect on the general movement toward peace in Iraq.

Now the challenge in Iraq is the path to democracy and the implied task therein of reconciliation between Sunni and Shia, Arab and Kurd. Department of Defense contractors have been critical to the mission here.... The time is drawing near when the role of contractor combatant will fade away, hopefully permanently.

A common joke among the 7,000 or so American and British contractor combatants in Iraq is that we are working our way out of a job. But just as when I became a federal whistle-blower, and lost my job while getting Custer Battles banned from government contracting for fraud, the need for Western contractors in Iraq to be held accountable for criminal violations of the rules of the use of force is critical. This is important not only for justice to be served, but to set an example of the U.S. rule of law for the Iraqi people. And there is a mechanism for this purpose: the Military Extraterritorial Jurisdiction Act (MEJA).

The problem is the new legal status of the contractor combatant in the American way of war. No one has ever been prosecuted under MEJA for war crimes, though it is easy to attack us (I have been referred to as a "mercenary" countless times). In the context of the fog of war, and with the reality of the ease of finding witnesses in Iraq with an agenda against the U.S....This is a process that must be carefully developed....Contractors are serving our country's mission in Iraq; therefore they should not be beyond the law but accountable to the law, and at the same time, fully protected by the law.[7]

*　　　*　　　*

One of the leading indicators for us that the crisis had begun to recede—other than the fact that I could now snatch a catnap or two in the back of my armored car on the return from "zero-dark-thirty" trips out to al Anbar—was the nature of the contracts we were executing. The mission had now moved to second tier work for the Iraqi security services and away from building the bases from which forces conducted combat operations directly against the insurgency. This meant support for the justice system and the security bureaucracy. It also meant that we were taking the police and army to another level of sophistication on the path to self-sufficiency and the exit of U.S. combat forces from Iraq.

Forward Operating Base Justice in Kadhimiya in northwestern Baghdad was to house the Iraqi ministry of justice. CH2M Hill, one of the largest construction firms in the world, won an award to stand up Justice from the U.S. Air Force's Center for Engineering Excellence—yes, even the Air Force was in on the game. In turn, the construction giant subcontracted to AISG to build a series of barracks and office buildings to house the ministry and its supporting police forces. We had already built concrete barracks for CH2M at al Muthana airfield, near where we constructed the Kurdish base in record time at the beginning of the Surge.

Kadhimiya was the location of the tomb of and named for one of the greatest figures in Shia Islam, the Imam Musa al Kadhim, seventh of the twelve figures who make up the historical leadership of Shi'ism. The *mahalla* (city district) attracts an annual pilgrimage of tens of thousands who walk to Kadhim's mausoleum to pay homage. In 2005, the first such procession allowed after the fall of Saddam, who had prohibited the practice, essential to the Shia faith, resulted in the death of over a thousand pilgrims when the false rumor of a suicide bomber in their midst caused a stampede on the al-A'imma bridge. Many plunged to their death, drowning in the Tigris River below.[8]

We could see that bridge just up the river from the job site on the west bank of the Tigris. On the other side of the slowly flowing four-hundred-meter-wide river known in Arabic as the *Nahr al Dijla* stood Adhamiya, an island of pure Sunni in an otherwise Shia population (especially following the ethnic cleansing of 2004–06). Consequently, it was home to a support network for al-Qaeda, now rapidly degrading under the impact of the Surge. The U.S. military had completely surrounded the area with blast walls and closely guarded the perimeter and its few entrance points (walls work—as do all obstacles in military terms—only when patrolled and observed on both sides). As a result, the people of the district got protection and the bad guys inside were starved of external support, and those outside, of safe haven. Every day we experienced the effectiveness of our own walls at Apache and saw the same effect in channeling—controlling—movement and protecting neighborhoods in Baghdad. One can only imagine how a wall across the DMZ and Ho Chi Minh trail could have isolated the Viet Cong from the North's critical succor, as detailed by U.S. Army Colonel (ret.) Harry Summers in *On Strategy*, his retrospective book applying von Clausewitz's principles to the Vietnam conflict.[9]

The riverine divide in geography represented a chasm in religious terms. Adhamiya housed the Abu Hanifa mosque and the tomb of the founder of one of the four schools of orthodox doctrine accepted by the one billion Sunni Muslims worldwide, but not the Shia. And the Imam Kadhim tomb directly underscored the fundamental schism in Islam, for the *Ithna'ashariya* ("Twelver") Shia today consider Kadhim to be the rightful seventh leader of Islam after Mohammed. Sunnis categorically reject that position.

The heart of the Sunni Arab world beats first for the era of the *Rashidun*, the rightly guided deputies of the Prophet Mohammed—the first four leaders, or caliphs, of Islam after the Prophet's death in 632 CE. (It is interesting to note that the leader of the virulently fanatical Islamic State of Iraq and Syria, Abu Bakr al-Baghdadi, almost immediately proclaimed himself "caliph" of the recently captured territory.)[10] The fourth and last

of the *Rashidun* was Ali ibn Abu Talib, cousin and son-in-law of Mohammed, who was assassinated in Kufa, Iraq. Ali's death forced the great schism
in Islam and the name "Shia" originated from the term *Shiat Ali* or the
partisans of the Imam Ali. The Shia broke away from the Sunni on question of the importance of the deputies being of the Prophet's bloodline,
versus the learned of Islam alone deciding through *ijma* (consensus) who
would serve as next leader of the earth's Muslim faithful upon the death
of a caliph. After the martyrdom of the Prophet's grandson Hussein (the
son of Ali) in central Iraq, the Shia continued to demand that caliphs be
selected from among Mohammed's descendants only. The Sunni (Orthodox) went the non-hereditary way—at least as far as the Prophet was
concerned, for when a caliph died his sons and their sons and so forth
tended to follow in his stead thereafter until violence or the lack of a male
heir disrupted the line.

A significant majority of the Islamic world, including the Wahhabi of
Saudi Arabia and al-Qaeda's jihadis, followed the Sunni path. The Sunnis
were not the majority in Iraq, though, where there were many more Shia
Arabs—the Shia were three times greater in population than each of the
next two Muslim ethno-religious groups: the Sunni Arabs and the Kurds.
Thus Baghdad, once the capital of the Sunni Abbasid caliphate, the greatest Arab empire in history, stretching from Italy to Central Asia and lasting
five hundred years (750–1258 CE), ironically was now in majority-Shia
Iraq. Osama bin Laden openly strived to recreate this very caliphate
through his jihad to defeat the West and its minions in the Islamic world.[11]

Many Sunnis had the greatest trouble accepting that they were in the
minority in Iraq. Baghdad police colonel Talal, one of our advisors who
was the biggest Kurd I ever met—about 6 foot 3 inches, 230 pounds, dark,
and handsome—came into my office one afternoon to talk about security
in and around Kadhimiya and FOB Justice. As he sat down, Tony joined
us and began translating for full clarity.

Talal started out, "You know, Mr. Carter, the biggest problem we have
in that area is *Jaish al Mahdi* [the army of the Mahdi, Moqtada Sadr's

Iranian-supported militia] for it is a Shia area and the Iranians control the situation there. They are the biggest threat to your operations."

Knowing where this was going from past experience with the good colonel, I asked, "Iran is the biggest threat to us in Kadhimiya or in general?"

"In general," the Sunni Kurd (90-plus percent of Kurds are Sunni) answered.

"Come on, Talal, you know that's not true. The real problem for us is al-Qaeda; that's who are primarily doing all the killing out there. You just don't like it now that the Shia are running the show because we have democracy in Iraq."

"You're right about the Shia. Why is it that only their religious leaders take a political role?" he asked somewhat rhetorically. Not expecting an answer, Talal just wanted to use that statement to indict the Shia. For many Sunni, and Iraqis in general, this all boiled down to fear of religiously oriented oppression.

But I had an answer: "That's because Saddam suppressed the Shia so that the only organizations they possessed were associated with their *husseiniya* [Shiite religious centers named for the martyr Imam Hussein]. They are the only known leaders left to the Shia."

Surprised, Talal mumbled something to Tony, who translated, "Talal understands now."

Talal regained his footing quickly though, and rejoined, "Why do the Shia control in a democracy? There are more Sunni in Iraq than Shia!"

Given that blatantly false but unshakeable belief, I could never win this endless, circular argument with Talal until a few months later when his wife, Susan, one of our lawyers, finally told him when we were all together that I was correct that *"al Shi'iaat al akhthariya fi Iraq."* After Sunni rule of Iraq since the Middle Ages, even educated Kurds who sided with the Coalition had tremendous trouble acceding to the legitimacy of a Shiite national government. One can only imagine how difficult it was for the Sunni Arabs who had actually held the reins of power for more than a millennium (during the Ottoman empire they still served as the elite among the indigenous people of Mesopotamia, even though subordinate to the Sunni Turks). This was at the core of why so many fought long and hard against the rise of democracy in Iraq.

The well-connected Talal was right, however, to believe that the main hazard to us *in Kadhimiya* did involve the Iranian-supported *Jaish al Mahdi* (JAM) the army of the Mahdi. But it wasn't a physical threat so much as a business challenge. As usual, projects in the war zone started out with hair-on-fire immediacy. In good faith, we mobilized onto the site before our subcontract was fully negotiated with CH2M Hill. It took a lot of time for paperwork to emerge out of the large corporations. The problem arose when we went to order stress "T" panels, a pre-manufactured material made of reinforced concrete, for the roofs of the buildings at FOB Justice. Unfortunately, only one functioning factory in Baghdad manufactured the panels—the others were bombed out—and we didn't have the time to import. We had learned that the plant was controlled by Sadr and his "army of the Mahdi." (In Shia belief, the Mahdi is the occulted Twelfth Imam whose return to an earthly manifestation will coincide with the Second Coming of Jesus and the Day of Judgment.)

We felt sure that the JAM wanted to put us out of business, at the least. So how could we price the panels, which in the quantity the project required would cost millions of dollars and might not get delivered on time or at all, causing us to fail and never get another government-backed contract? The factory had already shown us, on our earlier project in Muthana, that they would use their monopoly to jam us when they could. We had managed to slip by that through a straw buyer (someone not associated with the Coalition), but now the Shia militants were on to us at FOB Justice.

Problem presented, resolution developed—after all we called ourselves American-Iraqi *Solutions* Group. Carlos Flores, our chief operations officer and a civil engineer with decades of experience, came up with a new roof design using a peaked structure and fiber board that would last as long as the stress "T" panels; weigh less, thereby requiring less of a foundation; and facilitate better drainage from the winter rains—all of which we presented to CH2M with the passed-on cost savings and an explanation of the situation with the concrete plant and Sadr.

The CH2M Iraq country manager, a retired Navy Seabee officer, seemed to agree in principle and then presented us with a contract that left the roof design undetermined. This was a real red flag, as it meant we were financially exposed, as we couldn't know our costs. Like almost all our contracts in Iraq, this was firm, fixed price, which meant if we estimated correctly AISG made money and if not, then we lost money. No one's in business to lose money. We couldn't depend on getting the "T" panels from Sadr's people. And we were a cash-flow business without any source of credit to cover losses. We had only one client—the U.S. government—so if we failed to deliver in a timely manner and defaulted for cause then we had a great chance of never getting any further work in Iraq, which would mean the end of AISG. Plus, I didn't like doing business with the Sadrists anyway—it was counter-productive to the mission. CH2M refused to modify the contract. They offered us three choices: accept the original stress "T" panel roof; sign the agreement with the roof design undetermined; or demobilize off the site. So we left FOB Justice, never to return. CH2M finished the work by going around us to one of our Iraqi subcontractors; they got it done late.

This outcome was a perfect example of what it was like working as a contractor in the war zone of Iraq. We had to simultaneously overcome political-military, business, and technical challenges. *And* stay profitable.

On a more fortunate note, and as further evidence of the rapid development of the Iraqi security services, we won a bid to construct a building for training Ministry of Defense bureaucrats—the civil servants required to manage and sustain a modern 250,000 man army. The steel-framed, pre-engineered building, which would have fit in on any American military base, certainly contrasted with the adjacent Ministry of Defense (MOD) headquarters shoe-horned into one of the Saddam family's concrete, marble, and gilt palaces now inside the Green Zone's heavily guarded perimeter. We snapped the training facility together in no time, with wall-to-wall carpeting, drop ceilings, and air conditioning. The contracting officer, John Jensen, was great to work with, mostly. (I ran into him several years later near Waziristan on the Afghan side of the border with Pakistan—it's a small world, the war business.)

The building's completion was a big deal, however. The groundbreaking included a nice sign stating "Built by American-Iraqi Solutions Group." The Iraqi minister of defense, Abdel Qadir Obeidi, attended, along with Lieutenant General Martin Dempsey, the commander of the Multi-National Security Training Command–Iraq (MNSTC-I), later to rise to the most senior position in the American military, chairman of the Joint Chiefs of Staff. I had put on my best suit in Baghdad, "UPS brown," supposedly Italian-made according to the label, and given to me by Iraqi military police Colonel Firas, another one of our advisors. The jacket almost covered up the bulge of the Colt .45 on my hip.

I got to watch Spicer's Aegis security guys in action. They circled around General Dempsey in an otherwise Iraqi crowd of mixed military and civilians milling about in the courtyard between our building and MOD HQ on a beautiful fall day of pale blue skies and palm trees bursting with sweet dates. And they watched me back, not exactly sure who the hell this American was—not with them, but obviously armed. The Aegis bodyguards would have fit in a James Bond movie, particularly in the starring role. I guess they had put their best-looking guys on a high-profile client such as Dempsey. They said nothing to me, and I did the same to them.

Of course, Abdel Qadir was standing on his home turf, and he acted that way. So I walked up to him in the respectful space allowed to him and the MNSTC-I commander.

"*As-salaam allaikum, siyeedi wazir!*" I greeted the defense minister. "The peace of Allah be upon you, mister minister!"

He responded reflexively, "*Walakum salaam.*" ("And peace upon you.")

I then said: "*Rakhmat-allah, wa barakato…*" the rest of the greeting, not often spoken by foreigners, which means, "And the mercy of Allah and his blessing."

He smiled and immediately said in fluent English, "Your company constructed this building. Thank you." The man did not miss anything. General Dempsey leaned in on our conversation.

"Yes, sir," I said to the minister. "We have built and operated a lot of bases for the Iraqi military, including the East Fallujah base during the second battle in December 2004. I remember that you were there, in command."

"Those were challenging times, that's when we started the Iraqi Army we see today."

He then turned to Dempsey at his side and said, "He must have been a soldier, yes?"

The American general looked at me and I nodded affirmatively. He replied to the man leading the army of a nation in an existential war for its future, "He was a soldier once but now works as a soldier in a different way…."

CHAPTER 8

SADDAM'S YELLOWCAKE

"WE'VE GOT A MAN SHOT, CARTER," Tony stated flatly. He had just walked into my wood-paneled corner office with the sandbags still stacked outside the floor-to-ceiling windows, allowing just enough space at the top to tell if it was day or night. He continued, "Our first supply convoy into Besmaya got ambushed in Narwan, a town just after the Diyala River bridge [over a major eastern tributary that met the Tigris south of Baghdad] on the way to the Iraqi base."

"How bad?" I asked, a bit stunned. "Since Baghdad and Anbar turned so quiet and our convoys out there are now milk runs, I'd hoped we'd be finished with the bloodshed, Tony." This was December 2007. It had been several months since anyone had gotten hurt for the company, other than that time our site manager was pistol-whipped by a rogue Sadrist police officer on the way to Basra. Earlier in the week, just before this firefight at Narwan, Tony had announced over five hundred missions without anyone from the company being killed. This contrasted sharply with the period between my firing and our takeover of AISG (July 2005–October 2006), when the company suffered more than sixty employees killed on the job.

"According to the report I just got over the cell phone, as the convoy was driving through Narwan several men fired on the escort suburbans and our fifteen-truck convoy. Of course, our guys opened up in return with the PKs [Soviet-design, belt-fed machine guns that threw rounds the size of a finger downrange at a rate of seven hundred a minute]. The bad guys didn't expect it and broke off quickly, but Adel [one of our longtime Iraqi security men] got hit, but in the butt, so he should be all right." Tony couldn't conceal his smile.

I laughed out of relief, "You're messing with me, he got shot in the butt?!"

"Sure enough, so I guess he'll be fine. The convoy made it to the camp without any loss. They're taking him over to the American Army clinic at nearby FOB Hammer [a brigade-size combat base bordering and securing the newly developing Iraqi base at Besmaya]."

"OK, well, how do we make it through Narwan next time; it straddles the only viable truck-capable road on that side of the city, doesn't it? We've got tons of materials and equipment we've got to get into Besmaya, hundreds of truckloads." Our contract at Besmaya involved the first significant new Iraqi Army base on the eastern side of Baghdad, dead center of Tehran-allied Sadr territory on the edge of the flat, featureless desert stretching over a hundred miles to the Iranian border. We'd won contracts for the construction of a warehouse, rifle range, and medical clinic in what was to be the major armor-training facility for the Iraqi Army. Progress in the development of a modern military for the new Iraq had taken another major step forward. Once the Iraqi government fielded properly maintained and operated main battle tanks, no internal oppositional groups would have the capacity to withstand a firefight with Baghdad's security forces. Armor would also serve to deter aggression from Iraq's many less-than-friendly neighbors.

"We've got some connections into Narwan from our past work and we're now employing people from the area for construction at Besmaya. So I'll see what we can come up with," Tony answered.

Sure enough, Tony found a way into Narwan. From that time on, whenever one of our convoys entered the Shia town, a white Toyota sedan would take the lead from a side road, as coordinated earlier by our ops center. That signaled the gunmen that we were all "friends," and we never had another problem. We'd put a number of Narwanians on our security payroll—an investment that paid off, time and time again, especially on probably the most dangerous large-scale logistics move of the entire Iraq War, post-invasion.

But first we had to get through a mobilization to the al Kasik Iraqi military base just outside Mosul, where the last remnants of al-Qaeda had fled after the Surge and the Sahwa had forced them out of al Anbar, Baghdad, and Diyala provinces. Al Kasik was the largest Iraqi Army base in the north and represented the singular success of the Arab Shia–controlled government in integrating the Indo-European-speaking Kurds into the national security services. The U.S. Joint Contracting Command–Iraq (JCC-I), our primary interface with the Pentagon, had awarded us the operations and maintenance contract for the U.S. military training team at the base. Strangely, even though it was hundreds of miles distant from the nearest sea, a Navy submariner commanded this infantry training mission.

Our mobilization team departed Baghdad on a four-hundred-mile route to the east around still-dangerous Mosul. The route, well known to us from our days running the Mosul Public Safety Academy (2004–06), then entered autonomous and safe Kurdistan before turning to the north of Mosul and then back to the west, dropping in on the Iraqi base on the west side of the sprawling metropolis, third largest in Iraq by population. The problem was that our team got in a hurry and George, who was leading the convoy, decided to cut it short—skipping the usual overnight in Irbil, Kurdistan—and headed closer to Mosul. Then he ran into a roadblock on the convoy's self-chosen new route.

From Fort Apache, we were watching the convoy move in real time on Tapestry, the satellite monitoring system transmitted through the contractor-operated Logistics Movement Control Center to our ops center via secure website. Several of the vehicles carried tracking devices so they would appear on a map displaying the Iraqi road network, each route coded by the U.S. military in different colors according to threat level. The ratings ranged from green "good-to-go"—seen only in Kurdistan—to yellow "caution," meaning low-level insurgent activity, to red "medium risk," to black "no go." Next thing we knew, our convoy had shifted onto a black route headed straight into Mosul. Tony picked up the satellite phone and called George to find out what the hell was going on. George quickly told him that they were "in contact" and then hung up—with automatic weapons fire crackling in the background.

The next report came an hour later: two of our people had been wounded and part of the convoy had broken off to take them to a hospital in Irbil for treatment. A couple hours after that, the rest of the convoy reached al Kasik and began to set up our work site. I concluded then that I needed to travel up to the site to ensure that everyone was OK and that our people knew they were always connected to us at Apache even though they were hundreds of miles away. We looked at a map to determine the route. Rock, our recently hired Jordanian-American deputy security director—an Army infantry combat veteran who had left Triple Canopy to join AISG, said that he knew the best and fastest way. He advised that we head up to Baiji, the oil refinery town north of Samarra, and then get on Pipeline Road, which ran straight up past Mosul and on to the Turkish border. From there, Iraq's sole northern oil-export pipeline, often interdicted by insurgent attacks, went to the port of Ceyhan on the Mediterranean for shipment worldwide.

So we left the next morning at "oh-dark-thirty" (about 4:30 a.m.). As we got to the northern outskirts of Baghdad we had to pass through the three concentric belts of Iraqi-manned checkpoints intended to protect the capital. Approaching the first checkpoint, Rock—who was controlling the vehicles via radio—noticed and anticipated that the guards would be asleep. So we breached protocol and blew right through, as we did the second set of mandatory stops. But as we passed through the third, our four-suburban convoy finally roused one of the guards who stumbled out into our wake and took a wild shot at us as our vehicles accelerated away in the darkness. What Rock had done surprised me, but I put the thought away and focused on the hundreds of miles before us.

Six hours later we arrived on the road leading into al Kasik. Running along both sides of the blacktop were Iraqi men in t-shirts, underwear, and sandals. These were recruits stripped of any baggage and extra clothing a mile before entering the base to ensure they had not strapped on explosives. A couple days earlier AQI had exploded a suicide bomber next to the main gate. As we cruised along, we could look off to the right (the east), and see the mountains of Kurdistan. The scenery had a dark, almost black-green tint—quite the contrast with the sandy-beige desert of the south. The army division at al Kasik constituted the only major unit in Iraq with a joint Kurdish and Sunni Arab contingent. The unit was working well with American forces fighting the last remnants of al-Qaeda hiding out in densely urban Mosul. The city's population was mostly Sunni Arabs, but the remainder was quite polyglot, with Kurds, Turcomen, Assyrians, and even more esoteric groups in the surrounding Iraqi province called Ninewa (Nineveh in the Old Testament).

The attack on our convoy to Kasik had been part of the last stand of one AQI safe haven. Once we entered the base, I offered my gratitude and congratulations along with hugs and handshakes to the twenty or so AISG men who had braved the passage across an urban battlefield undeterred and completed the mission. Otherwise, because of the tight mobilization time schedule allowed by JCC-I, our contracting officer might have placed us in default, once again putting AISG at risk as an ongoing concern.

Then I pulled the mobilization convoy commander aside.

"George, *ahooya* [brother], how are Ayman and Iyad?" I asked.

"They are both doing good," he answered. "Ayman [a Baghdadi Kurd who had been with AISG practically since the beginning] has an injury to his hand, a bullet wound, and will need surgery. But the doctors are saying it will be okay. Iyad got some glass from the car window shattering in his face, so he will be okay also."

My next question: "What happened?"

"I know you told me not to go into Mosul at all costs and that was the plan, but when we got to the split in the road, the U.S. Army had a tank there and soldiers were directing us the other way. It looked like there was some sort of IED explosion up the road we planned to take. There was a huge traffic jam and we had to go toward the city; there was no turning back. The soldiers would not let us go any other way. I talked to them. As soon as we got into Mosul, I started noticing Wahhabi-looking men with long beards everywhere. Then the bullets started to fly out of—it seemed like—every single window of all the buildings. We returned fire and tried to get out of the ambush zone, but the trucks were too slow. I can't believe that all of us were not killed. Finally we made it out."

"*Alhamdulillah* [praise to God]," I said to the Lebanese-American. "Great work, George. I'm just glad we can now source everything locally from Kurdistan and do not need to go into Mosul again."

After a couple hours on the site, we jumped back into the vehicles and headed south for the six-hour return. Everything went smoothly. We got to Samarra, where we had to pick up one of our suburbans we had left at an Iraqi Army checkpoint after it had overheated. Then we hit the first of the Baghdad security belts and immediately Iraqi soldiers surrounded us, weapons drawn, demanding we get out of the vehicles. Not a pleasant experience, having multiple machine guns pointed at you. I jumped out; Rock tried to get me to get back in the armored vehicle. I walked up to the checkpoint commander and asked, "*Leish entu twagofoon-na?*" ("Why are you stopping us?")

The commander's translator answered in quite good English, "There were four suburban car-bombers who ran the checkpoints this morning without stopping and we understand they will be coming back into Baghdad and your vehicles fit that description."

Knowing now why we were being stopped—I would castigate Rock about this later, but not too seriously, as we had to remain aggressive—I emphatically demanded, "*Wen al-haqi?* Where is my right? I am an American with the Department of Defense, this is my security. We are able to go now...you are prohibited from stopping us! This is the *law.*"

The commander looked confused and started back to call higher up his chain of command when he saw an American Humvee patrol drive onto a side road nearby. He then directed me to go over and get the patrol commander to confirm my status. It had been a long day; by the time we got back to Apache the mid-winter sun had long since set.

As a footnote to the mission, I strived to ensure that the security team conducted an after-action review (AAR), as we called it in the Army, whenever they engaged in a firefight or had some other significant incident. This was a sort of Chinese communist self-criticism session, where leaders specifically got to admit their mistakes and to hear—from even the lowliest member of the team—how they had screwed up and how they could have done better. I used AARs especially to check training and confirm that everyone was following the rules in the use of force and understood that this was serious business. Consequently, our security force knew that their individual actions received close attention from the very top of our organization. So a few days after our return, we all gathered together, including the al Kasik mobilization security and my protection detail.

From the start, I felt a tension rarely seen among our security force. A rumble of anger rippled below the surface. And as I looked across the Apache team room while George repeated what he had told me up in al Kasik, I could sense the source of the ire. Arman, a baby-faced PSD (personnel security detail, the new term of art for warzone bodyguards), was exhibiting a conflicted expression of outrage and dismay. He appeared obviously agitated. I looked directly at him in the seated ranks of over thirty Iraqis and asked, *"Indkum akthar su'al?"* ("Do you all have another question?")

He stood up and said in Arabic with an accusatory tone, "Why did you leave us at the checkpoint in Samarra? We could have disappeared!"

Arman had been in the suburban that had overheated on the way to Mosul. Samarra was a Sunni Triangle city infamous for the February 2006 AQI attack on the Shiite Golden Mosque that had precipitated the sectarian war that had only now begun to subside. And yet Rock and I had trusted that the Iraqi Army at the checkpoint where we left Arman and two other PSDs would not turn on them just because our guys were Shia. The Iraqi Army, well trained and vetted by the U.S. military, was nonsectarian. For example, Abdel Qadir, the minister of defense, was a Ramadi-born Sunni Arab, whereas his army balanced a majority of Shia and Kurd. Now our security men would learn the same reality. This represented great progress for us and for Iraq.

After we got through that lesson, a discussion began about the traffic situation in Mosul that had forced the convoy into the city. Rabih, one of our top Lebanese security managers who had come over to us from the Virginia security firm MVM, began to talk about how he got blocking vehicles to move by discharging his AK in the air. Not long before the AAR, he had realized that one of his fellow MVM PSD teams had almost killed me in a friendly fire incident in front of a Green Zone checkpoint several years before, in mid-2004.[1] He then told me, apologetically, how he had criticized the first shooter—a fellow Lebanese—for missing me, saying, "I would have got him [meaning me]." I laughed and said, "No way."

But now I turned on Rabih a bit abruptly: "What did you say? You shoot in the air! Where do those bullets land? On the heads of innocent civilians, possibly…We do not shoot in the air; we only fire when we need to kill someone who is threatening us. If I find out about anyone shooting in the air again, you will be fired!"

✳　　✳　　✳

Now that we could flow materials, equipment, and personnel in and out of Besmaya as the result of our safe passage through Narwan, the next project came much easier. With the new supply chain mastered, the rest would follow pretty much as a matter of course. We needed to construct, supply, maintain, and feed a base for U.S. Department of Energy scientists and their military security team at Tuwaitha, the Iraqi nuclear weapons research facility just twelve miles south of Baghdad. That didn't seem far, but it was located in the "Triangle of Death." Utilizing his well-worn strategy of ethnic cleansing and population transfer, Saddam had created a zone dominated by Sunni tribes. This area, formerly Shia Arab like practically all of Iraq south of Baghdad, included the towns of Mahmudiya, Iskandariya, Yusifiya, and Salman Pak, in which he placed the crown jewel of his weapons of mass destruction program.

One can get a feeling for how bad this area was at the height of the insurgency from journalist Jim Frederick's *Black Hearts*, about a unit of the 101st Airborne Division's 502nd Infantry Regiment that the Triangle of Death nearly consumed in 2005–06. Overstretched and under tremendous pressure to secure this al-Qaeda safe haven, members of the unit committed one of the worst war crimes of the entire conflict in Iraq: raping and killing members of a local family.[2] They then had a checkpoint completely overrun by insurgents.[3] By late 2007, however, the Surge and the Awakening had opened the door for us to be able to get the camp at Tuwaitha done.

The work required involved housing for six hundred personnel, including a hundred scientists and their staff, along with a reduced company of armored infantry detached from FOB Hammer next to Besmaya consisting of about one hundred men and ten or so Bradley fighting vehicles. These numbers signified a serious combat unit, reflecting the priority of the mission and the still high, though receding, threat level of the surrounding Triangle of Death. Brigade command in FOB Hammer had sliced the company there out of the 3rd Infantry Division's 1st Battalion of the 15th Infantry (World War II hero Audie Murphy's unit)—the same regiment I had served with when in the Army almost twenty years earlier. It was neat when Rock got their first sergeant to give me a unit coin emblazoned with the motto: "Can Do!" Even cooler was the name "Task Force Dragon," the symbol of the regiment from its more than twenty years of service in China, beginning with the Boxer Rebellion at the turn of the twentieth century.[4] A ring around the edge of the bronze coin listed the bases the task force operated out of, including the one AISG had built at Tuwaitha: "Combat Outpost Cache."

✶   ✶   ✶

The name Cache derived from what Saddam had stored at Tuwaitha: 550 metric tons of yellowcake uranium, enough low-grade material, if enriched, to create approximately fourteen Hiroshima-size nuclear bombs. When traveling down to the Tuwaitha site, the first thing one noticed— after passing through a wasteland with a couple weakly manned police checkpoints—were the ninety-foot berms that backed the rear of the camp. I trudged up the steep manmade ridge, which stood out starkly against the flat surrounding desert, to look over the edge. The immediately visible smashed concrete dome identified the site as the French-supplied Osiraq nuclear reactor, caved in on June 7, 1981, by Israeli F-16 fighter-bombers that easily avoided the protective dirt walls. Saddam had announced that this site would begin the drive for the first Arab atom bomb. Tel Aviv took him at his word and resoundingly pre-empted that development.[5] The view from the top, hazy in a dusty desert day, was to the jagged remnants of the reactor amid tall berms framing a decades-old scene surreal in its apocalyptic finality.

Part of our work at Cache included providing static security for the storage sites of the uranium. This protection was not so much against insurgents as *for* hapless potential looters. Right after the invasion, locals, as they had in much of Iraq, pillaged the facility. At Cache they stole barrels containing radioactive uranium; many were sickened as a result of their ignorance. The universally recognizable yellow and black radiation warnings appeared all over the bombproof concrete bunkers, with their ripped-open steel doors now dangling from their hinges. When I visited the storage areas the first time, it jolted me back to a 1995 visit to the Chernobyl exclusion zone north of Kiev, Ukraine, where I had escorted a couple of U.S. scientists interested in helping remediate the environmental disaster. This was the last place on earth *I* would want to loot.

Other contract requirements involved feeding the scientists and the troops. Patrols braved the roads from other outposts just so they could eat the food prepared by our well-trained chefs. We even ran a jazz-style twenty-four-hour coffee bar with internet hookups. Those who want to criticize how well the troops lived on base or ate in Iraq have a point in the case of the "fobbits" (troops stationed in the Green Zone or other large forward operating bases) who got fat on the good KBR fare. But for the soldiers out in the field and humping seventy or more pounds of body armor in 120-degree heat, the better we could ease the challenges outside the wire with tasty food and reminders of home, the better we could live up to our obligations as a nation for due care of these intrepid volunteers.

In early 2008, after we had been on the job for several months seamlessly supplying COP Cache, a senior contracting officer for JCC-I approached us about a logistics movement from Tuwaitha without telling us any details. We said, yes, of course. Although we never saw any paperwork other than from our contracting command, this turned out to be a U.S. Defense Intelligence Agency project: the door-to-door transport of every last speck of yellowcake uranium at the Tuwaitha nuclear weapons complex to Baghdad International Airport. It would be a highly dangerous move—transporting the densely heavy material in over one thousand barrels in 140 truckloads over four nights during a period of two weeks.

DIA had observed the way that we did business. They understood that moving the material with an all-military convoy would increase the likelihood of attack. This was an especially valid concern given that the route to the airport was via AQI- and Iranian-allied territory out of the Triangle of Death and then along the eastern flank of Sadr City via Narwan. The consequences if radioactive material were scattered about an Iraqi road after an ambush or simply an accident could substantially set back the progress of the Surge and Awakening that was only now solidifying for the Coalition and the Iraqi government. Given the high volume of traffic and dense population on the route, the entire world would know of the failure to execute as soon as the sun rose at the end of the night the Americans spilled Saddam's yellowcake.

This AISG mission highlighted a revolution in the American art of war. The U.S. was successfully prosecuting the Iraq War through extensive use of private military contractors in high-risk areas to execute any and almost all work that did not require the special and very expensive training required for the limited number of available soldiers. Here in the uranium move, however, the use of contractors went even further. The highest levels of Central Command in charge of the entire war effort out of Tampa, Florida, controlled this critical contract.[6] The U.S. Army could have easily provided the trucking, as they did provide the security for each movement. (Eight heavily armed and armored Humvees accompanied each convoy.) But after observing our relationships with the surrounding tribes, developed over years of employing and paying their members millions of dollars, DIA wisely advised Tampa to do this mission with contractors. Why? First of all, it made for a lower-profile move. Our trucks would draw less attention than a U.S. military convoy would. But most importantly, our connections to the civilians along the route would ensure their buy-in for the move, and thereby further guarantee security.

We rented Swedish-manufactured and Iraq-ubiquitous Scania tractor trailers from the three tribal groupings on the route—two Shia tribes aligned with the anti-American firebrand Moqtada al Sadr and one al-Qaeda-leaning Sunni tribe. Then Tony gathered senior representatives from these tribes in the Green Zone during every movement of the nuclear material, with the unspoken but implied warning that if something happened to the convoys the tribal leaders would end up in Gitmo. The value of the trucks would itself have kept the tribes from allowing an attack. We rented four or five new tractor trailers capable of carrying twenty-five tons, each costing more than $100,000, from each tribe. And all our contracts for trucking, not just for yellowcake transport but in general, mandated that the truck owners self-insure, which meant that if something happened to the vehicles along the way—including being blown or shot up—then the owner took the loss, not us. (The truckers built this risk into the rental price, which enabled us to see how the local market estimated threat levels on different routes.) So when we moved along the route, each tribe in its respective territory positioned its people looking out (watching for threats) from the road traveled by the convoy instead of looking in (watching for the chance to attack). That's what you call "buy-in" by the people in support of the mission—the end game for the counterinsurgency that we won in the Iraq War.

After weeks of training and preparation by AISG in coordination with the Army, the yellowcake transport went off without a hitch. Our locally rented trucks, driven by Filipino drivers hired by us and vetted by DIA, which unfortunately had mandated "no Iraqis," delivered the uranium to Baghdad International Airport. The U.S. Air Force then flew it to the joint Anglo-American base in the Diego Garcia archipelago in the Indian Ocean. From there, the yellowcake went via ship to a breeder reactor in Canada for processing into fuel for U.S.-based nuclear reactors. As I understand it, the Iraqi government received $10 million for the purchase. No matter the debate about WMD as a pretext for invasion, the world could not trust Saddam with yellowcake uranium—a precursor for nuclear weapons—which AISG helped remove, in the most significant warzone logistics operation ever executed by a contractor.

CHAPTER 9

THE RAID

BAGHDAD'S STABILIZATION achieved growing solidity once the last bastions of the Sadrist movement became targets of the Maliki government, when the Iraqi security forces went operational on a national scale. This development followed on extensive U.S. efforts to recruit and train the now Shia-dominated Iraqi Army and police force. Sadr City, within easy rocket and mortar range of the Green Zone, had continued to be a problem, with areas denied to U.S. access because of Maliki's sectarian loyalties. The Iraqi prime minister gave approval for the cleanup of the densely populated, primarily Shiite slum of over two million people only in early 2008—after it had been a no-go area for Coalition ground troops for five years. As soon as the Shia-led government allowed American forces to enter the urban sprawl named for Moqtada's martyred father, Army engineers constructed a blast-wall barrier with U.S.-controlled access points around a large section of southwest Sadr City.

From 2004 until the enclosure of Sadr City, Shia insurgents had regularly launched rockets and mortars—supplied primarily by Iran—from this area into the U.S. military–protected Green Zone that provided the buffer for the largest American embassy in the world. Compounding the risks from these Iran-facilitated attacks—and underlining the lawlessness of the national capital—Iraqis would celebrate each victory of their highly competitive national soccer team by shooting their AK-47 automatic assault rifles. During the Coalition Provisional Authority, L. Paul Bremer had allowed each household to possess one assault rifle for self-defense, a policy that continued after Iraqi sovereignty returned in mid-2004. This policy resulted in massive firearms displays of literally thousands of high-velocity 7.62 mm rounds fired into the air simultaneously, with seemingly all of them angled to rain steel on the Green Zone—home not only to the American Embassy but also to the Iraqi government and national parliament. These celebratory shootings ended only in 2007, when Maliki's *Fard al Qanoon* (Enforcing the Law) program asserted Iraqi government control over local security in the capital city *mahallaat* (neighborhoods).

Even as the threat from Sunni Arab al-Qaeda in Iraq diminished in 2007, the Iranians continued to stir the pot. The *al-Quds* (Jerusalem) paramilitary special forces controlled by the millionaire mullahs of Tehran infiltrated Iraq under several guises, including as pilgrims to the great Shia shrines of Karbala and Najaf. Iran supplied explosively formed penetrators (EFPs) that shot a molten slug of metal able to pierce all armor except the frontal glacis of an M-1 main battle tank—and EFPs could and did cripple even these huge tanks by striking their sides or bottoms. The use of these weapons demonstrated that the U.S. was fighting a proxy war with Iran on the streets of Iraq over several bloody years. Extreme elements connected to the Iran-allied Sadr made deadly use of the anti-armor mines, and there were several months when EFPs killed the largest number of U.S. troops, especially around Baghdad.[1] Down south, the Sadrists launched rockets from Iran into UK army positions. Iranian revolutionary guards kidnapped fifteen British sailors off the Iraqi side of the Shatt al Arab waterway dividing the two ancient enemies. The word from London: hunker down and prepare to demobilize to Iraqi control as quickly as possible. By early 2008, the armed and radical partisans of Moqtada Sadr's Shia militia dominated Basra City. No longer could amorous couples walk the city's cornice at the confluence of the mighty Euphrates and Tigris Rivers, and women had to cover their hair with the *hijab,* if not wear the full-body *abaya.*

Al-Qaeda might be on the ropes, but for U.S. troops the war continued. Now the focus had shifted to shutting down the Shia militias. The hunt in Baghdad for the support networks of the Sadrist groups, however, misfired in its zeal.

*   *   *

The buzz of my cell phone ringing woke me. I looked at the time, 1:15 a.m, and registered the number, AISG ops in Baghdad. My first thought: "This cannot be good." And sure enough, it was not good.

I answered and my brother Kiffer, who recently had joined the company to run a due diligence and security project for the DOD Task Force for Business and Stability Operations, said, "The Army is raiding Apache and they have Tony and George tied up. They need to get into the safe in your room. What's the combination? We're in your bathroom right now."

When I was deciding to come back to Iraq to take over the company, I had known the one thing that would undermine my ability to perform under the stress of the war zone—combined with turning around a near-bankrupt business—was extended separation from my wife and two children: Callie, ten years old, and Henry, six at the time.

First of all, my wife Tanya, who had just finished her second Ph.D. in theoretical mathematics at George Washington University, told me, "No, we've already lived through that before and I can't take it again. You cannot go back to Iraq!"

After a great deal of introspection I responded, "I have to. The company will fail, the mission is failing. I need you and the kids to come with me. You'll live in Amman, Jordan, and I'll come see you at least a couple times a month."

Not an easy discussion, nor an easy decision. In the end, we have a strong marriage, so Tanya agreed to venture with me to the Middle East. When it came time to return home to the U.S. in 2009, neither my wife nor my children wanted to leave Amman. So I guess the plan worked out all right.

Consequently, the night of the raid I was in Jordan, having just flown in from Iraq that very day. We did all our banking in Amman, so I could kill two birds with one stone: take care of business and get to see the family. Being with them was a stress reliever, mostly, but life in the capital of Jordan served up its own challenges. Tanya had just moved us into a villa near the U.S. embassy after our earlier apartment's ceiling had collapsed under a foot of snow on the roof. Amman, at an altitude of about four thousand feet, actually got snow almost every year. The first night in the new villa, about 4:30 in the morning, someone started to scream in my ear so loudly I thought he was inside my head: *"Allahu Akbar*... (God is greatest)."

I nearly jumped out of bed. The Sunni mosque up the corner from us, which I had not really noticed before, had turned up the volume to "11" on the muezzin's announcement over the loudspeaker calling the faithful to ablutions prior to the first prayer of the day. (In Jordan, which is almost exclusively Sunni Arab, you have six, not the normal five, calls per day from the hundreds of minarets in the country.) I believe they wanted to make sure the American diplomats four blocks up the hill also got ready.

We quickly got a double-paned window installed and padded the door to our bedroom for soundproofing. I put the word out to our agents in Jordan that the mosque needed to turn it down, please. They did so shortly thereafter. The Jordanian people wanted to take care of the Americans. Our government's aid provided a huge percentage of their nation's revenue, probably second only to the money they earned from relabeling Israeli goods for re-sale to the neighboring Muslim countries, thereby circumventing the Arab boycott.

Nevertheless, the villa's location continued to test us. Directly across a boulder-strewn vacant lot stood a Palestinian refugee camp that must have originated in 1967 when Israel occupied all of Jerusalem and the West Bank. The camp had evolved into a mini-conurbation with winding alleys like those found in the centers of the older Arab cities of North Africa. Every day dozens of boys would emerge into the vacant lot to play soccer and chase each other around. Soon enough, my son, Henry, went out to play with them. Great idea, in theory. The Arab kids could not get over his blond hair and kept wanting to touch it. Finally he had had enough and headed back toward the house. The crowd of kids followed him and started to throw rocks at our villa.

I wasn't in Jordan at the time, but at that point the phone rang in my office in Baghdad. Henry was on the line, upset about the neighborhood boys. I immediately increased our Filipino gardener's hours (even though we really had no yard to speak of, just concrete and rocks). And one of our Jordanian employees went into the camp's casbah to inform the residents that there would be serious problems if something happened to Henry or our villa again. From then on, several of the male residents of the camp appeared every day to sit and smoke on the edge of the vacant lot and watch the kids. I worried that the clash with the Arab boys would traumatize my son and make him fearful of them. But several weeks later, when I was back at the villa for one of my four-or-five-day visits, I looked out the window and saw Henry marching with a few of his new friends from school toward the camp with sticks in their hands, looking ready for a fight. I called him back home quickly, but my worry about his fears had disappeared.

After transplanting my nuclear family, I thought, *Why not bring over my younger brother?* I really had not thought he would take the job, but when he did, I was fired up. Our father, on the other hand, a Navy Seabee engineering officer who had led the rebuilding of the Hue to Da Nang railway after the 1968 Tet Offensive, did not seem excited about having two sons together in the war zone (our older brother remained in Georgia). The project we had won with the DOD Task Force for Business and Stability

Operations at the end of 2007 entailed working with the high-end consulting firms—the McKinsey Group, Grant Thornton, SAIC, and Computer Sciences Corporation. And Kiffer, educated as a computer engineer, had worked for over a decade in business consulting, with his last job at the software security giant Symantec. Thus I thought he would be a natural to work with them.

The Task Force had invested about $100 million in U.S. taxpayer money in Iraqi state-owned enterprises as part of a plan to stimulate employment by getting these originally Soviet-inspired, command-economy factories up and running again by replacing missing or damaged equipment. The "Brinkley" Task Force, named after its leader Paul Brinkley, for whom I had worked briefly—he was the one who had video-conferenced with General Chiarelli about the giant drinking fountain in Sadr City—had struggled to actually account for the U.S.-purchased equipment. No one even knew if installations had taken place. All the high-end consultants could not travel to the factories without escorts by the U.S. military, which, of course, had other, more pressing concerns in fighting a war.

That's where we stepped in. Although our role was not envisioned in the initial funding, Paul saw the need. We established that AISG was able to send our vetted Iraqi engineers, who knew the sites and oftentimes the people managing the factories, to check on the U.S.-supplied equipment, such as generators, assembly-line conveyors, and looms. The Task Force enjoyed a 100 percent success rate on its investments from that point on. To paraphrase Reagan, now Brinkley's people would not only *trust* but, most importantly, *verify*.

✳   ✳   ✳

Interestingly—with me temporarily out of the country and Tony tied up by the U.S. soldiers who were searching Apache—our employees deferred to Kiffer, as my brother, even though he was not the next in line by the corporate structure. Luckily, at a strapping six foot two inches and with a generally calm demeanor, he projected the right presence for the Army guys—they turned out to be Delta Force—who were now aggressively searching through Apache, threatening to blow open every locked door and safe in our eleven-villa, three-city-block facility. Fortunately Kiffer got me on the phone and I gave them the combination to my bathroom safe, which held about $650,000 at the time, before they broke into it. The days of having millions of dollars of cash on hand had receded with the growing sophistication of our vendor network; by this time most of them accepted wire transfers from our bank in Jordan.

The keys to the locked doors to our information office, where we kept the records for all our thousands of local employees, weren't immediately available. So off they went via plastic explosives attached by Delta Force operators, who seemed to really enjoy blowing things up—so much so that they blew up our neighbors' floor safe even after Kiffer told them it was not a part of the company compound. The house was empty and so was the safe. The detailed planning that had gone into the raid on Apache included a map with numbers assigned to each of our houses. But the Special Operations Force–Delta (SOF-D or Delta Force) troops' numbers did not match our own internal labeling—and confusion reigned.

The U.S. military had launched a significant operation to take down Apache. It involved over four hundred troops inside the company's perimeter and in an outer cordon preventing anyone from entering or leaving our neighborhood. They didn't know if our heavily armed guard force of over fifty men behind Apache's fortified walls would resist—which of course they did not as soon as Tony recognized this had to be a U.S. operation. The AISG security director went out to the gate to meet the Army men and the spec ops soldiers grabbed him, cuffed him behind his back, and draped a red chemical light stick around his neck—identifying Tony as the prime target of the raid.

Meanwhile, the raiders had flex-cuffed all of our guards and live-in staff, in many cases leaving them face down out in the yards for hours while the search continued. With the exception of Tony and George, the Americans remained unshackled; but they were under close guard in the ops center. Over a hundred Iraqi security men, Filipino office personnel, a few Fijians, and one lone Brit, our business development director, remained handcuffed and scattered about the outside of Apache's several houses in the warm air of an early spring Baghdad night. Kiffer alone accompanied the Delta Force commander, who went by "Major Tom" with no last name on his camouflage blouse, as a normal military officer would have—while Kiffer opened doors around Apache and talked with our staff, trying to calm them.

My phone rang again after the brief first call about the safe combination. I had lain back down to try to get the rest I would need to deal with the situation, but all I could do was wait for the next shoe to drop. It was Kiffer again: "They're saying Tony is working for Sadr! There are two Treasury men here and they have taken over your office, where we are now. They want to talk to you."

Shocked, I could only squeeze out of my stress-constricted vocal chords: "*What*?"

One of the U.S. Treasury men came on the line and said, "Yes, we have information that Tony is involved in providing funds to Jaish al Mahdi through drug and weapons sales, extortion, and counterfeiting. How well do you know Tony?"

"I know him very well," I insisted, as my mind raced at the implications of what this federal agent had said. "You've been played! Whoever told you this is probably one of our competitors and planted that information."

He continued, "This is very serious. We know you personally are not involved—just Tony and his nephew George. Tony is the kingpin. No one can help Tony now, not even Petraeus." He had obviously seen on a shelf behind my desk the picture of me giving the commanding general a copy of my book.

Raising my voice into the cell phone, I said, "Remember Tony is a U.S. citizen. There had better be due process…you understand!"

Kiffer came back on the line and I told him, "This is bullshit! It *can't* be true."

Kiffer then proceeded to go outside my office and shout to everyone including Tony, George, and the Delta Force troops standing in our ops center, "This is all bullshit and not to worry, no one is going down. They have it all wrong about Tony."

In one of my proudest moments, Tony later told me, "I lay there tied up...seeing them in my mind taking me to some dark place, but the fear passed because I knew that you would come looking no matter where they took me." When he said that, I had a flash of memory about our trip to the belly of the beast of the National Police to rescue our employees.

Rock, who kept it cool in the ops center during the entire raid, told me the next day when I arrived from Amman, "I was thankful the whole time you were not here, because you would have been doing cheetah flips!" No doubt. I hated to imagine. I think, in retrospect, they waited until I had left Baghdad to act against us.

Lying back down to reflect on the conversation—if you can call it that—I pondered the surprising fact that the federal agent I had spoken to was from the Treasury Department. Why would a domestically focused agency have a presence in the war zone? I started to put it all together. We had completed the yellowcake movement just a few days before. Under Pentagon authorization, Tony had engaged with Sadr's Jaish al Mahdi-aligned tribal leaders via cell phone in order to rent the trucks to ensure safe passage for the nuclear-weapons precursor. The NSA picked up these conversations, of course. Additionally, someone—most likely one of our competitors—must have planted information about Tony (a well-known lynchpin of AISG operations) with the Iraqi ministry of defense claiming all sorts of criminal activity, including counterfeiting dollars—the very reason for the Treasury men's presence in Iraq. (The Iranians and Syrians had reportedly counterfeited U.S. money on a large scale in the early 1990s.)[2] I surmised that McChrystal's people, who were now focusing on the Shia militias in Baghdad, had told the wannabe-soldier Treasury guys something to the effect that they could have one SOF-D raid. Given the information about Sadr and counterfeiting from MOD and NSA, they jumped on Tony and AISG.

The phone rang again at about half past 3 a.m. Kiffer's voice boomed over the connection, exhausted but ecstatic: "They're gone! They left and they took nothing with them. Not Tony, not George, not anything at all. The Delta commander told me this was the first time they've ever done a raid and not taken anyone or anything out with them. *Zero.* I shouted at them the whole time as they picked up their crap and left, 'You got nothing. I told you!'"

Given the operational tempo of Delta Force—five to six assaults per night in Baghdad alone during this period—this was a clear example of the fog of war and one hand not knowing what the other hand was doing. In other words, the Treasury guys and SOF-D did not know about the yellowcake move, or at least not about our role in the secret operation. It was within this blinding fog that we had to operate.

The next morning I flew back into Baghdad. Tony met me at the airport. "I can't believe this happened to you, Brother," I said to him. "You are the rock upon which AISG's success in the mission is based. You know that you're my hero. Go to Lebanon and take some time off. I'll deal with this and get it all cleaned up."

Obviously pained but unbowed by the events of the night before, Tony responded, "I'll go to my father's village in the mountains up north. Maybe I'll be able to find some peace there. This was not right."

When I got back to Apache, it turned out that not only American troops had occupied our houses during the raid but also Iraqi special forces. During the search, the Iraqi soldiers had looted the rooms, taking anything of value they could find, including thousands of dollars and jewelry that our employees kept under their beds. They trashed my room, taking my .45 pistols, my heavily worn Austrian mountain boots, and a couple non-functional cell phones. The entire compound, which our people had already begun to clean up, looked like a tornado had hit it. Nevertheless, nothing critical had gone missing and, most importantly, no one had been injured or killed during the operation. Our Filipinos, in particular, took a very stoic approach to the theft and nighttime shackling. And the Iraqis knew what state-sanctioned brute force could do, from their lives under Saddam, and now from the Americans fighting pitched battles and running snatch-and-grab operations in and around their homes in war-torn Baghdad. All in all, our workforce took the whole operation in stride and never seemed to look back on it with rage, as I had feared. Because of the shared trauma and the fact that we came out of it unscathed, the raid even further unified us.

Nevertheless, I could not let this egregious blunder go unaddressed. Rock and I immediately went down to Delta Force headquarters outside the Baghdad airport to demand an accounting. Two senior Special Forces sergeants came out in the parking lot in front of the gate guarding a fenced compound centered on a manmade hill topped with a crusader-style castle, apparently built on a whim of Saddam's. The stocky, fit men with wraparound Ray-Bans heard us vent about everything stolen during the raid. One gave me his email address but did nothing more than acknowledge receipt when I sent him the list of everything pillaged. I never heard anything further from the Delta Force guys, although I felt some satisfaction in that they knew we knew where they lived…and could come knock on their door anytime.

After the Treasury agents went into hiding and did not respond to my emails or calls—they had left their contact information with Kiffer after he demanded it—I brought in Mike Waddington, a former Army lawyer well-known for his outstanding legal work defending soldiers accused of murder on the battlefield. Something I had learned early in my entrepreneurial career in the former Soviet Union: attorneys trump guns every time (because long-term business requires rule of law). And you should always hire a "brain surgeon" experienced and trained to deal specifically with a complicated legal issue. Waddington fit that description. I figured if he could handle capital crimes within the military justice system, then he could deal with this misuse of the Army's wartime power to raid and detain. He advised that I go to the judge advocate general for U.S. forces in Iraq. Through Mike's superb representation, U.S. Army Colonel Mark Martins, a Harvard Law grad and senior legal advisor to General Petraeus, agreed to see me. The main reason I wanted to have this meeting was to ensure that Tony and AISG had no remaining taint from the radically unjustified action taken by the U.S. government in raiding Apache—no presumed guilt driven by the adage, "If there's smoke there must be fire."

As I sat down at a conference table in the al Fao palace with a couple of his aides, Colonel Martins answered that question: "No, we realize SOF-D made a mistake. AISG is cleared to continue on with your role in the mission, which we appreciate here at MNF-I headquarters. Do you want to take it any further?" He meant further legal action.

"No, sir," I replied. "We understand that mistakes are made. We have no desire to take this to the press—that would undermine the mission. Yet we are missing quite a bit of our people's possessions."

"OK, we'll send out an investigating officer to check into that," offered the man who later would take over command of the briar patch that the Guantanamo military commissions had become.[3]

U.S. Army Colonel Thomas Huckabee, a cousin of the long shot 2004 Republican presidential candidate, contacted me asking for a ride from al Fao to Apache in order to undertake the investigation of the stolen items. I thought, "Hey, they *really* trust us if they want Tony's security team to transport the investigating officer across Baghdad." At the end of the daylong investigation, the good colonel interviewed dozens of our employees and agreed with our claims, but could only advise us to go to the nearest American Army unit for compensation. Yet his quite pleasant visit—he seemed a fine gentleman from Arkansas with old-school Southern manners—dispelled any question in our workforce about our continuing close relationship with the U.S. military. No one doubted now that it had all been a mistake.

In a funny footnote to the raid, one of the aides to Martins who was present at our meeting, a young captain, asked a few weeks later if he could teach a seminar about AISG to the other Judge Advocate General officers at MNF-I HQ. I said, "Of course," and gave him a copy of my book.

He reported back after the class, "Your role in Iraq is that of a hybrid, part military, part commercial, which is one that deserves further study. But we all respect what you do."

After that exchange, I slept easy, knowing that no hangover from the raid remained for me to worry about from the U.S. military in Iraq.

*　　*　　*

The situation with Moqtada Sadr and his Jaish al Mahdi had come to a head—it was a reflection of that fact that the most elite troops of the American military had taken down Tony in what they had mistakenly thought would be a direct strike on a major player in Sadr's support network. The battle for Sadr City, an underreported yet critical event, raged during this period. Even I didn't know the full extent of the vicious street fighting in the massive slum just across town until I read *Stryker: The Siege of Sadr City* by Konrad Ludwig, an Army Infantry sergeant who fought in the battle. Ludwig lays it out straight: "This was going to be the grand finale. This was their last stand and the entire war was at stake. Nowhere in the city had the fight become as bloody and bitter as in the streets of Sadr City. If they lost their footing in the city and the two million voters that came with it, Sadr's regime would become a thing of the past. Once we got control of their city nothing would save them."[4]

The battle did not go well for the Iranian-supported Jaish al Mahdi. In response to the U.S. assault on his home ground, a couple days after the Delta Force raid Sadr called forth all his minions throughout Baghdad to take to the streets and seize control of the capital. When he had done the same thing in April 2004, five years earlier, JAM shut down the city for two weeks, and blood ran in the streets.[5] Our Iraqi security liaisons and our Shia workforce warned us. We shook off the lingering shock of the raid, and got ready. The day broke with automatic weapons fire off in the distance from

every direction. This city had Shia districts in all parts. Tony had left for
Lebanon, so I threw on my flak jacket and the web gear holding six additional 30-round magazines for my AK, put on my Kevlar helmet, which I
never wore, grabbed my rifle and a radio tuned to our security network,
and proceeded to walk the perimeter. I went up on the rooftops of all the
houses where we had our machinegun positions. I chatted with all the
guards at our six gates, including the Ugandans taking care of our Belgian
Malinois bomb dogs.

Nothing happened. As the day stretched into night, the gunfire died
off. Sadr's call to arms had failed. Sadr City soon fell to the U.S. military,
and the Iraqi Army took over its mean streets. Moqtada declared a ceasefire for his Jaish al Mahdi that lasted until the mid-2014, anti-Shia jihadi
invasion from Syria. The time for politics had arrived for the Shia firebrand. He had failed with the gun.

CHAPTER 10

"DEATH TO AL-QAEDA!"

WITH THE EXISTENTIAL THREATS of al-Qaeda and the neo-Saddamists snuffed out by the Sahwa and the U.S. Surge, and the last remnants of the once-powerful Sunni insurgency fighting out of the alleyways and mosques of Mosul, Maliki felt able to move to consolidate national power. So he had ordered Baghdad's Sadr city fully open to U.S. operations, and then gone after Sadrist-controlled Amarah, near the Iranian border. In the south at Basra he took personal command of Iraqi forces in March 2008. With the British now hunkered down at the Basra airport and Amarah changed over from UK responsibility to complete Iraqi control in 2006, Petraeus had to launch U.S. support from the Baghdad area to quickly aid Maliki, who had set out personally to lead the fight for the city, nearly getting killed or captured in the process. The American-trained Iraqi forces, operating on their own in a large operation for the first time, floundered until the arrival of U.S. airpower, signals intelligence, and command advice.[1]

The lesson learned in the second British withdrawal from Iraq—
termed a "defeat" by UK generals when it was completed in April 2009[2]—
was not to lose the political goodwill of the majority Shia, as the British
had the first time, in the 1920s revolt against their League of Nations
mandate. After that mainly Shia rebellion, Iraq became ungovernable, at
least by a Depression-constrained exchequer. The British asserted a semblance of control over the Shia tribes of southern Iraq by using the Royal
Air Force to drop poison gas on rebellious desert villages in order to create
space for the establishment of a minority Sunni monarchy as political cover
for the first UK withdrawal in 1932.[3]

From the beginning of the preparations for the 2003 invasion of Iraq,
the Defense Department leadership, led by DOD undersecretary for
policy Douglas Feith, resisted State Department involvement in the plans
for post-invasion Iraq. The Pentagon civilian leadership and the vice
president's office believed that Foggy Bottom's diplomats and senior
management were not sufficiently supportive of the president's plan of
attack on the Saddam dictatorship. Nevertheless, the U.S. Foreign Service
stepped up and successfully negotiated the fraught passage of Iraq into
and out of the Coalition Provisional Authority. American diplomats then
handled a multiyear electoral process and negotiated a status of forces
agreement for the peaceful withdrawal of U.S. troops from a security-
capable Iraq with a UN-certified democratic government. Equally
important, the U.S. Agency for International Development, under the
control of State since the Clinton administration, achieved significant
accomplishments to the benefit of the Iraqi population as well, keeping
a low profile in the press but earning a positive *fatwa* (religious ruling)
from the top Shia religious leader, Grand Ayatollah Ali Sistani. The *fatwa*
stated that Iraqi clerics could work with USAID officials, alone among
all U.S. government and military personnel.[4] (Sistani, who was absolutely
successful in his efforts to force the U.S. and UN to conduct the earliest
possible national elections, had refused even to meet Paul Bremer, in
order to appear neutral.)

Ryan Crocker, the Arabic-speaking U.S. ambassador to Baghdad, and David Petraeus, the Iraq Surge commander, formed an especially effective partnership. Their credible reports of progress before Congress in September 2007 bought time for the Bush Surge strategy from the now Democratic-controlled House and Senate, where many members of the newly ascendant majority were howling for immediate retreat from the Iraq quagmire. The hearts and minds of the American body politic—the territory at issue in the second front of the war—thus remained adequately supportive for the final chapter of the insurgency during the Iraq War.

The war had begun with a conventional invasion, with key battles fought by my old unit, the 3rd Battalion of the 15th Infantry Regiment, a Bradley fighting vehicle battalion working in concert with tank units as a part of the Army's 3rd Infantry Division, which along with the 1st Marine Division, overthrew the Saddam regime in a classic *coup de main* by seizing the enemy's capital. (The much-maligned Bradley, a hybrid light tank–personnel carrier, proved its worth throughout the Iraq War.)[5] Then the war mutated into an insurgency under heavy influence from Iran and from what became al-Qaeda in Iraq. The defeat of these enemies required a population-centric counterinsurgency strategy and the effective training of Iraqis (the "host-nation forces"). The insurgency nearly reached the level of a civil war in 2006 but never escalated to that status—defined in international law as both sides bearing arms openly with identifiable uniforms or markings or both—only Coalition and GOI (Government of Iraq) forces ever met that standard. By mid-2008, American combat troops no longer needed to enforce the peace in Iraq. An enduring security had emerged on the horizon to those of us in-country with the vision to see it.

*   *   *

I had just begun our morning breakfast meeting. (Something an old CEO had told me when I asked him what created the biggest challenge to running a company effectively: "Communicating clearly, making sure everyone understands what the plan calls for on a daily basis.") So with the challenges of running ten job sites and employing thousands scattered about a war zone in a foreign country, I knew that my American management team had to talk regularly, both to each other and to me. We needed to be "on the same sheet of music," as they used to say in the Army. Events moved fast and unpredictably with lives at risk confronting the "friction"[6] (to quote von Clausewitz on what makes war-fighting more than a mechanical exercise: fatigue, weather, terrain, human error, the role of chance, and so forth) and the fog of war that was constantly gumming up the works.

Another principle I learned as a young Army officer involved span of control. Best leadership practices limit effective, direct management to five people. So I never had a secretary or a personal assistant, other than Abu Hind. The prematurely old but loyal and brave Baghdadi Kurd, who had been with AISG from the beginning, had started to lose his eyesight—he was working as a company driver—and got shot in the leg by the U.S. Army when he spaced out and got too close to one of their convoys. (After being shot, he drove to the company compound, not to a hospital, because he knew AISG would take care of him.) So he sat outside my door waiting to escort me on my daily walkabout. He ran errands for Rock and Tony, too, but otherwise I just let him hang out because I knew he listened to and talked with our Iraqi workforce and would give me the inside chatter. You have to manage a secretary, and that would inefficiently take away one of the five executives in my effective span of control. Those four or five executives, depending on the number in-country—our expats had nineteen days of vacation for every ninety days in Iraq—ran the company: chief operations officer, director of security, chief financial officer, human resource–travel director, and vice president for business development.

A Google email alert might pop up on my computer screen as I started a staff meeting sitting at my desk with the leadership team on the divan or in over-stuffed arm chairs arrayed in front of me, backed by an eight-foot-wide mahogany woodcarving of a jungle landscape including elephants and tigers. (I often stared at that dense jungle forest, looking for someone or something peeping out at me through the heavy foliage. Probably not an unusual thought in a house that had been owned by a now-deceased minister of the interior—a.k.a. secret police chief—under Saddam. Saadoun Ghaidan, one of the few members of the early Baathist leadership in Baghdad to escape Saddam's executioners, had two sons and a daughter who rented the largest villa at Apache to us.) Today, the email informed me that National Review Online had published another one of my op-eds. In order to check veracity and flow, I always read the last draft to my leadership team before I sent it to NRO and then the final article after it came online.

I opened the link to the website and started to read it aloud. I stopped, and the blanched look on my face brought Rock (Tony was on leave) to his feet. He quickly slid around my desk to see the computer screen. After a glance at the headline, he turned to me and exclaimed, "There'll be five car bombs at the gates tomorrow!"

I calmed my voice and read aloud the title, which was open for viewing by the entire world: "Death to al-Qaeda!" In her exuberance, the editor of NRO had decided to change my original comparatively bland title for the article.

June 24, 2008: Death to al-Qaeda! The View from the Red Zone
    Baghdad, Iraq – The war in Iraq is not yet finished for U.S. combat forces but you can almost see the end, just over the horizon, from my office perched in the Red Zone of downtown Baghdad. This last May saw the lowest monthly American military deaths of the entire war: 19 to include four non-combat fatalities. Attacks on U.S. Department of Defense contractor convoys have dropped by a phenomenal 20 times from one in five incidents at the beginning of 2007 to approximately one percent of cargo movements today. Oil production has

exceeded pre-war volumes and the Iraqi government is on its way to financial self-sufficiency. Provincial elections are sure to happen this fall—which will further reintegrate the once-estranged Sunni minority back into local governance.

Over the last three months, the Iraqi Army has successfully taken the lead in major security operations in Mosul against the last in-country stronghold of al-Qaeda, and against Iranian-supported Shia militants in Basra and Baghdad's Sadr City. The political will now exists in the democratically elected Iraqi government to finally rid the country of all militias. Among the hundreds of Iraqis with whom I work, a common refrain is: *"Bes jaish wahid bil Iraq—jaish Iraqi!"* (Only one army in Iraq—the Iraqi Army!) This is a direct counterpoint to the Jaish al Mahdi of Moqtada Sadr and evidence of a growing faith in their nation's ability to protect itself. Here is the exit strategy writ large: Get the American-trained Iraqi security forces stood up and U.S. combat units can come home.

The impact of the Iraq mission on world security is also dramatic and counter to what is commonly heard in the media and academic elites. The Iraq conflict has drawn fanatical Islamists to fight nearer to home, and as a just-released Canadian institute's study details, overall international terrorism fatalities—outside of the Iraq war—have plunged by 40 percent since 2001. The Simon Fraser University *Human Security Brief* records that, due to "the humiliating recent defeats experienced by Al Qaeda in Iraq," popular support in the Islamic world for the perpetrators of 9/11 has fallen off precipitously. For example, in Pakistan (where al-Qaeda is arguably most deeply entrenched): "support for Osama bin Laden has dropped from 70 percent in August 2007 to 4 percent in January 2008."

After going from success to success over the past three decades, from destroying a super power (the Soviet Union) in

Afghanistan, to blowing up American embassies in East Africa and the USS *Cole* off Yemen, onto 9/11, and nearly pushing Iraq into civil war in 2006, the Islamic extremists have now failed dramatically. Their jihad to dominate the Islamic world and beyond has smashed against the twin rocks of a steadfast American will and the Iraqi people's natural desire to live free of tyranny, whether from Saddam, al-Qaeda, or Iran. Nothing dissuades recruiting like catastrophic failure.

Strongly held arguments challenge the Iraq conflict as central to the war on terror with the claim that the "real" al-Qaeda of bin Laden is not present on the battlefield here. That statement ignores the nature of jihadi extremism as a pan-Arab ideology. Iraq is central, if not the key nation, in the Arab world. Baghdad is ground zero. Not the mountains, caves, and isolation of the Afghan-Pakistani border. When Robert Baer, former CIA operative and now commentator for *Time*,[7] states that "al Qaeda is an idea, a way of thinking," when he argues against our taking the war on terror to Iraq, he is right on, but not in the way he uses that statement. What is the death knell of the efficacy of an idea? When reality proves it does not work. Bin Laden himself has said the war in Iraq is central to his jihad, and we are taking him at his word here. The Muslim world sees that the al-Qaeda idea kills far more Muslims than infidels. The Muslim world sees the failure of the suicide bomber—the only significant weapon of jihadi terrorism—to force out the American Army from one of the greatest lands of Islam. The al-Qaeda idea has died a violent death on the battlefields of Iraq.[8]

✫   ✫   ✫

We waited for a response. After consultations with Tony, Rock increased security, to the extent possible given our available resources and already super-high protective measures, which would almost rank with those of the U.S. embassy in Baghdad. No one came in and out of Apache without being searched under CCTV camera observation monitored in our ops center. No vehicles entered the compound without being sniffed by our bomb dogs. We had stand-off and blast walls that would protect us from the most powerful truck bomb. Our footprint, although large, did not take up enough space for the highly inaccurate mortars or rockets—fired mostly by Iranian-allied militants, not Sunni insurgents—to effectively hit us. Nevertheless AQI knew where we lived. You could find us on the web, and Apache took up a significant portion of a high-profile neighborhood on the primarily Sunni side of town. No attack came. I guess that fact proved the point of the article. Or maybe no one from al-Qaeda read National Review Online! (Although UPI also picked it up.)[9]

Meanwhile and in consequence of the decline of the twin insurgencies of AQI and the Iranian-supported militias, Iraqi civil society began to emerge to the point where we believed that maybe the company could begin to find legal recourse in commercial transactions through use of the Iraqi court system. AISG had won a contract to build maintenance facilities for the new Mine-Resistant Ambush Protected vehicle—the MRAP—at five key bases in the Sunni Triangle: Camp Taji, just north of Baghdad; Camp Speicher, outside Tikrit; Taqqadum (TQ) next to Habbaniya; FOB Anaconda at Balad; and Camp Victory, inside the Baghdad airport perimeter. The MRAP demonstrated the power and quick reaction time of the U.S. manufacturing base, along with the ability of the American military to adapt to battlefield conditions by changing industrial design.

The IED roadside bomb was the number-one killer of U.S. troops during the Iraq War.[10] After seeing Saddam's *fedayeen* (irregulars carrying only small arms and no armor) slaughtered during the invasion, the insurgents understood—just as the Viet Cong came to understand—that you did not want to get into a direct-fire slugfest with the Big Green Machine. The well-trained U.S. military could shoot straight, unlike the preponderance of our opponents in Iraq. And you'd really get chewed up once air power and artillery came into play, such as the 155 mm satellite-guided Excalibur howitzer round. So you had to go to an asymmetrical battle— guerrilla warfare and terrorism. In this case, use the population and urban jungle to hide in and plant remote-controlled makeshift mines. The initiator could flee before U.S. troops could "find, fix, and finish" the enemy combatant. Once the war devolved into an insurgency mostly fought in the cities (known as MOUT, military operation–urban terrain), the American military in large part stopped deploying the M-1 tank, the Bradley, and other heavy armor in combat patrols. They went to the Humvee, which the Pentagon had originally deployed in significant numbers without any armored version. But early on, the soldiers jury-rigged armored Humvees by bolting or welding locally procured plate steel to the frame. Then, as combat continued into 2005, DOD fielded a specially manufactured armored version that reached almost every unit, but even it could not stop the larger IEDs.

The Pentagon, in direct response to the IED threat, searched for an answer and by the end of 2006 had decided to order thousands of MRAPs, which began to flow into Iraq by mid-2007. The original design came from Rhodesia, and then the South African army had further refined it in order to protect against Soviet- and Red Chinese-supplied antiapartheid guerilla mine attacks. While the Humvee's square sides and flat bottom directly absorbed the shock from a ground blast, the MRAP's high center and V-shaped hull deflected it. Although not fully protective against the explosively formed penetrator (EFP) metal slug provided by Iran, the MRAP cut the number of IED deaths dramatically by the end of 2007 and until the withdrawal of U.S. troops in 2011. The new vehicles reduced casualties by "roughly 75 percent" compared with the Humvee and to "less than half" compared with the M-1 Abrams tank and Bradley and Stryker armored vehicles.[11]

The new vehicles, however, required specialized maintenance facilities and service people. AISG came in on the construction of the workshops. For the service people, the Army and Marines needed to be trained and supported by civilian personnel. The MRAP was basically a big-wheeled armored truck, but its fire-suppression system and electronics required specialized training. One weakness of the military personnel system of "up or out" is that a soldier barely had time to become proficient in maintaining sophisticated machinery before he or she either had to leave the service or moved up in rank to a leadership position and away from handling the equipment. This necessitated contractors who could spend decades working on a particular type of technology. So another additional role for contractors in the Iraq War—and in past conflicts such as the Gulf War, with the Patriot anti-missile systems—was a significant part in the maintenance and repair of new or highly technical equipment such as the MRAP. On every base where we constructed the repair facilities, numerous civilians—many of them employees of the manufacturer—worked alongside the military to keep the behemoth vehicles running.

With the full deployment of the MRAPs in 2008, Coalition casualties began to plummet—even with the greater number of U.S. troops in country. The technological innovation of the American forces had dealt another deadly setback to the AQI-led Sunni Arab insurgency. Their principal weapon against the military—the IED, cheap and formerly highly effective against the casualty-averse Americans—now was severely blunted by the new V-hulled armored truck that had become the primary transport vehicle for the U.S. infantry, the primary hunters of the elusive insurgent. This third blow to al-Qaeda, coming on top of the Surge and the Awakening, sent the terrorist group into a death spiral in Iraq.

As usual, our contract for the MRAPs had "pants-on-fire" urgency, for obvious reasons. The MRAPs needed repair and needed it now, as by the time we were bidding on the contract many of the vehicles had been in country for a year or more. Rough roads and aggressive driving put the vehicles through a lot of wear and tear. But we entered this contract with the expectation that we could count on the same flexibility as with our previous contracts in Iraq; we'd accept the mission with its usual unrealistic timeframe and either get it done or receive an extension due to circumstances of the battlefield. But this time the Army Corps of Engineers (USACE) had control of contract execution.

There were inevitable delays. Of course, the Marines wanted something special. Their electrical equipment at TQ (Taqqadum Base) had to be similarly powered to the U.S. system—120 volt at 60 hertz—versus what the region used—230 volt at 50 hertz—which the Army and Air Force accepted on the other MRAP sites. We had thirty days to deliver in-country and got the generators retrofitted by having the distributors re-wire the equipment, but the real challenge came with the air-conditioners.

By contract, the industrial-size AC units required to cool huge repair bays in Iraq's summer heat had to be manufactured by the U.S. company Carrier. There was no way we could deliver in thirty days; and due to industry-standard long lead times for special-order equipment, the contracting folks had to know that.

Meanwhile, as we got into constructing the warehouse-size garages and auxiliary buildings, the USACE inspectors began to make their presence known. These civilians were highly knowledgeable and completely inflexible. In rapid contingency warzone contracting, time and effectiveness—not the letter of a hastily drawn up contract—normally define compliance. The Joint Contracting Command officers, who were often out of their depth on the technical side of construction, worked under tremendous time pressure. With them we could always count on resolving issues because of our shared goal of mission completion. We wanted the opportunity for the next contract, so we would never deliver a shoddy, non-functional product. Our interest in continuing to do business with the government was its own incentive for contract performance and quality work.

Now that USACE had taken charge, that collaborative attitude turned into a costly mistake for us. Instead of cooperating with us to get the job done, the Corps of Engineers were sticklers for the letter of the contract. As a construction manager from the world-class design-and-build firm KBR, then working on the LOGCAP contract at TQ, remarked to his boss in an email about AISG's MRAP work, which he blind copied us on: "The Army Corps of Engineers representative assigned to the job was overly demanding on every specification. For instance, he made them [AISG] move the forms for a massive concrete septic tank 6 inches because it was not exactly in the correct spot on the prints (on a 3 acre job site) which would have no bearing on the functionality of the system.... The SOW [statement of work].... is far beyond what is required in theater. The requirements were similar to the requirements in the United States for a suburban sub-division."

We searched high and low for the air-conditioning units manufactured to U.S. standards for the Marines. One of our local vendors—we now had more than a hundred of these, after starting out with just two or three in 2004—told us that he could deliver to spec. As time was running out for us, finally the vendor's supplier, with whom we had never worked in the past, said he could get our order to us, but only by dropping the units off in Sadr City because bridge closings from AQI explosions and the ongoing GOI curfew related to the fighting in the Shia slum would prevent him from getting the AC units across town. So Rock blasted out on a security team with trucks and picked up the eighty or so heavy-duty air condition-ers in a dusty lot on the edge of Sadr City. They seemed to fit the bill, but as they say, "Haste makes waste." These turned out to be extremely high-quality counterfeits with flawless Carrier specification plates; all func-tioned correctly even though, as we later discovered, an illicit factory in the lawless areas of Hezbollah- and Iranian-controlled Lebanon had actu-ally produced the units.

We needed to get the AC units to the five sites yesterday. So we loaded them up the next morning and shipped them from Apache to the bases. Our construction folks at the jobs started to set them up and noticed some did not fit the exact specs, to include having only one fan and not two. We looked at all of them more closely and realized that we had been duped in our haste. And, even more stupidly, we had already paid the supplier, per our agreement. Total cost: $285,000. My brother Kiffer—now, with the departure of Carlos Flores, he had just taken over as chief operations officer for the company—immediately reported the error to the contracting officer.

Time to get our money back, I thought. We knew the supplier's location in Karrada along the east bank of the Tigris, just over the bridge from us. The urge to go down there and thump him almost overcame me. But I decided we couldn't resort to mafia tactics; that's not what we are about. We had a clear case of fraud, and it was time to see about recourse in the Iraqi legal system. We figured, now that Iraq has begun to stabilize, let's test that stability and go after the supplier in the Iraqi courts—a justice system primarily designed and established by the British. AISG police advisor Colonel Talal's attorney wife Susan represented us on Baghdadi regulatory issues, such as business licensing. She also served on a committee that chose the capital's municipal judges, one of whom our suit would end up in front of for adjudication. I got Talal to ask Susan (interestingly, though she was an Iraqi, she had an English-style name), whom I had never met, to come and have lunch with us and then afterwards discuss the case.

We all sat down for lunch at the main house in our company compound. The dark mahogany table sat twelve with Susan to my immediate right and Talal next to her on her right. I sat at the head with Rock, as senior security manager present (Tony was on leave), at the foot of table, nearest the entry door per company protocol (an additional but hidden door led into a narrow alley between the neighboring villas, also part of Apache). Kiffer and the other managers filled up the remainder of the spaces. Habitually we did not talk much business at lunch; discussion mostly revolved around current events and family or old war stories. The breakfast and evening meetings along with an average twelve-hour-plus workday were enough. Lunch was quick, normally only thirty minutes long.

After having just finished reading Hanna Batatu's massive *The Old Social Classes and the Revolutionary Movements of Iraq*, the definitive political history of modern Iraq, I noted that Susan's last name identified her as a member of the Turcomen people, not Arabs, but a Sunni minority group favored greatly by Saddam. (Furthermore, her surname was the same as that of the commander of the Iraqi air force who as a leader of the 1958 coup participated in overthrowing the last king of Iraq, Faisal II, massacring him and his family.)[12] We started off with some pleasantries as I introduced her around the table to everyone as "our lawyer for the air-conditioning case." I then turned to Susan and said, "AISG is working in the reconstruction of Iraq. All of the men here are far from home and have sacrificed being with their families to help your country."

Susan then baldly stated, "Iraq was better off before you, the Americans, came here...."

I checked myself, looked hard at this fortyish woman with long flowing brown hair, stylishly dressed in chic London *haute couture*. Susan gazed back at me equally hard. We were off to the races. I began to speak Iraqi Arabic, to her great surprise. I said, "What about the Shia and the Kurds that Saddam and the people around him—that it looks like included your family—kept from power? What about Halabja? When Saddam and the Iraqi air force dropped poison gas on women and children. What about the Iran-Iraq war that Saddam started that killed hundreds of thousands of Iraqis? The Shia are the majority now in this democracy we have created. That is what you fear, is it not? You especially want the power back. That's why it is worse now for you and the other Baathists!"

At this point, Talal stepped in and said, "The Shia are not the majority!"

Susan turned to him and said, "Yes, they are. But why does he continue to call me *Suzanne*? Does he not know my name is Susan?"

Talal, who had been listening to my street-learned Iraqi Arabic for a year and half, replied "*Huwa galltich 'khusuussan' la Suzanne.*" ("He was saying to you 'especially,' not Suzanne.)

The heated discussion went on for almost forty-five minutes as my staff sat quietly around the table, other than Arabic-speaking Rock and our Jordanian-American HR director, not understanding much that was being said. In the end, Susan apologized back in my office. I hired her to go after the fraudulent supplier, assessing that she was one tough lady and that her kindred Baathist judges still ran the municipal courts. Maliki had not had time yet to replace them. The judge in the case, however, ruled that because we as DOD contractors had immunity from judgment in Iraqi law as written by Paul Bremer and the CPA, AISG could not use Iraqi law to go after Iraqis. We seized money from the vendor who had recommended the fraudulent supplier and would have benefited from the transaction, convinced the contracting officer to accept some of the counterfeit but fully functioning AC units under a yearlong warranty we provided ourselves, and ate the loss after air shipping the replacement units from a U.S. factory into Iraq.

In the end, we barely made any money on the MRAP contract, but our other ten ongoing projects churned monthly revenue of more than five million dollars. In fact, 2008 would not match 2007, when we grossed almost $100 million, but the AISG net profit had increased, indicating that we had gotten more efficient at our work. So business was looking up, just as the military situation began to turn ever more positive. We could start to look to the future in Iraq at peace with a huge upside of oil reserves that some predicted would outstrip even Saudi Arabia, making Iraq potentially the largest oil producer in the world. This would require tens of billions of dollars in infrastructure development, of course.

On reflection, it is interesting to consider the example of Susan, our attorney. The aggressively secular Baathist regime worked hard to cobble together a counterweight to the religiously conservative Sunni and Shia populations. Gaining power through a military coup, the Baathists emerged out of a post-colonial pan-Arab movement that mimicked Western political structures such as president and parliament, without an underlying democracy infusing those institutions with their true meaning. Ironically, this benefitted the country by helping to bring it into the modern world. As a result, the Baathists encouraged talented and well-educated Iraqi women toward success in the professions and academia, a rare achievement in the Arab world—one that Iraq continues to struggle to sustain and grow after the extensive violence of the Iraq War and its aftermath.[13]

＊　　　＊　　　＊

On January 1, 2009, after Sadr City had been pacified and the Iraqi government presence in the capital at large had solidified, the U.S. military handed over the gates and blast walls dividing the Green Zone from the rest of Baghdad to Iraqi security forces.[14] The fit Iraqi soldiers who took charge of the gates looked sharp and well equipped, with U.S. Army–standard armored Humvees, helmets, and ballistic vests. This tremendously symbolic transition indicated not only the maturity of the Iraqi military and police but that the U.S. government now trusted them to protect the largest American embassy in the world, located dead center in the Green Zone.

Furthermore, this transition effectively marked the victory of the United States in the Iraq War. The war-loving Saddamist dictatorship, dead and buried, and the twin insurgencies of al-Qaeda and the Iranian-allied militias had failed to derail the establishment of a democratically elected Iraqi government, aligned with the U.S. and the West, and, most importantly, able to protect itself. Iran retained influence, of course, as befits a neighbor that shared a thousand-mile border and had harbored and supported the current Shia political leadership in their long exile during the thirty-year Saddam regime. Nevertheless Tehran did not control Baghdad—the defeat of Sadr had insured that. The greatest impact of the U.S. victory in the counterinsurgency that arose was the utter defeat of al-Qaeda on the battlefield by the American infidels and the absolute rejection of the jihadis by the Sunni Arabs of al Anbar and throughout Iraq. With a continued and active American political and security presence in Iraq and the greater Middle East, al-Qaeda would never again be able to claim the mantle of a popular movement in the Arab world.

CHAPTER 11

THE OILFIELDS

IN THE JANUARY 2009 REGIONAL ELECTIONS, Prime Minister Maliki's State of Law coalition took a plurality in nine of seventeen provincial legislatures. Unsettled Kirkuk did not have elections. The Sunni Awakening, supporting the Baghdad government, gained control in al Anbar; and Maliki's Kurdish allies easily sustained their grip on power in the three northern provinces of the autonomous Kurdish Regional Government. Maliki, the former exile and second-tier leader in the Shiite Dawa party, had become a truly national figure. Beyond his provincial presence, he continued to lead the national Assembly of Deputies. (The national presidency, held by a Kurd, was largely ceremonial but possessed some powers, such as delaying executions.) Then in 2010 Iraq had UN-certified democratic parliamentary elections, with U.S. combat forces treaty-bound under the status of forces agreement to remain outside the cities during the voting. Very few security incidents occurred in the first Iraqi-protected *intehab* (election); the incidents amounted to only several minor explosions around the capital.

The approximately 90 percent drop in violence since 2006 had engendered a sense of optimism among the Iraqi people.[1] The number-one weapon of asymmetrical value to the al-Qaeda insurgency was the car bomb—with an impact both at the terrible points of explosions, slaughtering tens of thousands of Iraqi civilians, and on TV screens, sapping the will of the American people to vote for more war, as the U.S. economy peaked and then went into a radical decline, arguably second only to the Great Depression. During the voting, the Coalition and the Iraqi government banned all cars and trucks from driving in the cities, except a closely limited number of security-related vehicles. Thus, at every election from 2005 through 2009, the quietest days in the capital were the election days themselves.

Fuelling the internal stability necessary for a functioning democracy are Iraq's oil reserves, possibly the largest in the world, which also constituted the last of the untapped "sweet crude" reserves—low-cost, low-sulfur energy, easy to extract and refine. In 2008, oil production had shot up to provide the Iraq GDP with $80 billion a year to circulate among the country's approximately 28 million citizens. The potential of $200 billion in oil revenues inside ten years with additional, facile discovery and exploitation encouraged the Iraqi people with a vision of even greater economic prosperity. As Iraq came on line with additional oil, now that it was freed of the Saddam-era sanctions, the entire world—including the U.S.—benefited from lowered costs due to increased global supply. Iraq surpassed Iran in 2012 to become the second largest exporter in OPEC,[2] continuing the diminution of Tehran's place in the world.

The petrochemical wealth of the nation, however, became the key fracture point between the national government in Baghdad and the Kurdish Regional Government, which otherwise had been a reliable partner to Prime Minister Maliki, and also to his predecessors, Ibrahim Jaafari and Iyad Allawi. The most significant, super-giant fields are located in south

Iraq, but there is also commercially available crude in greater Kurdistan, including Kirkuk, on the ethno-political fault line at the heart of the Kurd-Arab split within Iraq.

*　*　*

By the beginning of 2009 I had worked and lived in the Iraq war zone for four out of the previous five years, and a changing of the guard at AISG was called for. It was early in 2008 that our chief operations officer Carlos approached me with the message that Kiffer should step in and take over the role of chief operations officer, the number-two position in the company. A few months later Tony told me the same thing. Carlos, who had served ably with AISG for four years, had had enough. We tried a couple qualified outsiders who did not work out. Probably our fault, as I told one when I asked him not to return to Baghdad from leave: "This is a strange place and we're strange people; this is more about us than about you...."

I tried never to add insult to injury when I terminated someone, which unfortunately the high-stress work environment, long hours, and isolation of the job caused me to have to do more times than I care to remember. I respected these men—and a woman or two—for coming out to the war zone in the first place. The nature of the company, though, as a flat structure with no expatriate middle management and a preponderance of local employees in our thousand-plus work force, necessitated a special type of leader. With no superior looking over their shoulders and hundreds of Iraqis watching their every move, our American (and a few British) managers required initiative, integrity, and competence. The minute we began to get an inkling that one or more of those qualities had gone missing in an individual we quickly sent him home. Or sometimes, they just didn't return from quarterly leave. Given life and reputational risk, along with the possibility of alienating our Iraqi employees, we could not take any chances with AISG's highly paid expats. With families absent and ever-present weapons at hand in our living quarters, depression that might be spawned by a sacking could turn deadly. Our long-serving expat employees even came up with an ominous joke about our standard termination process: "You go on the 'AISG vacation' and never come back."

At our dozens of remote job sites over the years, we developed another technique to ensure none of our American managers "went Colonel Kurtz" (the Green Beret officer in *Apocalypse Now*—a film inspired by Conrad's *Heart of Darkness*—who goes over the edge and embarks on a rogue operation). The potential for these AISG men to become little tyrants abusing their responsibility for hundreds of lives, millions of dollars in equipment and materials, and hundreds of thousands of dollars in petty cash, stood out as a singular risk of our standard operational methodology. We put an experienced American manager on every site, no matter the threat or location. In addition to the site manager, we would have a site security manager, typically a Lebanese Maronite (an Eastern rite Catholic), who worked directly for the site manager but also reported back to the company director of security. Tony not only recruited these men in the first place but also knew the security managers' families back in the Old Country. This way we established dual communication channels. If Tony's man began to report suspicious activity from his American boss, we would immediately investigate.

The AISG site manager position required three assets: comfort with insecurity (hence most of these men had prior military service), technical competence, and—the most difficult to find—patience to work with the locals in "on-the-job" training. From the beginning, all our Iraqi employees and subcontractors required—and even as the years went by, a significant number of them continued to require—skills training on the job sites. One of our greatest challenges, and one we were proudest of overcoming, involved getting U.S.-standard construction and equipment maintenance from a primarily Third World workforce. Teamwork under fire between Americans, Iraqis, Lebanese, and Filipinos defined AISG and our over eighty contracts for the U.S. mission executed without a single failure during the Iraq War. With that set up, we could deliver the services that became our hallmark: American transparency, accountability, attention to detail, and timeliness with an Iraqi workforce.

Four years in the war zone and I'd had enough, so my brother Kiffer took over the reins of the company. He had worked for AISG for two years at that point and earned the respect of our employees, most importantly Tony, especially after the way he had handled the Delta Force operators during their errant raid on Apache. Consequently I think the Iraqis, who are very family oriented, saw this progression as natural; I had not really left them, but assigned family to stay behind. So there was continuity. Kiffer, however, had one last test to pass before he could become CEO. Every other evening, I brought members of the AISG senior management team to the roof of the main house in Apache to lift free weights—great bonding and one of the best stress relievers you'll ever find. It took a little while before our guard force finally got used to the shouting as we pushed each other and ourselves. After he had accepted my offer to run the company, I told Kiffer: "Before you can become CEO, though, you've got to bench more than three hundred pounds."

He looked at me like I was crazy, which he already knew from our over forty years together, but responded simply, "Okay," with a slight look of doubt on his face because of all the surgery he'd had on his shoulders—the results of wrestling and football injuries.

On the eve of Christmas leave—the last day we'd all be together before the start of 2009—here we were on the rooftop working at the weights. I had developed a pyramid technique: three steps up, lift just a few times to stretch on the first two levels, increasing weight between levels. On the third step do the maximum weight possible (if capable of more than three reps, time to increase weight the next time). Then do two steps down at max reps at the same weights as going up. It was quick but it did burn, and you built strength pretty damn fast. On the same roof in Baghdad on my forty-fourth birthday, I benched 374 pounds—twice my own weight. We slid 304 pounds on the bar (the metal plates were metric). Kiffer stared for a couple seconds at the slightly convex steel rod bending under a heavy strain, then stretched out on the bench and pushed the bar up over his face like a roll of paper towels. He was ready....

✶   ✶   ✶

In 2009, oil production in Iraq exceeded pre-war volumes, with the Iraqi government now on the path to financial self-sufficiency. Exxon, Shell, and BP had established operations in the southern Iraq oilfields, reportedly the richest reserves in the world. Basra would become Houston East, with practically all the U.S. oil services companies present.

With the insurgency rapidly waning, the focus for our business had now shifted south from the Sunni Triangle and Baghdad to Basra. My vision for the company had always included working long term in the oil fields after the war. We knew that there would be a tremendous need for reconstruction in the south of Iraq in order to fully exploit the nation's mineral resources and take the country on the path to rapid development. Iraq should eventually surpass its neighbor Saudi Arabia. Iraq has more long-term potential because of the lack of a middle class in the Kingdom of Saudi Arabia prior to the oil boom. In contrast there is a deeply rooted middle class in Baghdad and elsewhere in the major cities of Iraq which would allow the Iraqis to diversify and make better use of the vast capital generated by $100-a-barrel oil. Fortuitously, the U.S. mission also headed to the south at this point. As the British troops departed, American forces needed to step in to ensure nefarious Iranian influences did not take hold, imperiling Baghdad's control over the Iraqi national patrimony—the hydrocarbon riches of the south—along with the nation's sole deep-water port, Umm Qasr. Thus the U.S. Army took over the old British base at Basra airport, where I had met with Colonel Rob Ryder about our captive employees in Samawa.

Looking down from our perch at Apache in the capital on the vast potential in the southern oil fields, we often talked about how AISG could make the leap from DOD contracting and into the more stable and long-term viability of the peacetime commercial sector. The company had some deep experience in Basra given our construction of the Shaiba Iraqi Army base in 2007, which would become the cornerstone of "Energy City." This complex in the desert outside Basra became the headquarters location for the South Oil Company (SOC), the government entity controlling the oilfields in southern Iraq, and also for practically every major international oil company involved in the country, along with major oil services companies such Halliburton and Fluor. As we would find out, SOC and the others crowded their facilities around the Iraqi Army at Shaiba for security. And all the Iraqis knew we had built the base during the violent struggle with the Sadrist militia.

Where the flow of the American mission in Iraq went, there went AISG. The takeover of the British base at the Basra airport came on March 31, 2009, with the complete UK withdrawal of forces from Iraq (except for a small training mission sent home by the Iraqi government in May 2011 after they rejected the British request for an extension).[3] A brigade-plus of American combat troops moved onto the base. In all past large bases in Iraq, KBR would have taken over the base operations under the LOGCAP contract that paid out almost $40 billion to the massive contractor.[4] This time, however, the military went another route, apparently interpreting the worldwide military logistics contract with KBR to cover only FOBs (forward operating bases), not the new-style "contingency operating base" COB Basra. Hey, if KBR did not challenge the tricky semantics, why should we? Especially considering that DOD went to the Joint Contracting Command-Iraq/Afghanistan and had the contract put out to bid to the pre-selected companies on the Omnibus Life Support contract, which included AISG, along with five highly experienced Iraqi and Middle Eastern companies. With the public animus toward KBR for its connection to Dick Cheney and charges of "war profiteering" from the newly ascendant Democrats now holding all three elected branches of the federal government in Washington, KBR wisely decided to let the Basra base contract pass.

Kiffer and his team jumped right on it, putting together the bid for the highly complex project. (The proposal exhibited several hundred line items costing power, waste management, water treatment, laundry, and security services—but not "anti-terrorism and force protection services," as the vast majority of our Iraq War contracts had.) As if by some great design, we came out on top; the company would occupy the catbird seat in the richest undeveloped oil fields in the world. DOD awarded AISG the operations and maintenance of five American bases in Basra servicing seven thousand U.S. military and State Department personnel through 2012. This $50-million-plus O&M contract included U.S. facilities at Basra International Airport (COB Basra), the Port of Umm Qasr, and the Safwan land-border crossing from Kuwait—the main points of entry into the Iraqi oil fields.

AISG still operated bases in the badlands as well. At COP (combat outpost) Shocker at the Badra border crossing used by most Iranian pilgrims entering Iraq to visit the great Shia shrines of Najaf and Karbala, the U.S. government took biometrics (retina scan, photo, fingerprints) from every "pilgrim" who transited there. We provided dining, operations and maintenance, and supply for a couple hundred American troops stationed at Shocker. FOB Cobra, a hundred miles or so northeast of the Iraqi capital, where we ran one of our outstanding coffee shops among a full suite of support services, sat right between a Baghdad-controlled military unit and a Kurdish Peshmerga force that was ostensibly part of the Iraqi Army. The base straddled the fracture line between Iraq and the territorial claims of the autonomous Kurdish Regional Government near the volatile mixed Arab-Kurdish city of Khanaquin. Among other smaller projects, we also ran O&M at and catered the Baghdad-based FOB Justice, the Iraqi training academy for prison guards under a U.S. Department of Justice program. Nevertheless, the war was waning and so were the DOD contracts associated with the military. Kiffer therefore decided to take a leap of faith in the future and move our headquarters out of Fort Apache, where we had been safely ensconced for six years against all sorts of trials and tribulations, and head south to Basra.

*   *   *

The shifting of material, equipment, and personnel to Basra took several months and cost more than a million dollars, primarily because we had to build from scratch the housing and offices we had leased back in Baghdad. On top of that, our reception in Basra did not bode well. A local contractor who had previously worked directly for the British and then the American military was now out in the cold, and not happy about that. So that company left the more than one hundred generators used to power the entire base drained of oil, hoping that when we started them they would disintegrate. We caught that in time, but our local *Basrawi* hires, of whom we planned to bring in several hundred, reported threats against them for working for us. Our workforce also included, evidently, some provocateurs. Labor strife, which we had never before experienced on an organized basis, now raised its ugly head.

Tony, who had seen a lot of death in his life and never got comfortable at COB Basra—he said the trailer-like luxury executive living quarters we had built reminded him of a tomb—came down from Baghdad to resolve the situation. He got out among the workers, explaining to them in fluent Iraqi Arabic, albeit with a Baghdadi-Lebanese accent, that AISG would treat them with dignity, just as we had the thousands of Iraqi *shabaab* (guys) before them. At the same time, he used the interrogation techniques he had honed at Fort Huachuca (the home of U.S. Military Intelligence) to uncover the labor agitators. The workforce quickly quieted down. But the mortars and rockets kept smacking around our compound.

Next door to us at COB Basra was the headquarters of OGA ("Other Governmental Agency"—the well-known pseudonym for the CIA). They told Kiffer that the old Basrawi-owned contractor was launching explosives at our facilities in order to cause us to fail. Having OGA next door provided information benefits, but their high-powered communications gear jammed our cell phone frequencies. No big deal: we got on VOIP (voice-over-internet protocol) to talk with the world. The interference did, however, run off the Samsung Engineering executives who came to visit in order to see if they wanted to stay with us while checking on opportunities in the oil fields. The Korean businessmen couldn't handle the unpleasant reality that their smart phones wouldn't work reliably at our facility; they never came back.

Mortar rounds landed randomly for more than a year. Obviously, the Sadrists supported by nearby Iran—the border stood less than twenty miles away—did not want the U.S. military to get comfortable in Basra. I had just arrived for my first visit back, after purposefully giving Kiffer the time to solidify control outside my shadow, when all of a sudden: "*Brrrrrrrrrrrrrrrrrrap! Tinkle, tinkle, tinkle,*" as metal rained down on the steel roof of my brother's office where we sat talking.

I exclaimed, "What! Are they shooting right over our compound?" The U.S. military had placed Phalanx 20 mm Gatling guns, originally designed for protecting Navy ships from missiles, to serve as anti-mortar and -rocket defense at bases throughout Iraq. The radar-guided automatic-firing guns could shoot an incoming projectile out of the air more times than not. I had heard them before at the U.S. Air Force's super-FOB Anaconda. Kiffer had told me months earlier that we'd actually repaired gratis for the Army the worn-out British generator running the Phalanx that the Royal Navy, I guess, had installed prior to our taking over the base.

"Well, I'm going to need to report this again. They keep test-firing in our direction after promising not to," Kiffer said nonchalantly. Just another day at the COB—it proved you can get used to anything.

The next morning, Kiffer and Tony guided me to our waiting convoy to meet with the *sheikh ash shuyukh* (premier leader) of a significant local tribe that wanted to work with us. The *al Bataat* numbered tens of thousands of members who owned thousands of camels on the territory stretched along the desert frontier with Kuwait. We drove across Basra, a mud-brick town that seemed like it would wash away into the Persian Gulf given a strong enough rainstorm. The Sunni-centric Saddam had nearly starved the second largest city in Iraq—almost completely Shia and formerly known (in the nineteenth century) as "the Pearl of the Gulf." Oil gushed out of the Basra region south to the waiting super tankers, and payment flowed north to the capital. To a certain degree, this reality continues until today, even under a Shia-dominated government: the center (Baghdad) rules.

We entered a *diwan* (a traditional area for leadership audiences) on the first floor of a large mud-colored brick house. (All the houses and low-slung buildings in Basra were the color of mud.) A feast fit for twenty people was spread out on the carpet surrounded by pillows, but there were only eight of us. Two barbequed *tulley* (lamb) lay splayed out on a bed of lettuce, onions, garlic, and tomatoes. *Khuubas*, freshly baked flat bread that no Iraqi could live long without, lined the table, with hummus and other tasty Arabic sauces arrayed for dipping. We sat down and dug in— Tony, Kiffer, and I surrounded by various sub-leaders from the sheikh's greater family, all dressed in flowing white dishdasha. The three of us finished eating last, out of conscious courtesy to the host. I felt so stuffed that I almost dropped into a satiety-induced stupor. I rallied, though, after a couple cups of bitter Turkish coffee and started to talk with the al Bataat sheikhs.

As I wiped the last of the succulent lamb fat from my hands, I said: "*Kullen hella*"—the Basrawi way of saying, "All is good."

They nodded in response with shades of smiles on their faces at this American trying to speak their language.

I then started to tell a story about my dream of wanting to cross the *Rubh al Khalli*, the "Empty Quarter," on a camel. This infamously treacherous, vast, and absolutely waterless area between Saudi Arabia and Yemen and Oman begins—for all intents and purposes, except for the vast oil fields—southwest of Basra. They listened closely but just stared somewhat quizzically at me when I said *jamal* (camel in Arabic). I repeated it, thinking my pronunciation must be incorrect.

Then Tony returned. He had been talking to the main sheikh at his couch at the other end of the room in preparation for my discussion with the tribal chief. Tony quickly corrected, "They don't know *jamal* here; they use *ba'ir* for camel."

Now they all smiled and one said in Arabic, "If he can do the business he has done in Iraq, it will be no problem for him to cross the Empty Quarter on a camel."

The sheikh of sheikhs motioned me over. About eighty years old, he looked at me kindly, touched my grizzled beard and said, "*Min win hatha abyedh?*" ("Where does this white come from?")

I responded, "*Min khibra*"—from experience. The white in my beard had not existed before I came to Iraq, that's for sure.

The sheikh laughed knowingly, and I thought we did all right with him, but we never did any business of substance with the tribe. We employed some of their people for the COB. They had developed their own connections with the South Oil Company, which controlled everything in the oil fields. That meant that Exxon and the other oil companies came to them for that access, so they had no need for us.

*   *   *

We stalked Exxon, just wanting to be a remora to the great white shark that the largest company in the world represented. Crumbs from its mouth would feed our families for generations. I was now back in Washington again, mainly involved in strategic business development along with supporting Kiffer and AISG in any way possible from the United States, including both recruiting and lobbying. I targeted Exxon immediately on my return home to the Washington area. Kiffer kept me updated about the Houston-based oil giant's activities in Iraq. We came to understand that AISG could not contract directly with Exxon for our standard services of construction and support. (There was more potential in security.) Our competition had it all wrapped up from London, where Exxon had launched its operation into Iraq. We would just have to get contracts with one of its engineering, procurement, and construction subcontractors—such marquee firms as Fluor, Halliburton, and Baker Hughes.

As a first step toward that goal, I brought Bob Kelley onboard my U.S.-based business development team. He had been a strategic advisor to Paul Brinkley and his Iraq business task force and was among the longest serving American diplomats at our embassy in Baghdad during the Iraq War. Bob, a Washington lawyer and Foreign Corrupt Practices Act expert, had been recruited by Notre Dame in 1958 to play quarterback. He knew almost everyone, and if he didn't, he could find a way to get to them. We discussed the plan and the targets. He went out to his network and came up with a name and a contact: Houston-based Nabors, the largest land oil-drilling company in the world. I traveled down to their headquarters and pitched the CEO of the international division and seven of his senior staff. I went in alone; in those face-to-face situations, it's not so much what you say but whether you "vibrate" the truth. I vibrated the truth. We knew Basra and Iraq. Nabors did not. They wanted in, and we could help them establish operations. Their CEO, Siggi Meissner, traveled to Baghdad and stayed at Apache (which we were in the process of downsizing) before going to Basra. And after days of tough negotiations with Nabors' Russian-American lady oil-contract attorney, they hired us.

Next step, I engaged Patton Boggs, the top lobbying firm in the U.S., through my Washington mentors, Mario Mirabelli, a then-Patton Boggs partner who had settled the Lockerbie Libya case, obtaining over $1.4 billion for the victims' families from Muammar Gaddafi, and Judd Gould, a securities attorney who had helped take my export/import company public in 1998. Patton Boggs led us to Fluor, the largest construction company in the world, who hired us to do an O&M contract at COB Basra. I then traveled down to Houston for a meeting with the folks at Fluor, who now at least knew about AISG from the O&M contract. I got the invitation to this meeting, to discuss the plans for Exxon going into Iraq, because of my friend Frank Guffey, who had shown me around Baghdad at the beginning of my Iraq adventure in January 2004 and now worked for Bertling, a German-owned logistics firm that had a preferred-vendor contract with Fluor.

The meeting, titled "Route Recon," took place in late March, 2011, in a conference room packed with over twenty Fluor people and a few Exxon types arrayed around a large polished table and seated along the walls. This was a big deal, representing a huge piece of business for the construction giant. The Fluor managers detailed a $65 billion initial expenditure to get Exxon's super giant field at West Qurna pumping at peak production. Frank gave a presentation on the proposed logistics route from West Qurna to the port of Umm Qasr. Bertling had sent out one of their German engineers to do a route recon from Umm Qasr to West Qurna. The report had only reached Frank the morning of the meeting (in German) and arrived not fully complete, but it was impressive, nonetheless, in that Bertling had sent an experienced and qualified man out into the field in a post-conflict zone, spending Bertling's own money to get the recon done.

One of the Exxon engineers said, "We're very concerned about the load capability on the bridge directly to West Qurna."

Frank responded, "On our route, we're proposing to use pontoon bridges over the first two waterways. We don't assess that the existing structures can carry the one-hundred-fifty ton generator loads required, but the third waterway [the one of greatest concern to Exxon] had a bridge that might work."

The Fluor and Exxon engineers looked skeptical and continued to grouse about the lack of exact load capabilities. So I interjected, "The most critical aspect here is that we can get anything accomplished if we work with the Iraqis and guarantee that we have their buy-in by ensuring that they know there will be mutual collaboration, investment, and employment. Otherwise, we might have problems."

More skepticism emerged, with some of those present questioning why AISG had a seat at the table. But Mike Morris, the head Exxon guy there, closed the meeting agreeing that "we need to have local content."

We assessed that as a victory for our pitch that working hand in hand with the Iraqis would prove more critical to success than load calculations.

(Meanwhile, Patton Boggs also led us to Smiths Detection, for whom we selected and vetted Iraqi engineers to travel to Germany for training on the company's first-class explosives and metal detectors. The U.S. government had funded a program to install that equipment at all international points of entry—meaning the twenty-plus airports and border crossings into Iraq. The newly trained Iraqi AISG engineers returned from Frankfurt and succeeded perfectly on the technically challenging task of installation. We worried, however, about operations and maintenance, which were not part of the contract. For example, when our team returned for a follow-up visit to Mosul airport, the customs chief there had taken the metal detector off the passenger line and put it over the entrance to his office. He said, "I'm not from around here, so I want to make sure no one comes into my office with a weapon....")

As time went on, we noticed things slowing down on the Exxon deployment schedule. Spring dragged into summer. We came to understand that the Iraqi government's South Oil Company was continuing to give Exxon a hard time, not approving purchases of production-required equipment. Unfortunately, the Iraqi government had awarded only production service agreements, not concessions. Not only did this preclude the oil companies from booking the reserves on their balance sheets—a standard practice worldwide—because they did not "own" the fields they had to get written acceptance from SOC for all purchases. The Iraqis got hung up on their own nationalist rhetoric with the reserves issue—for obviously the oil companies could not move the assets from under the ground without Government of Iraq approval. (I think that this Iraqi mistake originated from the psychological trauma of past Western imperialist abuse. For decades prior to the Baathist regime nationalization of oil production in the early 1970s, the British-controlled, minority-American-owned Iraq Petroleum Company paid pennies on the barrel to the Iraqis and restricted output to enhance

UK production in Iran.)[5] Yet the IOCs—international oil companies—could have taken the booked assets and raised capital that in turn would have made investments in post-conflict Iraq even more attractive. The initial value to the IOCs on the awarded fields was not much more than a measly $1.50 a barrel, hardly worth the trouble. However, they did come; the Big Oil men did not want to miss out on the greatest hydrocarbon bonanza of the twenty-first century.[6]

We watched a $400 billion energy company that had conquered giant waves in the North Sea and overcome an insurgency in Indonesia[7] founder on the shoals of Iraqi intransigence and shortsightedness. At last, I received the invitation to come to Houston again to meet a senior ExxonMobil executive to discuss Iraq. We sat down to a steak dinner in a white-linen fine eatery. The executive, a top graduate of a first-class engineering school, as were almost all Exxon managers, exuded a tough-minded confidence and technical expertise that could intimidate anyone. After finishing our supper, where the small talk spanned the globe, we ordered scotches and then got to talking business.

The thirty-five-year ExxonMobil man asked, "So what do you think about what's going on in Iraq?"

You don't get very many open doors like that in this world, and certainly not a second whack at it. I responded directly, speaking quickly for fear of getting interrupted and sidetracked. "The South Oil Company is corrupt. This is the reason that you are not able to move forward at West Qurna. This is coming from the highest levels in Baghdad. So I propose the following: The people of Basra are seeing no benefit from the oil flow. Unemployment is still sky high. In order to break through the corruption at SOC we need to bring political pressure on them from the tribes. In Iraq, as in most of the developing world, there are no individuals in the Western autonomous sense, only collectives. The collectives we are talking about now are the tribes." I paused, choosing my words carefully. "AISG has vast experience with them, having employed over ten thousand Iraqis in every corner of the country and from practically every tribal grouping. We can take Exxon representatives around to meet the sheikhs, inform them of your plans including how many members of their tribe you will train and employ. Then they will realize, with our prompting, that SOC is holding up tens of billions of dollars in investments into the Basra region, with commensurate employment of their people. The consequent pressure, I strongly believe, will break the corrupt log-jam at SOC."

We talked a bit further, with the sophisticated executive never either denying what I had said about SOC or agreeing with my proposal. But I could sense that the radical concept had some traction. Of course, my plan was the Full Monty: there were possible lesser gradations to it that we could implement collaboratively. At the end of a most gracious dinner, the Exxon exec said, "I will have my director of security for Iraq reach out to you to discuss working together." And he did ...

CHAPTER 12

THE LAST OF THE OCCUPIERS

AFTER THE IRAQI-RUN 2010 parliamentary election, Maliki's State of Law coalition managed to maintain national control after coming in second to Iyad Allawi's Sunni-dominated *Iraqiyya* party. Allawi, who had won a plurality of one seat, never gained an additional parliamentary vote, as then–U.S. ambassador to Baghdad Christopher Hill stated. Maliki took eight months to assemble a majority while running a continued anti-terrorism campaign against al-Qaeda, neo-Saddamists, and Iran-allied militias. The insurgency was over. No longer did a guerrilla force capable of insurrection threatening the existence of the state hold safe haven inside or along the borders of Iraq.

The 2008 Status of Forces Agreement (SOFA) negotiated between Maliki's government and the Bush administration moved along with cold efficiency as the contractual December 31, 2011, end date for all U.S. troops to exit Iraq inexorably approached. No security threat on the ground indicated a need to change the process, but everyone involved assumed that there would be an extension to allow for stay-behind American forces to help in training and counter-terrorism. Then–Secretary of Defense Robert Gates noted in his autobiography *Duty*, "In December 2008 and thereafter, I believed we should and would have a residual military presence in Iraq after 2011…even though that would require a follow-on agreement." (Gates went on to be Secretary of Defense under President Barack Obama, an unprecedented example in American history of serving in that critical position under consecutive administrations from different political parties.) Casualties among civilians, Iraqi, and U.S. forces continued to remain low. The new Obama administration, installed in office in January 2009, had picked up the ball on the talks for a continued U.S. military presence in Iraq after the SOFA expired. Not an easy task, as we always joked: "The Iraqis have lost a lot of wars, but never a negotiation."

No combat forces of any consequence from any other Coalition nation remained. Spain, Ukraine, and Italy had initially deployed infantry brigade–level forces, but they had all departed by 2006 after being run out of their central-Iraq operational areas by a combination of an al-Qaeda terrorist attack in Europe (Madrid, March 2004), local Sadrist resistance, and anti-war protest at home. Japan and South Korea had provided military reconstruction assistance in the less kinetic areas of south Iraq (prior to 2007) and Kurdistan. Several "new" European states, as Rumsfeld would put it, had also contributed, with Poland staying until 2008 and Romania departing in 2009. British combat forces left in 2009 except for a small training mission departing May 2011. Georgian troops manned the gates of the Green Zone until 2008, just prior to turnover to Iraqi forces, when Bush ordered them airlifted back to their homeland to confront an invading Russian army.[1] All the Latin American nations left with Spain, except for El Salvador, which had not forgotten American help in their own recent guerrilla war; the Salvadorans stayed until the end of the insurgency in 2009, running convoy security.

The drawdown of U.S. forces in Iraq did not come without cost. Among the last combat bases turned over to the Iraqi forces was COP

Shocker, on the Iranian border, where the arid Iraqi flatlands push against the Zagros Mountains that form the western front range of the vast Iranian plateau that extends over one thousand miles to Afghanistan. Never before had I seen a change in geography more distinctly delineating a political and ethnic frontier. Our site manager at Shocker, John McCulley, ran a tight ship, winning an Iraq-wide Army award for small-unit (non-KBR LOGCAP) dining facilities. Before becoming a contractor in Iraq, he had served in the Marines and then joined the peacetime Army afterwards for greater opportunities, but I think he still thought of himself first and foremost as a Marine.

Shocker was due to shut down on June 30, 2011. The area had been quiet for several months, if not longer, with no one killed during the entire yearlong deployment of the U.S. Army unit occupying the base, the 2nd Squadron of the 3rd Armored Cavalry Regiment (famed for its COIN tactics in Tal Afar in 2006). The Pentagon had rebranded the 3rd ACR an "advise and assist brigade" to comply semantically with the commitment to get "all U.S. combat forces out of Iraq by August 31, 2010" and fulfill Barack Obama's campaign promise.[2] Thus ended Operation Iraqi Freedom and began Operation New Dawn (reminiscent of a dishwashing soap ad— "New and Improved!").

John had co-located the AISG site headquarters tent (with power, AC, and a raised floor) next to the base's tactical operations center (TOC); that's how integral his operations had become to the local Army command. In preparation for demobilization, the unit had evidently already pulled down the "eye-in-the-sky" aerostat balloon providing over-watch for the combat outpost when on June 29, Iranian-sponsored Iraqi Shiite militiamen—in this case apparently the *Kataib Hezbollah* or "Battalions of the Party of God"—launched three or four IRAMs (improvised rocket-assisted munitions, basically IEDs on rockets) into Shocker from a deep wadi just a few hundred meters away. The projectiles impacted directly on the TOC, killing two Army officers and a senior sergeant, and severely wounding John. (Fifteen U.S. soldiers would die from enemy action in Iraq that month—an isolated peak in the middle of several months of low single-digit losses from combat action.)[3]

As a part of our contract with DOD, the U.S. military air-evacuated John to Landstuhl (Germany) Army medical hospital where they managed to save all his limbs and get him up and moving around after months of surgery. He will continue to need several surgeries. A real blessing in all this: his wife, Stephanie, an Army medic and nurse who had served in Iraq with an infantry brigade out of FOB Hammer, now worked at Landstuhl in the obstetrics ward, delivering the babies of military families. So they were able to be together with their two young boys from the beginning of his treatment and recovery. John is a tough man with a lot of courage, no doubt—when I went to visit them in Germany on my way back from a trip to Iraq and Afghanistan, the only real question John had for me was "When can I get my old job back?"

*　　　*　　　*

Iraq asserted full sovereignty by forcing U.S. troops to withdraw completely in December 2011, leaving AISG as one of the last of the American DOD contractors still present from the Occupation. The negotiations between the Obama administration and the Maliki government for a follow-on Status of Forces Agreement had broken down ostensibly over the immunities issue—protection for U.S. soldiers from prosecution under Iraqi law for actions in Iraq. But others describe the failure to reach an agreement differently. Vali Nasr, a high-level staffer inside the Obama State Department during the negotiations, judges harshly in his memoir, *Dispensable Nation*, "The administration responded to the collapse of its halfhearted negotiations by declaring victory.... But it was a Pyrrhic victory, a testament to American fickleness—a break-it-and-bolt that will be tough to shake."[4]

New York Times reporter Michael Gordon's *Cobra II* and *Endgame* constitute the first attempt at a comprehensive look at the Iraq War. In

Endgame, he details a tortuous process within the Obama administration in which the minimum number requested by the Pentagon and the president's commanders in the field—ten thousand American soldiers remaining in Iraq—was whittled down to an offer to the Iraqis of around five thousand troops. Gordon reports, "The inability of the two sides to negotiate a new SOFA was not a setback, the president's advisers concluded, because the White House never considered it a requirement."[5]

On October 11, 2011—just before the collapse of the status of forces agreement—Leon Panetta, the new secretary of defense, who had replaced Robert Gates in the summer, finally addressed the issue publicly when answering a U.S. service member's question about the immunities issue in salubrious Naples, Italy. He stated that the SOFA "is in negotiation.... But—as secretary of defense, if I'm going to put a significant or large group of forces in place, I've got to have protection for you."[6] Secretary of State Hillary Clinton, who traveled the world, but not to Iraq, during the negotiations, said hardly a word in public about the SOFA talks. And during the 2012 presidential debates, after the SOFA negotiations broke down and the last troops had been withdrawn from Iraq, Obama himself seemed to disagree with the position his own administration had taken in those negotiations, criticizing Mitt Romney—who said he agreed with the president's plan to have stay-behind forces but disagreed with the number of soldiers, wanting more than the five thousand proposed by the White House negotiators—and asserting that Romney "wanted to keep troops in Iraq as of today [October 22, 2012—less than a year after the final American forces departed Iraq]. That is not a recipe for taking advantage of the opportunities and meeting the challenges of the Middle East."[7]

On the ground in Iraq, we sensed that the Iraqis realized they needed U.S. troops to stay in country but to be acceptable the offer had to be serious, reflecting a real commitment, because keeping the "occupiers" would come with a political price. The Sadrists in parliament agitated against the agreement, and the Iranians were dead set against the plan. On August 11, 2010, the senior Iraqi Army officer, Lieutenant General Babakar Zebari, observed to the Western media, "If I were asked about the withdrawal by the politicians I would say: the US army must stay until the Iraqi Army is fully ready in 2020."[8] "If the Americans leave, the training here will fall apart or become fake training," said Iraqi Army Colonel Abbas Fadhil Sahib, the commander at Besmaya armor training center, in early 2010. "We will have to put a sign on the gate that says, 'We are very sorry to accept you for training.'"[9]

After years of working with the Iraqi security services, and especially the Army, we knew that the respect and bond established by the shared loss and risk with the U.S. military need not be broken. The Iraqi politicians feared each other almost as much as AQI and Iran, and they had seen first hand the non-political role the U.S. military had played in keeping the peace. The Iraqis remembered their close brush with all-out civil war in 2006. Plus, Iraq lived in a tough neighborhood where blood enemies lurked beyond almost every border—Iran, Turkey, Syria, and even Saudi Arabia, terrified of the rise of a Shiite power in Baghdad given its own substantial Shia minority living on top of the kingdom's major oilfields. The thought of the might of the U.S. Air Force protecting the skies above and the American Army ready to return if the trip-wire of the remainder forces got sprung had put much ease in the traumatized minds of many Iraqis.

The earlier SOFA (2008) had skirted the immunities issue in an artful way, with language crafted by focused and motivated diplomats on both sides:

> Article 12
> Jurisdiction
>   1. Iraq shall have the primary right to exercise jurisdiction over members of the United States Forces and of the civilian component for the grave premeditated felonies enumerated pursuant to paragraph 8, when such crimes are committed outside agreed facilities and areas and outside duty status....

8. Where Iraq exercises jurisdiction pursuant to paragraph 1 of this Article, members of the United States Forces and of the civilian component shall be entitled to due process standards and protections consistent with those available under United States and Iraqi law. The Joint Committee shall establish procedures and mechanisms for implementing this Article, including an enumeration of the grave premeditated felonies that are subject to paragraph 1 and procedures that meet such due process standards and protections. Any exercise of jurisdiction pursuant to paragraph 1 of this Article may proceed only in accordance with these procedures and mechanisms.[10]

Therefore the Iraqis had authority over U.S. service members on paper, but not for all practical purposes, because no U.S. soldier would be out on liberty in Iraq, all would be on "duty status." Nevertheless, the Iraqis had a tangible concession to hang their hat on, and they saved face. Something along the same lines could have resulted in a new SOFA agreement—if the U.S. government had possessed the will to get the job done.

More than a year after the last U.S. troops departed Iraq, I was sitting in a restaurant on Capitol Hill enjoying a mid-Atlantic early spring day of budding green leaves and crystal-blue skies with Bob Kelley and Chris Shays, Republican former senior U.S. Representative from Connecticut and chairman of the Iraq War Contracting Commission. Talking about how to benefit from lessons learned from the war, I said, "We need to institutionalize the successes of contracting in Iraq. Just like with counterinsurgency, the American government has not done long-term memory effectively. We keep reinventing the wheel."

"Agreed," Chris responded, "but it seems like things are not going well in Iraq now politically and with the Syrian situation [the high-intensity civil war overlapping jihadis into Iraq]. It is so unfortunate that we did not leave troops there."

Then it struck me in the pit of my stomach: "You know it's hard for me to call for more war, even with Syria, after all I've experienced in Iraq and Afghanistan. I guess as a result of that, when the last troops crossed into Kuwait, I felt a sense of relief. They were no longer targets." I then caught myself and continued, "But the real problem came when we drew down the CIA to near nothing. The Iraqis do not have our technical intelligence-gathering capability, such as signals intercepts. We really beat al-Qaeda in Iraq because they loved to talk on the cellphone. So Delta Force tracked their calls with the help of the NSA and killed or captured them.[11] The Iraqi security forces do not understand a network-centric approach; their focus of stopping terrorist attacks is at the checkpoints, which is too late."

I could have added that retaining a significant training element and Special Operations force in Iraq would have made a significant difference—both politically (as evidence of continued U.S. commitment to Iraq's security and stability) and militarily (by helping kill and capture bad guys). This stay-behind force, however, would have required a SOFA.

*   *   *

Business continued. No matter what happened with the U.S. military in Iraq, we were in country long-term. I had said many times when asked when I planned to leave Iraq, "When the Iraqis throw us [AISG] out."

Back in Connecticut, Graham Wiggins, a reality TV producer, was friends with Dennis Blankenbeker, an IT guru who had served with AISG from 2006 to 2011, rising to financial comptroller working alongside Mark Walker, our longtime CFO. Graham had read *Contractor Combatants* and thought that Americans would get a kick out of riding along with us in Iraq—vicariously, of course. We met up in Dubai, flew into Kuwait City, and rode to the border with one of the al Bataat sheikhs. At the border we linked up with Tony, Graham filming the whole way. He did a short promo piece that begins with him and me crossing the border, where I say: "Now we're about to travel from one safe place into a not-so-safe place." He went out on a convoy movement and even let me say on camera, "We're as hard as woodpecker lips." All good fun. The entire Basra team really appreciated Graham's interest—everyone called him "Hollywood."

With the help of Frank Guffey, who had left Bertling amicably to come to work with AISG as vice president for business development, Kiffer won us a contract for the State Department building a $25 million air ops hub at Basra international airport. We had done a little work for State in the COB Basra O&M contract that extended out to four other, smaller bases in the province including for Provincial Reconstruction Teams. Foggy Bottom's real contribution to the reconstruction effort in Iraq, aside from the good works of USAID, emerged out of the PRTs. These civilian-led groups composed of development experts with substantial numbers of seconded military officers worked directly with the Iraqi provincial leadership to build capability on the public services side, with small construction projects included. The final report of the Special Inspector General for Iraq Reconstruction called the PRTs "perhaps the most innovative, and where it worked, integrative capacity-building initiative in Iraq."[12] These teams served as key components of the *civilian* surge, supplementing the overtaxed military's reconstruction efforts.

The Basra air ops hub, however, would support an entirely different level of work for the State Department, which was now, with the complete drawdown of U.S. military forces, about to take control of the post-conflict mission in Iraq. State's unprecedented role was planned to involve 17,000 personnel, mostly contractors, and their own airline, now that the military's massive helicopter fleet would depart the country.[13] The diplomats needed to be able to hop from one safe U.S.-controlled air facility to another, as land movement without the U.S. Army quick-reaction forces was too great an unknown to the risk-sensitive civilians from State. As a top USAID official had told me early in my tenure in Iraq, "We are not soldiers!"

Because of the extensive steel work associated with the 24,000-square-foot hanger, we brought in a billion-dollar Turkish conglomerate to joint venture with us on the facility. Working with the Turks presented its own challenges, including a more elastic sense of time, shall we say, than what showed up in black and white on the schedule. Their safety procedures also left a lot to be desired. When I came back to visit, Kiffer escorted me into the vast space of the hangar built to maintain and repair forty-passenger fixed-wing aircraft with a massive twenty-ton boom crane on tracks stretching from wall to wall. I looked up at the peaked steel-girder roof frame and saw a man-lift fully extended fifty feet in the air with a couple Turkish workers installing lighting and said, "They've got no safety harness on."

Kiffer responded, "I'll get with their manager right now." Whereas almost all our construction people onsite were Iraqi (many of whom we had worked with for years) with American site managers and master electricians—the lack of that technical expertise was a systemic weakness in Iraq and elsewhere in the developing world—our partner's workforce was entirely Turkish.

When he returned, Kiffer said, "They've improved. We keep getting on them. I can remember coming in here when the Turks had just assembled the hangar framework. There were two workers on a too-short lift; one stood on the top rung of a ladder resting against a side of the lift box, leaning out over the fifty-foot drop above the concrete floor welding a joint with an acetylene torch. The welder had on a safety strap attached to the *ladder*."

Nevertheless, we got it done together. As far as we could tell, this constituted the only State Department construction project in Iraq completed to spec and on time. The U.S. consulate being built not far from the air-hub by the giant Boston-based construction management firm Perini (think Big Dig), was still lagging several months behind when we completed our project. The design included two nine-thousand-square-foot office buildings with overhead indirect-fire protection from mortars and rockets, along with the full-service hangar, all linked with networked security systems and powered by three 1.7-megawatt generators. We constructed multiple aprons for rotary wing operations, twelve helicopter pads, and two fixed-wing aircraft pads along with a new passenger terminal and office building. The work also required extensive force protection measures such as security towers with automated entry control points utilizing hydraulic blocking mechanisms that would stop the biggest truck bomb.

By the end of the project, the place looked and acted like a fortress, run and protected by the U.S. Diplomatic Security Service—except for the airplane taxiway leading out to the Iraqi-controlled airport. State envisioned a retractable wall on wheels spanning the one-hundred-meter-wide space as defense against vehicle bombs or any type of ground attack *a la* Viet Cong. But no company in the world could design, manufacture, and deliver that size ballistic gate in the time required or, for that matter, within the budget available. Therefore one entire side of the U.S. diplomats' exclusive air hub remained completely open out into the vast airfield.

The whole thing seemed to upset the Iraqis a bit as, I guess, a criticism of their own security capabilities, given that the air hub stood inside an Iraqi military base. They got their revenge in a symbolic yet meaningful way. Per State's specifications, we had ordered bullet-proof windows for the looming guard towers from a specialized U.S. manufacturer in Maryland. Prior to paying for them, I had even gone to the factory to inspect the shipment of high-quality glass, capable of stopping a heavy machine gun round. But when the carefully crated cargo arrived via air-shipment at Basra customs, we could never get it to clear, even with heavy State Department pressure. It just sat and gathered dust for weeks, months, and then years until finally released in early 2014.

*   *   *

The diminution of American influence in Iraq with the failure of the SOFA talks and the final withdrawal of all our troops—just before deadline—on December 18, 2011, came with additional, insidious costs. The rule of law so assiduously preached (and enforced at a certain level) by the U.S. government to the Iraqis fell by the wayside. This impacted American business in Iraq and, even more importantly, the Iraqi people, who were only now beginning to see the benefits of an open society, free of tyranny and war.

On August 11, 2011, the journal *Middle East Oil & Gas* published an article called "In Depth: Iraq," which included my input as principal owner of AISG. I observed to the journal that as an old ExxonMobil hand had told me, "There are four types of business risk for international oil companies: exploration, technical, marketing, and cultural-political.... In Iraq, we only have one risk—cultural-political—as we know the oil is there, it practically burbles up out of the ground in Basra." The article referred to an assessment of the potential of the country's oil fields. "Harry T. Holzman, Jr., the man put in charge of estimating Iraq's reserves by the U.S. Army, thinks 230 billion barrels is realistic." That number, which other oil industry experts have also told me is not far off, would put Iraq at the top of the charts for oil reserves and represented over *$20 trillion* at current oil prices. This constituted a huge opportunity not only for businesses such as AISG but also for the Iraqi people to climb quickly out of the hole Saddam had dug for them and into the twenty-first century in record time. As a result, the article projected (using data from the International Monetary Fund) that Iraq would see economic growth of over 12 percent in 2011, and 11 percent in 2012[14]—rates seen by few other countries, especially considering that the world community had just started to emerge from the Great Recession.

The cultural-political risk, however, didn't need any help from the other business risks—that alone sufficed.

Exxon's Iraq security director reached out to us for a meeting at their offices in Dubai, United Arab Emirates. Ongoing security concerns strictly limited the actual number of international oil company (IOC) employees— not contractors—in Iraq. So most of the companies kept large staffs to support the Iraq effort in the desert megalopolis of Dubai—a city-state of glass skyscrapers and malls with the latest Milan fashion. Dubai had sprung up twenty years before out of nowhere along a creek off the Persian Gulf formerly best known for smuggling and pearl diving. The small emirate (one of seven making up the UAE) had become the new Beirut—the Middle Eastern international center for commerce and travel—after the Lebanese capital never recovered from the civil war, Syrian occupation, and Israeli invasion.

Kiffer and Frank showed up at the appointed time and place. They asked for the security director. The receptionist told them to wait. They waited. Finally, another man came out and said that the security director had left to go to Kurdistan. When Kiffer reported back to me on a Skype call, I said, "It sounds like they are messing with us, brother. Exxon has nothing going on in Kurdistan…"

The next call came shortly after I sent an email relaying the no-show to the Exxon exec back in Texas who had suggested the meeting in the first place. Kiffer and Frank flew back to Dubai from Basra—perseverance is the key to success. This time the director showed up. He was a Brit just like the majority of the security men, mostly contractors, associated with the oil companies in Iraq. All the top professionals were former members of the elite UK army special operations unit the SAS (Special Air Service), or "the Regiment," as they all called it—a very small and tight-knit group. Having heard about our intensive work with the Iraqis, Exxon wanted us to put together a network of observers among the local populations around their West Qurna "super-giant" oil field and along the logistics routes to and from the port of Umm Qasr, a hundred miles or so to the south—shades of the Fluor "Route Recon" meeting. These observers would report any and all threat situations back to us and then, after further analysis, we'd pass them on to Exxon's security team in near-real time.

Vetting was the key to why the world's largest company could count on us to provide sensitive information potentially affecting the life and limb of their workforce, along with success of a huge investment. By this time AISG had employed ten thousand Iraqi citizens from and in the most dangerous areas of the country without a single internal insurgent incident. We had several sources of information including the comprehensive Iraqi Ministry of Interior (MOI) database left over from the totalitarian Baathist

police state. Our information director, *Abu Malak* (father of Angel)—
responsible for managing all personnel records including conducting
pre-employment interviews—had served in a similar role for MOI, pre-
invasion. Abu Malak came from a *Faylee* Kurdish tribe, a small minority
of the Shia faith favored by Saddam, like other ethnic and religious minority groups, in an attempt to counterbalance the Arab Shia majority and
the rebellious Sunni Kurds. Nevertheless, Abu Malak hated the Iraqi
dictator—and he proved time and time again over the years that he was
more than happy to work with the Americans.

After the initial interview—in a house just outside the perimeter of
Apache—involving extensive questions about the applicant's parents and
home location, plus more directly employment-related questions about
past experience and training, Abu Malak's all-Iraqi team would cross-
reference the information provided with that from MOI and other sources.
We also submitted our armed bodyguards, who required MNF-I badges
to enter Coalition bases, through the DIA-CIA anti-terrorism database
located in the Green Zone. As the years went by and our workforce
expanded, we had every new hire guaranteed by an existing employee.
Thus if an employee stole from us or damaged anything negligently or
purposefully, the guarantor had to pay if we could not recover from the
employee directly involved. We had multiple family and tribal groupings
represented in the workforce, all carefully balanced by Abu Malak and his
direct supervisor, Tony. All of this served to effectively ensure the coher-
ence of our workforce, because if one member caused problems for the
company, then the guarantor and his group's reputation for reliability
suffered, and they risked losing out on further employment opportunities
with us. Additionally, AISG paid very well, in U.S. dollars, and on time.

From the beginning in 2004 we had helped pave the way forward for
what became DOD contracting law in Iraq (and in Afghanistan, where the
intent would be misinterpreted and undermine the mission): "Iraq First."
Section 886 of Congress's FY (fiscal year) 2008 National Defense Authorization Act (NDAA), which enabled annual funding of the $500 billion-plus

Pentagon budget, mandated a preference for Iraqi and Afghan goods and services in their respective war zones. Because of our Iraqi-focused employment practices and vendors (AISG had put over $300 million into the Iraqi economy), the Joint Contracting Command selected us to be in a pool of five or six contractors able to bid on two major multi-award task order contracts (MATOC) covering Iraq-wide construction and operations and maintenance. That resulted in the COB Basra O&M work.

Our compliance with NDAA Section 886 turned out to be not only good business but also good for the COIN mission of turning over the internal security fight—and all its support requirements—to the Iraqis. An Iraqi-American contracting consultant on the award team that developed the first MATOC told me, "I studied AISG's record on the ground and that helped us decide that we could be effective and do Iraq First at the same time." We transferred a great deal of knowledge through our on-the-job training, which generated an extensive cadre of supportive Iraqis. With this loyal foundation—representing all major facets of Iraq's population—already in place, putting together the Exxon network proved fairly straightforward.

Our proposal began with this introduction:

> Operating successfully and securely in Iraq requires local ground truth in real time. In order to provide this capability, AISG is prepared to stand up, within 30 days of notice to proceed, a proprietary network of vetted and trusted local sources of information embedded throughout ExxonMobil's areas of operation to include logistics routes in Southern Iraq. We propose to manage and prioritize the resulting flow of information through a secure Internet interface.
>
> AISG's proven ability to execute such precise and challenging work is the result of operating effectively nationwide in Iraq for the past eight years while employing over 10,000 Iraqi nationals. We have demonstrated our commitment to the host

nation through our "Iraqi First" policies as AISG aims to provide comprehensive solutions not only for our clients but also for the social and economic development of Iraq. Our successful contract execution—primarily using Iraqi employees, subcontractors and vendors—has led to our direct investment of over $320 million into local economies, establishing AISG's trustworthiness and cultural acceptance. Our tenured presence in Basra has led to the development of an extensive and active Iraqi workforce, with over 80 percent coming from the immediate area.

If the "unthinkable" occurs, whether an accident or a deliberately caused event, AISG can put you in the best position possible to minimize the impacts and respond effectively. In short, we can help ExxonMobil resolve situations and keep critical issues from spinning out of control and becoming a full-blown crisis, by identifying and offering solutions to problems prior to reaching critical mass.

The AISG risk mitigation approach is not just focused on threat identification and resolution. We also propose to assist ExxonMobil in developing goodwill among the locals such as advising on workforce employment to reflect proper balance in regional demographics helping to ensure maximum political support among the Southern Iraqi populace while fully complying with your business and skills needs.

With Tony in the lead, under Kiffer's guidance, and utilizing Frank's extensive knowledge of the oil company's activities in Basra Province, we could now say confidently that our network included at least one trusted, vetted, and indigenous observer in over sixty locales adjacent to Exxon's oil fields and logistics routes. These towns and villages, large and small, had mostly obscure names such as al Hayy al Markazi, al Hadi, Bani Malik al Shamaliya, and al Najibia. The information-gatherers would report back to us on several different areas that could impact the energy giant's business operations, such as insurgent and terrorist activities, Iranian or other malign external influences, criminality, labor unrest, and political agitation.

When we got the proposal to the Exxon security director in Dubai, he said, "Looks good; we're studying it." Kiffer and the team went back to keeping operations running in Basra and elsewhere. And we waited. Several weeks went by and then: the headlines blared, "Exxon signs oil deal with Kurdistan."[15] We were shocked, knowing that this would cut the company off from doing business in Baghdad-controlled Iraq—that is, the parts of Iraq outside the autonomous Kurdistan Regional Government—including, of course West Qurna, an enormous field that represented hundreds of billions of dollars in potential revenue to the oil giant. But apparently they had had enough of the corruption at the South Oil Company blocking their development of their fields. I can only surmise that the deciding factor was the SOC issue, because I've never had it confirmed directly by anyone inside the company. But as with the Platonic cave dweller who determines the existence of the world by the outline of the shadows on the wall, the circumstantial evidence and our own experience with the Iraqi government company with absolute control over the Basra oil reserves clearly points in that direction.

The Kurdistan Regional Government fields did not have near the volume of oil available to Exxon in the south, but the company could book the reserves there, and that meant a great deal to the publicly traded firm's bottom line. And the intransigence of the Iraqi government in how they handled the situation has in the end hurt them more than Exxon. One of the challenges of the south Iraq oil reserves is that they are massive and interconnected. You cannot just pump out the oil alone; you must inject something into the empty space left behind in order not to collapse the architecture of the underground reserve. The most effective replacement substance for that purpose is water, but it cannot be too saline because of the possibility of chemical reactions with salt already present in the reserve structure. Consequently, it can't come directly from the briny waters of the

Gulf. Considering that we were talking about millions of barrels of oil extracted *every day*, that's a lot of water—too much to take it out of the Shatt al Arab River bisecting the oil fields on its way south to the Persian Gulf. That could potentially turn the Shatt al Arab into an Iraqi version of the Colorado River, which dries up in the desert before it finishes its ancient route into the Sea of Cortes because of all the water siphoned off to hydrate Los Angeles and the farms of California's central valley.

Thus the water injection project for south Iraq involved a massive desalinization program and extensive expertise in hydrology and oil geology. Most important, though, the financial requirements were upwards of twelve billion dollars. That's why the Iraqis had been smart to choose Exxon to lead the team to undertake that multiyear project. Now the Iraqis, enraged by the Kurdistan move, kicked the oil giant off the team. No other company could step up. Only Shell might have, but they were bogged down in a similar-sized natural gas project in Basra. (The Iraqis did not have the technical capability to capture the gas byproduct of the oil production there; thus they had burned it off, creating flares that lit the fields at night like it was the Fourth of July *every day*. This waste also cost the Iraqis about a billion dollars in lost annual revenue.)

We watched from our headquarters at COB Basra as other oil and services companies, such as Russia's LukOil and South Korea's Samsung Engineering, tried to step into Exxon's shoes on a piecemeal basis—a billion dollars at time. This could not work because all the fields' underground reserves were interconnected, so that the solution required a holistic approach—thus the huge price tag, which only Exxon would have been able to handle. Endemic corruption also presented insurmountable obstacles to this program. Law-abiding and technically competent firms would not take large investment risks with tens of billions of infrastructure investment in Iraq. As a result, until 2014, the country's production had stagnated at around 2.5 million barrels a day (bpd)—a number achieved more than three years before—whereas it should have been well on the way to climbing to six million bpd. Finally in early 2014, Iraq saw a major total production increase to 3.6 million bpd,[16] but still well below where it could be—in the 5-6 million bpd range. Oil exports fell in June 2014, but only by approximately 150,000 bpd to 2.4 million bpd, reflecting the loss of the northern pipeline into Turkey to the jihadis of ISIS. Otherwise, exports out of south Iraq remained stable and unaffected by the ISIS threat, which was halted north of Baghdad at Tikrit, over three hundred miles away.[17]

CHAPTER 13

THE ARAB SPRING

WITH IRAQI GOVERNMENT FORCES now completely in charge of all internal security, Prime Minister Nouri al-Maliki secured a second term as leader of the country in UN-certified democratic elections—the first in the Arab world. Maliki's second government took the longest to assemble in history, but he did it in December 2010. Almost simultaneously with the near-unanimous approval of the new government by the Iraqi parliament—including support by the Sunni Arab bloc—the region-wide Arab Spring ignited in Tunisia, then Egypt, Libya, Yemen, Bahrain and, finally, Syria. Iraq saw limited political demonstrations. But the security services maintained order nationwide without resorting to massive violence.

Obama's State Department Middle East expert Vali Nasr writes, "When Tunisians and Egyptians revolted against corruption and misrule, many expected the Iraqis...would take to the streets to demand accountability and good governance.... but in Iraq the Arab Spring did not have any wind in its sails.... Saddam's dictatorship had also kept minority rule

giving Sunni Arabs a disproportionate share of power and resources, bru-
tally suppressing Kurds and Shias in the process. The US invasion ended
that imbalance."[1]

In other words, politics reflecting the will of a super majority of the
population (approximately 80 percent, counting both the Shia and Kurds)
served as the classic safety valve that ensures stability in a democracy—which
Iraq had now become. U.S. Army Colonel Peter Mansoor (retired), brigade
commander in Iraq and then Petraeus's executive officer, categorically asserts
in his memoir *Surge* that if the Pentagon's civilian leadership—Rumsfeld,
Wolfowitz, and Feith—had handled the de-Baathification process less
severely, not demobilized the Iraqi Army, and immediately reinforced the
invasion force, the Sunni insurgency would have been contained from the
beginning.[2] This counterfactual argument underestimates the impact of a
Shia-and-Kurd government—and the Government of Iraq had to be Shia
and Kurd, if democratic—installed in Baghdad through Western force of
arms on the predominately Sunni Islamic world where al-Qaeda still held
considerable sway in 2003. No matter if there were any early American
"errors" in tactics, there had to be enough "blood in the sand" to force the
Iraqi Sunni Arabs to give up their pretensions to continuing the minority
rule of the past 1300 years and accept the Shia-led government in Baghdad
as legitimate. The U.S. accomplished this in less than six years (2003–08),
which represents a historical achievement of significant note.

Mansoor does accurately highlight the critical role politics played in
relations between different Shia factions—and in Iraq at large—by pointing out the connection between the withdrawal of Moqtada Sadr's members of the Council of Representatives (the national parliament) from
Prime Minister Maliki's government with Maliki's willingness to allow
American forces to clean up Jaish al Mahdi–controlled Sadr City.[3] After
the Sadrist defection in April 2007, Maliki survived, weaker in parliament
but stronger in terms of his national position. And because of the Bush
administration's patience and understanding of the sensitivities of the
prime minister's relationship with his Shia brethren who had suffered so

much under Sunni rule, the Coalition also emerged much stronger. (To get an idea of what the Shia had suffered, one only had to visit the vast cemeteries of still unmarked graves where Saddam's minions had dumped tens of thousands of massacred Shia following the abortive Shiite rebellion after the defeat of the Baathist army in the 1991 Gulf War.)[4]

Step by step the Sadrist-led insurgency was destroyed. With the Shia giving their political support to the campaign against it, Moqtada Sadr, Iran's main ally in Iraq, was prevented from achieving his goals through violence and forced to the political table. From the beginning, the key strategy of the U.S. in Iraq that ensured Baghdad did not get swept up in the Arab Spring was keeping the Shia majority on our side (or at the least neutral) throughout the war and letting them handle internecine issues— as much as possible—through politics.

✷   ✷   ✷

The twin, sequential blows of Afghanistan and Iraq crushed al-Qaeda to the point that the Arab Spring offered no ideological or religious allegiance, nor even deference, to the now U.S.-martyred Osama bin Laden. The U.S. had succeeded in achieving the crucial intellectual objective in the war of ideas that was facing America post-9/11. No military effort alone could destroy the rising jihadi Islam determined to annihilate Israel and humiliate the West as it had the Soviet Union in Afghanistan; the U.S. had to prove the jihadis wrong not only on the battlefield but also in the minds of the Muslim world. By conservative estimates, the U.S. and local forces killed twenty to thirty thousand al-Qaeda in Iraq supporters[5]—six to ten for every person slaughtered in New York, Virginia, and Pennsylvania on September 11, 2001.

The killers, or would-be killers, in the name of Islam emerged from every corner of the Middle East from Morocco on the Atlantic coast to Beirut, Lebanon, from which a blonde woman drove alone across Syria to Iraq's al Anbar province just to blow herself up next to an American

military convoy. One of our local contractors supplying the isolated Iraqi
Border Patrol Academy at al Walid on the Syrian frontier—a place so
desolate among red-orange sand dunes that you could've been on Mars—
had driven past the aftermath of the explosion. The ambush site sat on the
highway five hundred kilometers in either direction from Baghdad and,
at the other end of the four-lane road, Amman, Jordan.

Abu Sally, an Anbari Sunni who had been with us from the establishment of the base at al Walid, told me, "The American Army stopped their
convoy as I drove by. I could see burn marks on the sides of a couple trucks
and a giant hole in the middle of the highway and as I looked down I saw
a head with long blonde hair. I thought at first it was one of your female
soldiers, but I later learned it was a Lebanese woman from Beirut—the
suicide bomber who attacked the convoy."

✳   ✳   ✳

The U.S. Defense Threat Reduction Agency, in conjunction with Science Applications International Corporation (SAIC), produced a study
titled "Why Have We Not Been Attacked Again?" This extensive paper,
published in June 2008, discussed various theories that might explain why
al-Qaeda had not attacked America since 9/11. The collaborative research
and conference involving dozens of terrorism and security experts from
the government and commercial sector called my assessment—they quoted
an NRO *View from the Red Zone* op-ed—one of the "most compelling
hypotheses."[6] I had argued: Why would al-Qaeda attack our distant homeland when the American military had occupied nearby Baghdad in basically a dare to "bring 'em on!" in the words of President Bush (rash words,
but they expressed something commonly felt by his compatriots in Iraq)?

Anbar posed the most serious challenge in defeating the Sunni insurgency because it offered safe haven to al-Qaeda so close to the capital and
strategic center of the Coalition war effort. Yet as a Hollywood actor playing a biologist once said, what appears to be a disease's great strength is

often really its most fundamental weakness and the source of the cure.[7] Soon after my discussion with Abu Sally, we lost our first employees killed—three men near Ar Rutba, a notorious Sunni Bedouin smuggling center and the nearest town (more a glorified village, really) to al Walid. Shortly thereafter, in June 2005, AISG had an entire convoy wiped out west of Ramadi, with eleven killed. A few weeks later, after continually challenging how the company was handling security, I was fired. From that point on, the company lost an additional forty killed in Anbar before my return in November 2006. So when I wrote in *Contractor Combatants* in late 2006 that we had to "calibrate our expectations of what the U.S. and Iraqi military can do" in Anbar, a region that had been lawless for millennia,[8] I was reflecting the consensus among the U.S. military at that time. I was wrong.

The Sunni Arabs turned against al-Qaeda because of the innate moral nihilism of the *takfireen*, those who claim other Muslims such as Shias are apostates and therefore only worthy of death. French historian Gilles Kepel first wrote of this phenomenon in his seminal *Jihad: The Trail of Political Islam* (English version published 2002) about the horrific war in Algeria against the radical Islamists in the 1990s, where the jihadis regularly massacred "apostate" women and children. The Islamists enjoyed enough popularity that they threatened to win power through democratic elections in 1991. The Algerian army stepped in, blocking the elections and establishing a dictatorship; the Algerian Civil War had begun.

Eventually in Algeria—and the lessons for al-Qaeda in Anbar during the Iraq War are clear—"the growth in violence and the indiscriminate killing—whether or not some were provocations or deliberately arranged by the security forces—were steadily eating away at the popularity jihad had enjoyed in 1993–1994. The final break between a population growing more and more tired of unending conflict and the armed Islamist groups was accomplished by the last amir [in 1997].... Thus the GIA [the Armed Islamist Group, the most prominent of the extremist guerrilla movements] had finally chosen the path of *takfir*, the excommunication of society as a whole." As a result, the Algerian Islamic movement lost all popular support and has never again had the potential to take power through democratic means.[9]

Fortunately for the United States, our greatest enemies in modern history have espoused totalitarian ideologies with fatal flaws. First the Nazis (with the Imperial Japanese) founded their expansionist military conquests on a theory of racial superiority, which only accrued more and more resistance as they occupied more and more territory with "inferior" peoples. The internationally aggressive Soviet police state embraced a centrally controlled economy that would fail of its own accord under continuous pressure from the more dynamic capitalist system. Now with the jihadis in Iraq, Afghanistan, and elsewhere, we face an enemy whose religious extremism allows for massacring those who do not submit totally—including women and children. With that Achilles heel or internal self-destruct mechanism, it only required time—and our continued presence—before the Anbari tribes would turn on AQI, just as the Algerian people had rejected the armed Islamic groups. Interestingly, the timeframe for Algeria's defeat of the jihadis (1991–1997) approximated that of the destruction of al-Qaeda in Iraq (2003–08).

In *Surge* Mansoor talks about linear thinking as the reason the U.S. military, particularly the Marines running the Anbar command, did not perceive the rise of the Sahwa. What developed with the Sunni Awakening could only be understood with non-linear or chaos theory analysis.[10] I often said that our role in Iraq was creating order out of chaos. One of the last pieces of advice I gave Kiffer before my brother took over for me as AISG CEO at the beginning of 2009: "We always have to understand our objective in any situation here, whether it be building a camp or ensuring the guard force remains loyal. That objective is point B and we're at point A. So we want to move from point A to B as expeditiously as possible. Anything that interferes in that path to B, you must deal with until resolved. If it does not, then you must ignore it. Otherwise, you'll get caught up in this world we live in Baghdad that is circles within circles—culturally, politically, familial, and tribal—that we will never truly understand. People will try to manipulate you. Just keep focused on the objective."

✳   ✳   ✳

The American art of war is linear by nature, not least because of the extensive requirements for supply lines for our mechanized and technologically intensive military machine, with its well-cared-for troops ensured of air evacuation if wounded. We as Americans are linear almost genetically; just compare how the Iraqis drive—the road-marking lines are mere guides—and how we drive: between the lines. Construction, which constituted a sector with tens of billions of dollars of U.S. money invested in Iraq, is made up of right angles and square foundations. Of course there are many, potentially uncountable, variables involved, and the direct actions the American military takes on the battlefield create chaotic flux in the liminal zone influenced by those operational lines. Therefore we must be prepared to anticipate and seize opportunities in those changing variables to facilitate and protect the mission. That, though, is more about Boyd's fighter pilot "OODA Loop: Observe, Orient, Decide, Act."[11] There was really nothing random or unpredictable—which by its nature chaos theory must be, otherwise it would not be chaotic—in what happened with the Awakening.

Other aborted Awakenings had taken place earlier in Anbar. Al-Qaeda crushed them, or they faded away from lack of response from the American side. The difference came with the presence in Ramadi, the capital of Anbar, of a unique U.S. Army unit, just before the Surge. The Ready First Brigade Combat Team (1st Brigade, 1st Armored Division) was organized around the M-1 tank, a truly linear instrument of power. The Ready First team had originally learned the lessons of counterinsurgency from the 3rd Armored Cavalry Regiment after relieving the pioneering unit and building on the 3rd ACR's discrete success—not widespread in the Iraq war zone—in protecting the population in isolated Tal Afar, west of Mosul.[12]

What became abundantly clear to me, when I went into Fallujah in mid-2008 trying to find an alternative route to supply Camp Habbaniya, was that the Marines had walled off the city and were engaged in drive-by patrolling; they certainly did not have troops living in and among the rebuilding population of the devastated city—which is COIN 101. But Colonel MacFarland and the Ready First Brigade Combat Team did exactly that in Ramadi. (This is well documented in former Marine officer and journalist Jim Michael's *A Chance in Hell: The Men Who Triumphed Over Iraq's Deadliest City and Turned the Tide of War.*)[13] Sheikh Abdul Sattar Abu Risha al Rishawi, the budding leader of the Sahwa, lived next to Ramadi. From the highway that bordered the sprawling city to the north, you used to be able to see the Bradley fighting vehicle that the U.S. military had put in front of his house, until Sattar's assassination by AQI in September 2007, just days after meeting President Bush at FOB Al Asad, a hundred miles or so west of Ramadi.

The Anbaris, part and parcel of the greater Bedouin tribal grouping, had lived in freedom for thousands of years, respecting no political frontiers—trading, smuggling, and raiding throughout the Arabian Desert that in modern times spans seven countries. The austere setting fostered an austere version of Islam that closely resembled the Wahhabism of bin Laden and his cohort, with its almost pre-Islamic treatment of women. (The Prophet Mohammed actually improved upon the position of women by granting them legal rights, while prior to Islam, during *jahiliyya*—paganism—the Arab tribes recognized none.) The Sunni jihadis also had a common internalized (and mutual) fear and hatred of the Shia—calling them the *Safawi* to imply that the Iraqi Shia were not even Arabs but Persians. (The aggressively Shiite Persian Safavid Empire had ruled over various parts of Iraq at different times during the sixteenth, seventeenth, and eighteenth centuries—virtually yesterday in the Middle Eastern time perspective.) Yet the most important moral aspect to life for the Anbari people was *sharaf* (honor), and the totalitarian regime that al-Qaeda attempted to impose on them generated deep resistance.

Finally, in mid-2006, the Anbari tribes produced a leader, Sheikh Abdul Sattar Abu Risha al Rishawi, willing to reach out to the Americans; and the U.S. put forth a commander, Colonel Sean MacFarland, willing to reciprocate and support the anti-AQI uprising. Then came the Surge and U.S. leadership in Iraq that fully embraced the concept of protecting the people. The necessary American commitment of time and resources to reach the objective of freeing Anbar from the terrorism of AQI and in the process free Iraq and end the war now existed.

In many significant ways Anbar was ground zero not only for the Iraq War but for the subsequent Arab Spring. The Arab people throughout the Middle East watched on Al Jazeera TV as the Sunnis of Anbar joined with the American military and, more importantly, the Shia-led, democratically elected Government of Iraq in order to do battle with al-Qaeda. This reconciliation between Sunni and Shia under the aegis of politics and against a shared enemy represented a radically new way forward for the Arab peoples, the conclusion of the Sunni resistance in Iraq—and groundwork for the end of al-Qaeda's claim to pan-Islamic relevance.

U.S. intelligence captured a 2005 letter from Osama bin Laden to Abu Musab al Zarqawi—the SEALs found a copy near Osama when he died on May 2, 2011—in which bin Laden pleaded (unsuccessfully, as it turned out) with the Jordanian extremist leading AQI in a scolding, almost wifely tone to change his *takfiri* ways (killing Muslims who opposed Zarqawi's narrow vision of Iraq and Islam). The massacre of thousands of Shia women and children in Iraq by *intehareen* (suicide bombers), bin Laden said, damaged the "good" image of al-Qaeda. As a result, he had even considered changing the name of his organization.[14] The brand had gone bad.

In sharp contrast to the dark vision of Zarqawi's AQI, what we saw in the Arab Spring were democratic and human rights–driven popular movements throughout the Middle East. In Egypt, the democratically elected Muslim Brotherhood looked to be following the moderate path of Turkey's democratic Islamic government—and when they seemed to be deviating from that path, the Egyptians elected a secular, albeit military-led, government instead. Post-Iraq American influences, indirect but real, clearly aided the largest Arab nation's turn from autocracy to democracy. These influences included Egyptian revolutionary leader Wael Ghonim, a Google executive, and Ashraf Khalil, the journalist who wrote in his *Liberation Square* of the inspiration of Secretary of State Condoleezza Rice's 2005 pro-democracy speech in Cairo,[15] along with Twitter, Facebook, and Egyptian protest posters displaying U.S.-deposed Saddam on the gallows.[16] Even in Baathist Syria, a secular, democracy-driven insurgency seized large swathes of the country—tragically sparking a bloody civil war as the U.S. and the rest of the West stood aside. With Bashar Assad's grip on Syria in danger, nuclear weapons–grasping Iran had stood on the brink of complete isolation in the Middle East with the loss of its lone regional ally—an unexpected postwar boon. Instead, war-torn Syria provided safe haven for the resurrection of mutated al-Qaeda and a subsequent invasion of Iraq.

*   *   *

At this juncture in history, we have an opportunity to assess the status of the three strategic goals of George W. Bush's Iraq War: 1) Saddam and his genocidal, predatory dictatorship were dead and buried in 2006; 2) in December 2010 Iraq's second UN-certified democratic government took office after an election participated in by all the formerly embattled segments of Iraqi society; 3) beginning in that same month the Arab Spring was launched throughout the Middle East—with al-Qaeda completely sidelined and Osama bin Laden soon dead. Most important for the security of the United States, the radical jihadis of 9/11 had evidently lost—in a brief decade—the crucial war of ideas. The ideology that underpinned bin Laden's terrorist praxis and formerly had global impact was now in retreat. But the United States withdrew from the contest, leaving a vacuum for the Islamic State of Iraq and Syria—an al-Qaeda offshoot—to seep back in and destabilize the Middle East once again.

One strategic goal of the Iraq War was a more sweeping challenge than the other two: going beyond the removal of the predatory Saddamist terror regime with victory on the battlefield to destroy al-Qaeda's credibility as a major force in the Islamic world. This involved standing up a democratic Iraq that would serve as an example to the rest of the autocratic Middle East, causing other countries to embark on a similar democratic path. Of course, all three goals overlapped and mutually reinforced one another: you could have no democracy in Iraq with Saddam still in power, and a democratic Iraq having defeated al-Qaeda in common cause with America would fatally undermine al-Qaeda in the Middle East. Now, there is no effective U.S. alliance with Iraq, or adequate support for the Syrian people seeking freedom and democracy, and the results are shockingly catastrophic.

*   *   *

From the apparently abrupt beginning of the revolutionary democratic movements sweeping across the Arab World in 2011, you could not help but see the underlying connection with the Iraq War. *If* you were ready to look. Then–Secretary of Defense Bob Gates, a traditional *Realpolitik* mandarin, counseled Obama to be cautious about pushing military dictator Hosni Mubarak out of power in Egypt. In his memoirs he says, "[T]he Obama administration—and everyone else in the world (including the Arab governments)—[was] surprised by the 'Arab Spring,' a revolution that shifted the political tectonic plate of the Middle East."[17]

*   *   *

About this time I met probably the most preeminent expert in the world on Saddam Hussein, history professor Amatzia Baram, chairman of Iraq Studies at the University of Haifa, Israel. We struck up a running email dialogue that included the following discourse on the connection between the Iraq War and the Arab Spring. When I had mentioned the connection

at a lunch in Washington, D.C., in February 2012, Professor Baram had
asked to see proof.

> From: Carter Andress
> To: Amatzia Baram
> Have you read Ashraf Khalil's book on the Egyptian Revolu-
> tion? See:
> Washington Post Book Review January 24, 2012: However,
> it was the Iraq war that led to the Bush administration's pressure
> on Mubarak, which Khalil believes also set the stage for the
> Egyptian revolution. In particular, he credits a "harsh speech"
> that Secretary of State Condoleezza Rice delivered at the
> American University of Cairo in June 2005, demanding that
> the Mubarak regime open up the political system. "Bush and
> Rice probably won't be remembered too fondly in Egyptian
> history," Khalil writes. "But this brief window—when America
> abandoned regional realpolitik—deserves to be remembered
> generously."

> From: Amatzia Baram
> To: Carter Andress
> Probably correct. The problem as I see it is that the Bush
> administration did not know how to make it happen gradually
> and Obama just couldn't care less. At the same time he dropped
> Mubarak cynically like a rotten apple the moment he all-of-a-
> sudden discovered what was "the right side of history". Gradual-
> ism is the secret for necessary historical deep changes to succeed.

> From: Carter Andress
> To: Amatzia Baram
> Agreed on the gradual approach and that the full results of
> the "Arab Spring" are as yet unknown. The thesis is that there

would have been no overthrow—not within the timeframe we are talking about—of Mubarak and the end of the old regimes in Libya and Tunisia, along with the potential for the same in Yemen and Syria, without the US invasion of Iraq. Khalil seems to agree with that, at least that's what it looks like from the review—I've ordered the book from Amazon. Thought you might find that interesting…

From: Amatzia Baram
To: Carter Andress
I am not so sure this is the case, though. In my book when every single year in the last 5–7 years in Egypt 1.6 million young people are joining the job market, but only 50–60% of them actually find jobs, that's the problem. The oil regimes so far escaped revolutions. They are no less authoritative than Egypt. Bahrain—this is a sectarian case. Syria—a combination of economics and sect (like in Egypt: 400,000 new job seekers every year, only 200,000 jobs). Add to this the 50–90% rise in food prices within 2–3 months and you have most of the immediate causes. The Iraqi example may have added to the revolutionary zeal, but the economic disaster is the root cause. How did those regimes survive till now? They learned how to paralyze the opposition through bribes, intimidation and surveillance and, sometimes: massacres (Syria 1982, Iraq 1991, Algeria 1990s).

From: Carter Andress
To: Amatzia Baram
No challenge on the root cause being economic with population growth and government corruption putting spurs to the final decline of a command system modeled in many ways on a long-dead Soviet Union. This is the death knell of a post-colonial system in the Arab world that retained the

trappings of republicanism but in reality the power was in the military because there were allowed no other independent centers of civil power. Herein lies the commonality of Egypt, Tunisia, Libya, Yemen, and Syria. (Do you really see an existential threat to the al Khalifas in the city state of Bahrain?) The question is why did these military-led authoritarian regimes come to their end, or the beginning of their ending, in 2011, when other such regimes had collapsed under their own corrupt weight in Africa, South America and Asia (with some significant exceptions) by the 1980s, when democracy became the principal form of government worldwide?

You know better than I, but there are some unique characteristics to the Islamic world such as the old political saying of "better years of tyranny than one day of chaos." This is where I see the successful establishment of the second Maliki government in December 2010 as the immediate catalyst for the Arab Spring beginning to get out of control in Tunisia and then Egypt in January 2011. Iraq had then achieved the first truly democratic government formed in the Arab world. That accomplishment, along with other elements of US involvement in Iraq once we made the tremendous commitment to re-order this core Arab country in a democratic manner with American blood and treasure, evidently inspired people throughout the Middle East as one can see with the Saddam-to-the-noose poster from Tahrir Square and the Khalil book. As an old FBI agent once told me during an investigation I was working on with him: "There are no coincidences...."

From: Amatzia Baram
To: Carter Andress
I think that we agree. You have the petrol all over the place but you also need the spark. Saddam's execution was very

probably part of the big spark. The democratic elections in Iraq too. The outcome not so much, but there was an example, yes, and MANY Iraqis are telling me that their elections were a road-sign for the Arabs. Now, as you know, I fully supported Bush on Iraq. But I had no hope for a domino effect: I just thought Saddam was a loose cannon. But yes, the "Spring" is very probably indeed a domino effect in an unexpected way.

Where is the "Spring" leading? You can know what you don't want but it is far more difficult to know what you do want. I see in Egypt and Syria chaos for very long, as there is no solution for the socio-economic problems in the non-oil states. Bahrain is indeed different: this is all about money. This is a clear-cut sectarian issue.

Even the Chinese government saw the connection, which worried the communist dictatorship. A December 15, 2011, *Washington Post* article titled "China warily watches U.S. withdrawal from Iraq" included an interview of Yuan Peng, director of the Institute of American Studies of the China Institutes of Contemporary International Relations, an affiliate of the Foreign Ministry. The *Post* observed, "But what was most unnerving may have been the prospect of seeing the United States send combat troops halfway around the world to overthrow a government and impose a fledgling democracy in the heart of the Middle East. 'Through the Iraq war, you've planted the seeds of democracy,' Yuan said. 'Then you can see the Jasmine Revolution [Tunisia], the Arab Spring.... It changed the mind-set of the young generation. In the long run, it's in your interest because there's a trend of democracy,' he said. 'No one in China thinks it's a big failure.'"

The real impact of the Iraq War on the Arab Spring was the dog that didn't bark. Where was Osama bin Laden in all this? The SEALs assassinated him in Abbottabad, Pakistan, at the height of the popular uprisings, in May 2011. He had become a *shaheed*, a martyr—the highest calling for a so-called man of faith, iconic of the jihad to rid Islam of the West. Where was the outrage? Where were the people pouring out into the Arab Street burning U.S. flags and calling out "Death to America"? Bin Laden and al-Qaeda were mere afterthoughts in the most radical political changes the Arab and Islamic world had ever seen. For the first time in history, popular movements overthrew governments in the Islamic Middle East. Before the Arab Spring, changes of ruling elites only came through military coups, assassinations, or imperial impositions.

*   *   *

I always noted how important religion and religious language were to the Arab people. So many terms in common use had *Allah* in them. For example, *allahaleak* (God be with you) is often translated as "please" or "thank you"; *maashallah* (with God) is used as "really?!" You could not help but be caught up in an awareness of the Almighty in everyday life just through normal conversation. So when I first noticed the absence of al-Qaeda in the Arab Spring, I reflected back on an exchange that had taken place at Apache in late 2007.

On my normal afternoon walkabout, accompanied only by Abu Hind as usual, I went into our logistics staging area, inside the protective perimeter of Fort Apache, which we had created out of an abandoned lot next to our local elementary school (we paid the school a very healthy rent every month). Nearly a hundred of our Iraqis worked in the staging area every day except Friday. You could just about fit twenty tractor-trailers in the gravel-covered yard. We had cranes, a fuel point, and cool food storage along with spare parts and construction materials warehousing. Each trade had a corner, with the welders, carpenters, and electricians coming together to build all sorts of accommodations—bedrooms, offices, kitchens, and shower-bathroom units—out of used twenty- and forty-foot ocean shipping containers. These eight-foot-tall and eight-foot-wide steel boxes, usually with wood floors, were portable, lasted forever, and were very low-profile on the road, as they looked just like standard cargo units until you opened up the back swing doors. Whenever I stopped by the staging area, my most lengthy and probing discussion was always with the mechanics. (I had learned early on how important these men were, because the last thing you wanted was for your vehicle to break down out on the hazardous Iraqi roads.)

On this visit to the shaded mechanics' corner, I immediately noticed Hussein, a diminutive Baghdadi who had been with us from the beginning of AISG. As he emerged from under one of our security SUVs, I asked him, "*Shakoo maku?*"—"What's happening?"—in highly colloquial Iraqi Arabic.

Hussein, who usually had a smile on his face, answered plaintively, "*Mishkala wiya mujahideen ala tareek!*"—"Problem with the holy warriors on the road."

I started to ask what kind of problem, when Fadel, one of our parts suppliers and a brother of Brahim, an Iraqi AISG founder, quickly interjected, "Mujahideen! They are not holy warriors. You and I are more holy warriors than them." Pointing at me, he continued: "He is a holy warrior! Not them, they are devils!"

The Arab world had caught up with that truth about al-Qaeda, beginning with the youthful progressives who led the early stages of the uprising. The people had deserted bin Laden, and the language of revolution was no longer the same vocabulary as the jihadi sheikh's. He and his ilk were no longer in the conversation.

CHAPTER 14

AFGHANISTAN: HOW NOT TO DO IT

WITH THE MISSION IN IRAQ WINDING DOWN, Afghanistan came calling. The U.S. had forced al-Qaeda and the Taliban out of the country at the end of 2001 in a rapid campaign fought primarily by local militias supported by U.S. Army Special Forces (the Green Berets), the CIA, and American airpower. But now the deteriorating security situation in Afghanistan required renewed focus by DOD, AISG's principal client. The Pashtun-based Taliban had regrouped as an insurgency instead of the ruling party, from its safe havens in the borderlands of Pakistan's lawless Northwest Frontier, and in 2004 had begun to aggressively recapture territory from the U.S.-allied Afghan government of Hamid Karzai. By the end of 2008, huge chunks of the country's Pashtun-populated eastern and southern provinces had shifted to insurgent control. The Afghanistan War had heated back up again, and it has not cooled down to this day, in 2014—with no end in sight.

We—the United States—have made so many mistakes in Afghanistan in recent years that it is difficult to know where to begin cataloging them. The mistake I am most familiar with is the Afghan First program, which represented a failure to learn from the successes of the Iraq First program. Both congressionally mandated programs were intended to encourage local economic development by funneling U.S. funds and purchases into local goods and services. In 2012, after firing General Stanley McChrystal for comments he and his staff had reportedly made impugning the character of the president and vice president in the presence of a reporter from *Rolling Stone*—although an Army investigation later cleared him—the Obama administration turned to Petraeus, the general who had saved Iraq, to save Afghanistan. But that precipitous move didn't amount to applying all the important lessons from the U.S. success in Iraq to Afghanistan, a mission then (and in many ways now) faltering and on the brink of failure. The key factor in the stable political situation in Iraq at the time the last U.S. forces withdrew in December 2011 was the success of the Iraqi security services in establishing and sustaining control nationwide. The low levels of violence realized during the American-manned and -funded Surge continued after our withdrawal. We had achieved the exit strategy for U.S. forces of "we draw down as the Iraqis stand up." How did this happen? It was only possible after tons of American taxpayer money (over twenty billion dollars from 2004 to 2012) and prodigious American efforts expended on "training [and] equipping" the Iraqi security forces.[1] But as the military saw goes, "Amateurs talk tactics, professionals talk logistics."

During the peak of the Surge, on August 11, 2007, General Petraeus wrote me a letter in which he stated, "Our nation is indebted to the services provided by contractors, and I appreciate your efforts in helping the Coalition bring safety and stability to Iraq." Yet DOD contractors, bringing all the experience gained in Iraq at great expense in blood and treasure, were unwanted for the Afghanistan mission. Across the board the U.S. contracting folks in Kabul told us, "You have not done work in Afghanistan, you're not an Afghan-owned company, therefore don't think you can work for the U.S. government here unless you have done the first or become the second." That was the Afghan First program in action and a Catch 22 for us.

DOD entrepreneurs—the small companies, not the KBRs or even the Blackwaters—were a few dozen companies with a few thousand Americans risking our lives in Fallujah, Baghdad, Mosul, and other places with names almost everyone would be hard put to find on a map. But we made a difference. We went where the mission took us, and we lost a number of good people along the way. The U.S. reconstruction focus began to change after the big American corporations such as Parsons and Bechtel, all with highly successful international track records, failed to operate in the rapidly degrading security environment in Iraq in 2004. The new challenge at that time was to support the development of the Iraqi security services.

The companies that built the Iraqi bases, fed the Iraqi troops, set up and staffed their medical clinics, ran their power, water, and waste systems, and developed the supporting network of suppliers and subcontractors included businesses often barely established prior to the U.S. invasion or spun up in Iraq itself during the occupation. And equally important, in the process we hired, employed, and trained hundreds of thousands of Iraqis. Thus, our role cut at least two ways: we built, operated, and maintained the infrastructure necessary for the Iraqi security services to develop into the effective force they are now, and we established an entire cadre of Iraqis and local businesses capable of sustaining their military and police without permanent foreign involvement.

This was exactly what was required both by the Afghan mission in general and by the people-centric counterinsurgency strategy of U.S. and NATO forces in Afghanistan in particular. Nothing is perfect, of course, and the contracting experience in Iraq had its problems, but not nearly at the level one might believe. Fraud consumed a small proportion of overall American taxpayer dollars expended—just read *Hard Lessons*, the seminal book on contracting by the U.S. Special Inspector General for Iraq Reconstruction. Waste was prevalent only in the early years, until the newly created system sorted itself out. The system worked. But the U.S. government unfortunately did not transfer the program wholesale to Afghanistan.

The Afghan First program is a failure while the Iraq First program delivered a success because the mission came first in Iraq, not the *pro forma* requirement for local-only firms. What DOD entrepreneurs brought to contracting in Iraq represented accountability, transparency, U.S.-standard business practices, and compliance with the Federal Acquisition Regulation. Billions of dollars have disappeared in Afghanistan on critical but unfinished projects. On my fourteen trips to Afghanistan, beginning in November 2008, the constant refrain I hear from contracting officials is that practically every single Afghan company looking for new American-funded work has already defaulted on a U.S. government contract. Now that may be an exaggeration, as there are some good Afghan companies, but there are certainly not nearly enough of them to undertake the massive challenge of the U.S. in Afghanistan, that graveyard of foreign armies.

Our government has invested almost $100 billion dollars of American taxpayer money in the reconstruction of Afghanistan.[2] What have we gotten for it? It's hard to say. A good example is the Ring Road, begun in 2002, shortly after expulsion of the Taliban and al-Qaeda from Afghanistan. The road plan called for connecting all regions of Afghanistan to ensure security and commerce via a highway that would parallel the border, avoiding (except in the east) the permanently snow-capped Hindu Kush Mountains that bisect the country, creating in many ways two Afghanistans by dividing the Tajik, Uzbek, and Hazara north from polyglot Kabul with a Pashtun south and southeast. As of today, in 2014—twelve years and billions of dollars later—the road is still not completed. The parts of the road remaining unfinished are in western Afghanistan, not a particularly dangerous area because they are outside the Pashtun homelands of the Taliban along the borders with Pakistan. But the *Kandahari* trucking mafia, purportedly, obstructs construction by intimidating local contractors in order to keep the traffic out of and into Iran from diverting to the north. And the completed parts of the road from Kabul to Kandahar have fallen apart to a degree that the potholes literally rip apart vehicles and kill people attempting to transit the route.[3]

The project reminds me of my favorite Doonesbury comic strip. An Afghan is advising the CIA character sporting a cowboy hat how the U.S. must build roads in Afghanistan. He says, "That's how the Romans controlled their empire—they were able to move both armies and goods quickly. It was all about the roads!" The CIA guy answers, "Which they lined with crucified slaves." The Afghan responds: "Yes, Rome was a robust brand, for sure."[4]

It's hard to estimate, but I would guess that over 50 percent of the money the U.S. put into Afghan companies under the Afghan First policy ended up in private bank accounts in Dubai, United Arab Emirates. Even though the Arabian city-state has no oil, it continues to boom even after the real estate collapse associated with the Great Recession. New glass-and-steel skyscrapers emerge girder by girder above the empty sand seemingly every week. Afghans, including President Hamid Karzai's family,[5] have heavily invested in properties in Dubai. U.S. money, in many cases stolen by the suitcase load because there are no currency controls at Kabul airport, must be a principal source of the continued boom.

The U.S. Army Corps of Engineers (USACE), our old nemesis from the MRAP construction project in Iraq, had control over the DOD reconstruction budget. USACE had somehow (we would learn later how, after much digging) twisted Section 886 of the National Defense Authorization Act of 2008, mandating a "preference" for Iraqi and Afghan goods and services, into a requirement for all funds expended to go to majority-owned Afghan companies. AISG had served as an example of how the Iraq First program should work, prior to the passage of Section 886. The preference had come into effect only when it did not interfere with the mission in Iraq, but it (especially as interpreted by the Corps of Engineers) was certainly interfering with the mission in Afghanistan—by keeping the job from getting done. Afghan companies simply did not have the technical capacity to do the work to the construction standard that the thousand-plus page USACE contracts required.

On my first visit into Afghanistan toward the end of 2008, Rock and I had come to set up company operations in Kabul at the behest of the Joint Contracting Command–Iraq/Afghanistan (headquartered in Baghdad's Green Zone) because of our success at achieving mission goals in Iraq. One of our contracting officers from Iraq emailed a counterpart in Afghanistan and copied us: "I want to introduce you to a great contractor [AISG] that always gets the job done to the highest standard.... Truly I would use these guys for anything, they're that good."

Through his connections from his days at the large security contractor Triple Canopy, Rock had hooked us up with a couple old Afghan hands, both former U.S. Army guys, who had been running the roads throughout the country since 2003. Their handful of team members included an Afghan *sayyid* (someone who claimed to be a descendent of the Prophet Mohammed and the Arabs that converted Afghanistan to Islam in the seventh century) who drove us around Kabul soon after we got there. As he took us on a tour of the city, I looked around, amazed at how secure it was compared to Baghdad—there were hardly any blast walls, and every now and then I could see Westerners walking the streets, apparently unarmed and without body armor. The sayyid would proudly intone as we passed a place, "This is Wazir Akbar Khan, named after an Afghan general and later emir who chased the British out of Afghanistan. That is named for Dost Mohammed, who defeated the British at Maiwand...."

When he got to the third place named for someone who had humiliated the UK, I got the point and interjected, "Hey, you know, we also have a lot of places named for people because they did a good job of killing the Brits, such as the capital of our country—Washington. Keep in mind, we're not the British, we're the Americans." I believed that he was trying to intimidate me, but I already knew the bloody history of foreign interlopers in his country.

After spending a few days in Kabul getting a feel for the city and setting up the legal process for getting our company established there, I wanted to head out into the field. So off we went to Jalalabad, the closest Afghan city to the famous Khyber Pass and headquarters for USACE in Regional Command–East covering the Pakistan border, where the autonomous tribal areas offered primary safe haven to what remained of al-Qaeda and the resurgent Taliban. We descended the winding, quite well built highway that paralleled the sharp fall of the Kabul River. It had been constructed by the Russians during their ill-fated occupation in the 1980s. Rock joked, "Once we have peace here, this would be a whitewater rafting magnet!"

As we passed through Sarobi, the only town until we got to the flat-lands around "J-bad," as the U.S. soldiers called it, one of the American Afghan-hands noted a group of men crossing the highway in front of us: "That's the Taliban going home to momma prior to winter setting in. They don't like to fight when the snows come into the mountains."

I said, "Look, they've got the classic *capri* pants cut above the ankles that the crazy jihadis think is Islam compliant!" We all laughed at the absurdity, a bit too nervously—we felt pretty damned exposed in our one-car convoy with only a couple of M-16s.

I then told a linguistic joke that Tony had told me just before I left Apache for Kabul. In Arabic, *talib* is "student"; *tulaab* is the plural "students." The Taliban got their name because in a self-created myth their initial recruits in the mid-1990s came from the *mudaaris* (religious schools) for the millions of Afghan refugees in Pakistan. Tony had asked, "Do you know why the Taliban can't win in Afghanistan?" And before I could launch into a geopolitical analysis, which he anticipated from listening to me pontificate for years now, the Lebanese Catholic cut me off, "Because there're only a couple of them!"

I laughed, getting the punch line, "Yes! Talib-*aan* is only *two* pupils in Arabic."

(Several days after we were there, U.S. Spec Ops raided Sarobi, killing and capturing more than twenty Talibs.)

Once we got down into the valley where Jalalabad sits, I looked to the right and could see the mountains around Tora Bora, the then–last known location of Osama bin Laden. To the left, even more impressively, the peaks of Kunar rose up over twenty thousand feet to the massive plateau, "the Roof of the World" that included the Himalayas and Mount Everest. We drove through orchard after orchard of citrus with locals on the roadsides selling some of the most brightly colored oranges I have ever seen (and I'm from Florida). As we approached the USACE compound we entered a forest of eucalyptus trees obviously brought from Australia by the Brits. Inside the compound, I asked one of the senior engineering sergeants, "How are things going?"

The sergeant first class responded, "We've got to work with locals on these contracts. And we never get anything done, because we spend the whole time teaching them how to do submittals (construction paperwork). The actual construction never seems to start. Everything is way behind schedule."

Even more important than the issues with the paperwork—involving design, cut-sheets (product descriptions used in the construction), and laboratory testing for soil, concrete, and leach-field percolation—I never once met an Afghan electrical engineer or master electrician trained only in Afghanistan. There were none, whereas in Iraq we employed some pretty damned good electrical engineers who had graduated from Baghdad Technical Institute or another Iraqi university; while they weren't so good at the equations, they could design and make a system work. (When DOD's "Task Force SAFE," created after faulty wiring had electrocuted sixteen American soldiers in Iraq, inspected one of our construction sites, Camp Phoenix, in 2008, they certified us as 100 percent compliant with the U.S. national electric code, which was beyond our contractual requirements at the time.)[6]

The Afghan companies to which USACE spent its time shoveling all this money simply could not perform the work for which they had contracted. Evidently, the metric USACE used to check the performance box for their contracting officers measured how much money they paid out to Afghan contractors—not whether contracts got finished. This reminded me of Soviet throughput statistics. The USSR had the largest steel manufacturers in the world, surpassing the United States in the 1960s (the goal) but they didn't have the customers to use all the steel. Yet they continued to increase production.

This metric certainly made the USACE contracting officers' lives easier. You could see ideally that this process made a lot of sense. In theory, if the DOD paid the Afghan companies directly, the money would enter the local market. But in reality, no absorptive capacity existed because the Afghans did not have the capability to perform. They had little or no acceptable services to sell. It was a classic American mistake: just throw money at a problem and that'll fix it. On May 2, 2010, in an article that also mentioned AISG's struggle to find competent local subcontractors from among "[o]ften completely different companies" that "come in with the same pictures," Associated Press reported, "'You can either have it done on time, or contracted to the Afghans,' says Colonel Kevin Wilson, the head of the U.S. Army Corps of Engineers in the south and west. He said his own office building took longer to complete because it was Afghan-built."[7] Even USACE knew that their misguided implementation of the Afghan First policy had proved detrimental to the mission.

So what would happen was this: the Afghans would take the mobilization fee, often 10 percent of total value of the project, and bill for as much work as possible before a USACE inspector would come out to the site. The last part of this equation could take quite some time, especially if the construction was in a dangerous area outside Kabul. The Army Corps of Engineers American-citizen civilians, who constituted almost all the contracting officers in Afghanistan, did not like to take a lot of physical risk (there were exceptions, I'm sure). Once the U.S. government would discover, yet again, that the contractor could not perform, USACE would terminate the contract, oftentimes for "convenience of the government," not for default. "T for C" required a lot less paperwork for the "KO" (contracting officer—"CO" meant commanding officer) than "T for D," but the former allowed the incompetent, if not fraudulent, contractor to continue to bid for U.S. government work. Even if terminated for default, the Afghans, whose owners' names confused the USACE contracting folks in any case because of the lack of last names and because the limited number of Islam- and Afghan-acceptable names caused vast numbers of similarities, would often just change the name of their companies and go back to bidding on contracts.

It's always good to recall Kipling's poetic adage:

> And the end of the fight is a tombstone white with the name of the
> late deceased,
> And the epitaph drear: "A fool lies here who tried to hustle the East."

*　　　*　　　*

In Iraq, AISG and other professional DOD contractors had provided the U.S. government with more subtle services, beyond just technical capacity. The Afghan First policy now forced the KOs not only to be competent in contracting rules—the infamous two-thousand-page Federal Acquisition Regulation—and knowledgeable about construction, but also to communicate and negotiate with, while performing due diligence on, Afghan companies and individuals. Afghanistan is, to say the least, a translucent, if not opaque, society to the outsider. The Army Corps of Engineers had asked its contracting personnel to achieve the near impossible under tight deadlines in the stress of the war zone.

What we provided to the mission in Iraq, and what was lacking during the peak years of American reconstruction awards (2009–12) under the Obama "Surge" to fix the "good war" in Afghanistan, versus the "bad war" in Iraq, was a vetted, reliable, and accountable interface between the KO and the local workforce. Whenever we undertook a project in Iraq and Afghanistan—and from 2008 until 2012, we'd only gotten one revenue-generating contract in Afghanistan—the key moment when AISG asserted control over the site, and the contract, was when we terminated the first subcontractor and hired a new one to take its place. Then we could usually count on performance because the shocked locals now realized they could be replaced. This was the principal reason we had always finished the job in Iraq, with over ninety contracts worth $400 million executed for the USG in the toughest places in the Iraqi war zone. And as a result, the KOs could do government contracting business and we could get the locals working on time and to spec with all the challenges that were involved below the surface of our stable contractual relationship with the Departments of Defense and State. It worked in Iraq, and it would have worked in Afghanistan.

✳   ✳   ✳

When General Petraeus took over command of Afghanistan, he brought along the friend who had helped us so much in Iraq, Colonel Mike Meese, to be deputy chief of staff for the International Security Assistance Force (ISAF, the NATO command in Kabul). When I found this out, I made arrangements to link up with him at the former Soviet officers' club in a tree-shaded park, now serving as NATO headquarters. It would be a break for me from the nitty-gritty of trying to get dirt moved and bricks stacked.

We sat down to dinner at the HQ's fully stocked chow hall, and after discussing AISG's frustrations, I asked Mike, an erudite PhD and son of Reagan attorney general Ed Meese, "Where does the strategy go from here?"

"We've got to get the Afghan security services stood up," he stated. "They're willing to fight, but the real challenge, unlike in Iraq, is the literacy issue. If we can get these soldiers trained to read at a third grade level, we'll win this war. In addition, General Petraeus has told me that he wishes he had the government ministers here in Kabul back in Baghdad. They've got a lot of energy and want to get things done."

Cause for optimism, no doubt, if the mission had enough time on the ground with the Afghans ...

✳   ✳   ✳

Prior to 2012, the one contract we'd undertaken in Afghanistan involved a small construction project in mid-2009 at FOB Shank in Logar Province, one of the most dangerous parts of Afghanistan—if not the world. AISG got into one of our few firefights in Afghanistan on the road back from Logar to Kabul; we'd been involved in dozens in Iraq, killing an estimated hundred-plus bad guys who tried to stop our convoys or assault our sites. In this incident, the Taliban had set up a fake police checkpoint. Our locals leading the convoy, however, knew an ambush when they saw it and drove through the kill zone as fast as possible. But the vehicle carrying the AISG country manager crossed the "X," as they say, at the center of the attack, both in time and space. Bullets sprayed the unarmored SUV through the windshield.

Rabih, our longtime Lebanese security manager, afterwards gave me the cap he was wearing with bullet holes on either side of where his face had been. But unfortunately for the Taliban, the old Lebanese warrior had seen this movie before and as he described to me, "Boss, I saw them try to shoot the vehicle in front of us as it flew down the road. So by the time they turned on us, I shot one, two, three.... They were close. Many dead Talibs."

The convoy made it home intact but we did have one wounded. Samir, a Tajik from Bagram just north of Kabul, had been hit in the leg by an AK-47 bullet. It took him a year or so to fully recover, yet he continued on with us into 2014 as manager and translator, even courageously accompanying a convoy carrying a high-value generator to one of our worksites in dangerous Helmand.

The U.S. Army contracting officer wrote a letter of recommendation in which he stated:

This is to express Bagram Contracting Office appreciation for the outstanding performance of AISG Construction. AISG was awarded a very difficult and short notice contract…at FOB Shank, Logar province, Afghanistan. Their professional staff and management worked around the clock ensuring timely delivery…. Their ability to react and deliver in just 10 days…is truly a major accomplishment for any contractor operating in Afghanistan….

Their quality of work and the ability to meet the U.S. Government's stringent standards were clearly shown on this project….

I commend AISG Construction for their exceptional duty performance and ability to support the U.S. Forces with their mission in Afghanistan…. I highly recommend AISG for future construction services in support of the U.S. Forces.

Primarily because of the distorted interpretation of the Afghan First policy being put in place around the time we undertook the Shank project, we didn't see another revenue-earning contract again until early 2012—while keeping a company office in Kabul with security team and staff in place running at a cost of about $100,000 per month. Our—*my*—frustration extended beyond the business loss because, once again, we were not there just for financial opportunity—if you could describe a hell hole like the badlands of Afghanistan that way—but for the mission. And we watched from the sidelines as the reconstruction effort struggled.

☆   ☆   ☆

To further compound our pain and give additional evidence of the Army Corps of Engineers' lack of ground truth in Afghanistan, in September 2010 we were awarded the construction of a police headquarters for the uniformed Afghan national police in Sar Hawza, Paktika province,

near the border with Waziristan, Pakistan, *the* safe haven for the Taliban
and its even nastier ally, the Haqqani terrorist group with close ties to al-
Qaeda. No Afghan-owned company wanted this project because of the
dangerous location and smallish size. So it sat unawarded for over a year.
We had raised so much Cain about not being able to get contracts because
of the Afghan First policy interpretation that USACE offered the project
sole source to us. We costed it; they accepted our price at just over two
million dollars.

I think in retrospect that they were setting us up for failure. The engineers at Qala House—the USACE HQ in Kabul—were probably laughing
in their coffee about giving us an undoable project. In July 2011, just up
the mountain from the site location, Taliban-allied Pashtun Waziri tribesmen poured across the border and beat back a company of U.S. Army
Rangers, forcing the U.S. Air Force to drop two-thousand-pound bombs
on the insurgents, killing over a one hundred of them.[8] During the entire
life of the project, there was an openly Taliban village standing just over
the next hill. And down the road a little ways, another police station
changed hands back and forth regularly between the local police and the
Taliban. Our final subcontractor—we had to fire the first two, having to
go beyond our normal practice because of the difficulty and delays of the
project—described the entire area around the job, composed of Kharoti
Ghilzai Pashtun "Kuchi" tribes, as Taliban. Of all the Pashtuns, the Kuchi
constituted probably the poorest—many were nomadic, rootless people.

Afghanistan is divided among four major groups: the Sunni Pashtun,
Tajiks, Uzbeks, and the Shia Hazara. Mullah Omar, leader of the Taliban,
and President Karzai are both Pashtun, and not only that, they're both
Abdali (Durrani) tribal members from nearby areas in southern
Afghanistan, and are probably related distantly. This is why I see similarities
between the Afghan war and the war in Laos, where half-brothers (both
princes) led the fight, one with the U.S.-supported royal government and
the other as commander of the Pathet Lao communists,[9] whom the North
Vietnamese backed until Hanoi assumed complete control of the

landlocked country after the fall of Saigon. In Afghanistan, we have brothers fighting brothers in an inter-Pashtun quasi-civil war. So unlike the insurgency in Iraq, fought between groups divided by a religious schism of over 1300 years (the Sunni-Shia split) or ethnic and linguistic differences (Arab-Kurd), real common ground existed between the combatants and, therefore, cause for optimism in the potential for reconciliation.

✶　　✶　　✶

After the project award, I flew into Kabul to undertake a visit to the site. We had gotten this "bassackward" and bid the job without a site visit first, outside our normal practice. The roads between Kabul and Sar Hawza offered numerous opportunities for Taliban ambush like the convoy attack on the road back from Logar, much closer to the Afghan capital. So we chartered a Russian helicopter, a Mi-17 cargo-lift craft with room for twenty. The bird was over thirty years old, but we'd had it inspected by a retired U.S. Marine helo pilot. So we were good to go. Nevertheless I asked the captain in Russian before boarding: "*Vertaloet khoroshi, da? Vii kho-teetye zhit tozhye?*"—"The helicopter is good, yes? You want to live also?" As all the crews originated in the former Soviet Union, whether Russia, Ukraine, Uzbekistan or Kirghizstan, they all spoke Russian. Every time before flying on one of these charters, I asked a version of those questions. Usually the pilots just laughed at an American speaking Russian to them. They were all old men, at least a decade older than I. So I felt pretty confident if they could survive until now flying these old warhorses around the high mountains of Afghanistan; another flight just meant another day at the office for them.

The big white bird shook like an off-kilter washing machine on full spin cycle when taxiing for takeoff and then picked up the agitation when taking flight. Travelling across eastern Afghanistan, you really got the feel for how empty large swathes of the country remained, interspersed with brown mud-walled homesteads with watchtowers forming mini-forts, crammed up into defensible crevices in the mountains. As we approached Sar Hawza, which stood at about seven thousand feet, you quickly noticed the looming mountains of the Pakistani border, nearly three thousand feet higher. The border between them was the famous Durand Line, put in place by the British toward the end of the nineteenth century, delineated precisely to award the high ground to the then-London-ruled Indian Raj. The Taliban now held that position, looking down on Sar Hawza and the rest of eastern Afghanistan.

On the helicopter with me were three of our Afghan subcontractors— the main guy, Haji Ayoub, an *Ahmedzai* Pashtun tribal member, claimed family in the nearby area. He had fought with Gulbuddin Hekmatyer, the Pakistani-supported warlord who had destroyed large sections of Kabul in the 1990s with Scud rockets, killing thousands of civilians during the civil war among the mujihadeen after the Soviet defeat in 1989 and the collapse of the Soviet-supported government two years later, when the USSR itself imploded. As Hekmatyer was continuing the fight against us, I had asked Ayoub earlier why he had broken with the warlord. The tall, lean, weathered Pashtun, the default look on whose face evinced the feeling that he wanted to kill you—until he smiled a smile that would light up the darkest room—said, "He was not a good Muslim."

The pilots opened up the door leading to the cockpit and motioned for me to come forward to look out the window. I did so and looked down at our site location, per the grid coordinates provided by USACE. There, arrayed in a defense perimeter, stood HESCO barriers interspersed with short wheel-based (for mountain conditions) MRAPs and plywood structures called "B-huts." The U.S. Army had built a combat outpost on our project location for the Afghan police HQ, without the Army Corps of Engineers even knowing it! Our chopper landed on the level gravel HLZ inside the fortified perimeter where we had thought we'd be setting down in a sketchy open area to be met by the local Afghan police. The 10th Mountain Division soldier standing on the edge of the landing zone showed his surprise—it was a surprise arrival both for them and for us.

Of course I knew then that we'd have to find another site. The Army would never give up what they had taken. Little did I know that it would take almost two more years before we could begin to actually build the HQ at a location more than two miles up the mountain (and closer to Waziristan) and at an altitude 1500 feet higher.

Meanwhile, we continued to shake the bushes for more contracts and found some in another garden spot of Afghanistan—Helmand Province, the most casualty-filled battlefield for Coalition troops during the entire Afghan War. The Marines controlled contracting for the area out of FOB Leatherneck. They didn't give a damn about the Afghan First policy—they just wanted to get the job done and go home. This demanded an even crazier contract than the Paktika job. We had our American site managers riding around on motorcycles; even Rock did the same when he went down to inspect progress.

It was a place so desolate and forbidding that even the Marines treated us as if they were happy to have visitors when I landed in another charter helicopter. The trip there was such a long distance that a third of the cargo hold contained an extra fuel tank. Whereas the Sar Hawza flight took just over an hour, travel time to Now Zad, Helmand, from Kabul required almost three hours. Afghanistan is a big country, the size of Texas, and made even bigger by numerous mountain ranges. I felt sorry for these young Marines left alone in the harsh desert north of Pakistan's Baluchistan province, which cut Afghanistan off from the sea. They had no hot chow and no shower until our site manager built them one. I can hear it now: Jim Jones, retired USMC 4-star general and then–National Security Advisor, might well have said to President Obama, "Those Marines—they're so hard, they can just eat sand!" So to save money, the White House gave them that exact opportunity in southern Afghanistan.

By early 2013, during the Marine pullout from Helmand, AISG successfully completed a permanent clinic in Khan Neshin serving four thousand locals, a high school in Marja where the epic 2010 battle between the Marines and the Taliban had taken place,[10] and four police stations in

Now Zad. We were probably the only American-owned firm to effectively work "outside the wire" (that is, off a military base) in Helmand using our tried and true methods perfected in Iraq of a U.S. or Western site manager and a predominantly local (in this case, all Afghan) construction crew trained "on the job."

As Frank Guffey, a former Recon Marine who had now taken over as AISG Afghanistan Country Manager, observed in a press release after he had led the completion of one of the projects in September 2012, "We have overcome the challenges of Ramadan in the hottest of summers and an extended Eid, followed by an increase in Taliban activities hindering the logistical support to bring materials to the site. We persevered, self-adjusted, and continued on the mission until completion." Kiffer added, "The people of Khan Neshin, much ravaged in the past by the Taliban, will long remember the gift from the American people of this urgently required health clinic, now open to all the citizens of Helmand."

The disarray present in the U.S. reconstruction program also reflected the lack of connectivity between the American and Afghan governments. The level of animosity between President Karzai and the Obama administration had become apparent to everyone on the ground in Afghanistan. The biggest bombshell of then–Secretary of Defense Robert Gates's book comes when he describes how Richard Holbrooke, Obama's special ambassador for Afghan-Pakistani issues, worked with U.S. Ambassador to Kabul, the retired Army lieutenant general and former Afghanistan ground commander Karl Eikenberry in leading "American efforts to unseat" Karzai during the 2009 election. Not only were these bizarre actions unsuccessful, Karzai "sure as hell knew what was going on in his own capital."

The whole treatment of Karzai by the White House reminds me of what we did to Ngo Dinh Diem in South Vietnam. After Kennedy acquiesced to a coup against the Republic of Vietnam president because Diem was difficult to work with, and his consequent assassination, the U.S. never again had a strong political partner in Saigon connected to the Vietnamese people—just a series of tin-pot generals—a key reason for our defeat.

When I originally heard that Ambassador Kai Eide, the UN representative for Afghanistan, had complained that "there was blatant foreign interference in the elections," I certainly didn't realize that he meant "the United States and Holbrooke."[11] Gates further states that he wanted to see the "insubordinate" Eikenberry fired but that "he was protected by the White House."[12]

So when one of our subcontractors from Helmand attempted to extort money from us through corrupt Afghan officials, I should not have been surprised that the U.S. government had no established mechanism to protect us. In order to attempt to gain control of our overhead, given the dearth of contract availability, we had moved from our twin villas next to the American embassy in Wazir Akbar Khan to the Green Village, a highly secure complex containing over two thousand expatriates. (It was not completely safe; the insurgents had targeted contractor convoys entering the main, heavily fortified "GV" gate with two car bomb attacks in the last couple of years, killing numerous bystanders and, reportedly, at least one of the retired Gurkha guards.)[13] In late January 2013, Afghan police started to show up daily at the gates to the Green Village with specious arrest warrants for Frank Guffey and for our Lebanese security manager, known to us as "GQ Joe" for his dark good looks. The Nepali guards shooed them away, but they kept coming, and the threat of arrest on the road or at the airport persisted.

I contacted USACE HQ and they said that this did not fall under one of their contracts, since the Marines owned it, but as they had no contracting presence in Kabul, the USACE advised us to go to Task Force 2010 for Afghan corruption. I exchanged emails with U.S. Army Major General Richard Longo, in charge of the task force, but he finally said to go to the U.S. embassy, that he couldn't help. The embassy folks had already basically said they would get an American citizen out of jail but not intervene in a dispute to prevent the arrest. Finally we got a summons from a general at the Afghan Ministry of Interior. This we felt we had to respond to, so down went GQ Joe for a meeting that Afghan police officials said was with

General Muhammed Nabi Majrouh, in charge of MOI criminal complaints involving forgery (*tazweir* in Dari), which had absolutely nothing to do with the dispute with the subcontractor. At that meeting in the MOI on January 20, 2013, uniformed Afghans detained Joe for two hours, and the ministry official representing General Majrouh, who we found out later was in India at the time, told him that unless AISG settled with our Afghan subcontractor within forty-eight hours, he would arrest both Frank and Joe.

This looked to be the end of AISG in Afghanistan, if we couldn't get this stopped. So Bob Kelley and I searched for legal assistance in Kabul that we could trust. We came up with Ward Scott, a retired U.S. Marine colonel and attorney practicing in Kabul. Ward jumped right on it. He took Frank down to the Afghan national attorney general's office. (The situation called for a lot of bravery on Frank's part because they potentially could have detained him right there, as they had done earlier to another American, whom some inmates then beat up in jail.)[14] A medieval quirk in Afghan law requires an Afghan citizen to act as a sort of bail bond, or else the foreigner being charged under the fraudulent and corrupt criminalization of a commercial dispute has to remain in detention as assurance that he or she will show up in court. Ward came up with an Afghan from his office, who later tried to go sideways on us as things got rough with the *Helmandi* subcontractor who had evidently paid off prosecutors at the Attorney General's office (AGO) to extort us.

In the end, with Ward's help, we did not back down. We got the case moved to commercial court, which potentially could take years to resolve it. This forced the subcontractor to come back to the mediation table, where we settled with him for substantially less than the claim he had put before the AGO. Part of the settlement required him to unwind what he had corruptly done at the AGO, which he cried about for weeks to Ward. It cost us a substantial amount in lawyer fees, but in the end the most important result was that the word got out among the Afghans that AISG could not be rolled. Otherwise, we'd get taken by our subcontractors on any future work. The most disheartening aspect of it all was the fact that no one in the U.S. military establishment in Kabul stepped up to protect us, even though this involved DOD contracting for the mission in Helmand. I could never have imagined being put through something like this during the war in Iraq, where the government in Baghdad did not want to mess with us in large part because we had mutual consent and respect for a shared mission.

Just as the illegal arrest threats began in Kabul, we'd finally gotten ourselves in the position to build the police headquarters in Sar Hawza—three years after award of the contract!—but only after a huge battle with the Army Corps of Engineers. They tried to default us for cause, which would have potentially put us out of business. We butted heads with every level of USACE, until finally I wrote a letter to the commanding general of the Army Corps of Engineers and had it hand-delivered to him through a mutual contact in Washington, D.C.:

April 23, 2013
LTG Thomas P. Bostick, USA
Chief of Engineers
U.S. Army Corps of Engineers
    Re: Contract No. W5J9JE-10-C-0039 Afghan National Police HQ, Sar Hawza, Paktika
    General Bostick:
    Our firm has loyally supported the United States in Afghanistan and Iraq for almost ten (10) years. I am requesting your office to review a current dispute as our firm works to construct and complete this critically needed project. We are currently constructing an Afghan National Police Headquarters in Paktika Province, but we have been stymied by site location problems, which continue to impact our firm. Paktika is a remote Taliban infested area in eastern Afghanistan beset with war violence. The project area is outside active U.S. military

patrols. We are constructing these security facilities to support the U.S. mission to transition the country to the Afghanistan government. Our firm has worked hard to solicit local support for this project to protect our operations from Taliban violence by coordinating the location of our construction site with local elders, the ANP and Ministry of Interior.

The Corps has changed the site numerous times and we have negotiated contract modifications for some of the earlier site relocations. However, we have not been compensated for the most recent site relocation, which the delay in relocation substantially impacts this project. We request that your office review this matter and provide whatever assistance that is proper and appropriate to assure that our firm is fairly paid for these changes and site location problems. We are continuing to perform this work. However, we did not agree to finance this project and would like this matter resolved during performance without resorting to a lengthy contract appeal.

AISG, Inc. has successfully completed over 90 projects in war zone conditions to support the reconstruction of Iraq and Afghanistan. We recently built 4 police stations in Helmand Province.

BACKGROUND: On September 3, 2010, the United States Army Corps of Engineers awarded Contract No. W5J9JE-10-C-0039 to AISG, Inc. for the construction of the ANP Uniform Police District HQ in Sar Hawza, Paktika Province. Various modifications to this contract extended the time for performance.

Originally, the site was located on barren land free of interferences and obstructions. After contract award, AISG deployed to the site and discovered that the location was no longer available as the U.S. military had expanded an adjacent base into the project footprint. The Corps changed the site location several kilometers away to a location near an Afghan village, which would place the changed construction footprint over an ANP Checkpoint and encroach on a security wall for the local village.

After the initial location change, the Corps was unable to provide the site to AISG since consents from the Afghan Police to demolish the Checkpoint (used by the ANP to provide security in this dangerous area) and local Village authorities (for site encroachment on their security wall) was not obtained. The Corps never obtained the necessary approvals to demolish the Afghan security structure.

Confronted with these problems, on February 28, 2012, the Project Engineer directed AISG to "site adapt" (per the contract) the project approx. 100 meters east to avoid these interferences. AISG negotiated and obtained approvals for the new coordinates that would not intrude on the Village's vital security wall or require the demolition of the needed ANP Checkpoint. These consents from the local tribal elders, ANP and MOI are the only known consents and approvals available to permit construction of the project. Pursuant to these approvals, AISG started work, swept, and cleared the area of any unexploded ordinance, and performed the site work. The site survey and geotechnical testing were completed long ago.

On April 26, 2012, with the assignment of new personnel (the contract administration staff is beset by frequent turnover), the new Project Engineer and ACO insisted upon returning to the site coordinates that were plagued by the security wall and Checkpoint conflicts. They never provided any reason, functional or otherwise, why the site covering the wall and Checkpoint was necessary to the project. Contract administrators pushed for AISG to start work even though these conflicts had not been resolved.

The Corps finally acknowledged the proper site to construct the facility, and after a short suspension of the work, issued a contract modification with the proper coordinates in late December 2012. AISG was unable to work from May to December as the Corps refused to acknowledge the proper site and doggedly insisted upon construction on the site opposed by local and national Afghan authorities. AISG was on standby at the project site this entire time and has requested compensation for this May through December delay. The Contracting Officer denied this request in total except for a nominal amount incurred during the time when the Contracting Officer had suspended contract performance. A large portion of these costs were for the local Afghan contractor that AISG was mentoring.

CONCLUSION: Providing the site was the Corps' responsibility, not AISG's. When the Corps relocated the site on top of the local village's security wall and Afghan National Police Checkpoint, AISG coordinated and obtained the approvals from the local population for a new site supported by them. As the ultimate customer for this facility and an essential partner for site security, the local and Afghan national approvals were critical. AISG obtained these approvals but was delayed when the Corps reneged on its approval of AISG's efforts to site adapt (as required by the contract) and only approved it in December of last year. AISG is steadily making progress to complete this work but should not be required to finance and fund this delay from May until December 2012.

Please review this matter to ensure that our firm is treated fairly and equitably.

Thank you,

Carter Andress

President

AISG, Inc.

Nothing happened, and I received no reply. So we had to sue USACE in the U.S. Armed Forces Board of Contract Appeals, where our case is pending currently.

By the way, we finished construction of the police HQ at Sar Hawza in April 2014, but USACE dragged out the final paperwork until July.

CHAPTER 15

CONTRACTORS AT WAR

AISG AND OTHER MILITARY CONTRACTORS created a revolution in modern warfare. In 2005, contractors represented an extraordinary 30 percent of the total U.S. force deployed in Iraq. Because of domestic American political pressure and financial constraints there simply were not enough U.S. forces available to fight the al-Qaeda-backed Sunni insurgents and the Shia militias supported by Iran. In 2006, America stood on the precipice of losing the war, and contractors helped win it. We played a vital role as counterinsurgents by employing and training host-nation citizens while providing critically needed services and undertaking construction during active conflict. Throughout the Iraq War reconstruction, contractor employees exceeded or matched U.S. troop levels. To reiterate what I've said before about the role we played in Iraq, private companies like AISG effectively assumed Geneva Convention–regulated defensive combat roles, relieving the limited number of trained Coalition troops able to take the battle directly to the enemy and thereby greatly enhancing the critical

239

"tooth-to-tail" ratio. Simply stated, contractors overcame horrendous odds to help secure victory in the most complex American war since Vietnam.

As a 2008 U.S. Congressional Budget Office study on the role of commercial entities in support of the military determined, "Although the use of contractors during military operations is well established, most experts agree that the scale of the deployment of contractor personnel in the Iraq theater (relative to the number of military personnel in the country) is unprecedented in U.S. history."[1] That study and additional studies have shown that contractors can do many warzone-related services less expensively, more effectively, and more quickly than the military or other government entities. The question, then, is what should contractors on the battlefield *not* do? The term of art is "inherently governmental functions."

Prior to Iraq (and Afghanistan), the demarcation between combatant and contractor in the American art and practice of war appeared straightforward. U.S. combatants were uniformed soldiers who engaged opposing forces with violent means in the service of the government's political goals. American contractors provided a variety of support services to the combatants, but took no officially sanctioned direct role in the exercise of violence in overcoming the enemy.

The need for a new definition of the contractor's role in modern warfare arose in the Iraq War when contractors took on controversial but mission-critical roles (see, for example, Blackwater and KBR) that revolutionized U.S. military logistics on the battlefield by substantially reducing the requirement for the limited number of available uniformed troops to undertake roles that contractors could fill. Military scholar John J. McGrath, in his authoritative paper "The Other End of the Spear: Tooth-to-Tail Ratio," estimated that in 2005 contractors amounted to 58,000 personnel directly supporting a military force of 133,000 in Iraq—thus the unprecedented 30 percent civilians in the total U.S. force deployed inside Iraq. Tooth-to-tail ratio traditionally means the number of combat-arms troops—infantry, armor, artillery, special forces, attack air—proportionate to combat support troops—such as engineers, transport aviation, military police, and intelligence units—and combat-service-support troops—quartermaster, ordnance (munitions), transportation, finance, acquisition, judge advocate general, and chaplain corps. In the Iraq War, the relatively large number of contractors redefined the term, while allowing a significant shift of the ratio in the direction of combat-arms soldiers.

As a result, *Wiktionary* and other online dictionaries now contain definitions for a new term:

> Contractor Combatant. Etymology: Author and United States Department of Defense (DoD) contractor Carter Andress coined the term "contractor combatant" in his book about the Iraq War titled *Contractor Combatants: Tales of an Imbedded Capitalist*. Noun: contractor combatant (*plural* contractor combatants) (military, US) A civilian in a war zone who performs the tasks of an armed soldier under Geneva Convention[s].[2]

What differentiates a "contractor combatant" from a mercenary? The Geneva Conventions define a mercenary as an illegal combatant working "essentially" for monetary reward and not a citizen of a "Party to the conflict," such as the U.S. or Britain, which provide the majority of contractor combatants in the Iraq War and the current conflict in Afghanistan. In the Law of Land Warfare, contractor combatants are civilians accompanying the armed forces of a lawful belligerent.

Some would challenge the claim that security contractors working in Iraq and Afghanistan for DOD and the U.S. Department of State are combatants. For example, in a review of *Contractor Combatants* in *Army Lawyer*, the reviewer, a U.S. Army Judge Advocate General Corps officer, asserts, "Andress...incorrectly refers to himself as a 'combatant,' even though his company's primary mission is to provide life support [food, water, fuel, spare parts] to the local Iraqi police and security forces."[3] However, as many have noted since the Jessica Lynch incident during the initial

invasion, convoy security is one of the riskiest military missions in a counterinsurgency, where there are no frontlines.

The confusion may originate in an anachronistic legal analysis. Modern warfare calls for the new term—contractor combatant. According to
the *Merriam-Webster* dictionary a combatant is "a person, group, or country that fights in a war or battle." Throughout the Iraq and Afghan conflicts, civilians armed with military-type automatic weapons, authorized
and contracted by the U.S. government, engaged in firefights with insurgents to protect critical supply lines and personnel for the U.S. and Coalition military effort. This is the very reason the U.S. government hired the
services of these individuals: to defend convoys and personnel traversing
the combat zone.

The question remains: What precisely are the inherently governmental functions that are outside the role of the contractor combatant? One
might think offensive operations—assaults, ambushes, raids, artillery fire,
and the like. But what about the state of affairs when the contractor offers,
in order to provide services, to rush into a situation where there is the real
potential of entering an area with active fighting?

In mid-2009, shortly after I had returned home from Baghdad, an
investment fund offered to back AISG in buying Aegis Defence, Ltd, the
Scottish company that had the DOD contract to provide bodyguard services to U.S. VIPs and establish and run the Reconstruction Operations
Centers in Iraq. That was bit of irony after our run-in with Aegis in Basra
when rogue police seized our team in south Iraq in 2007.

I sat in a conference room in a downtown Washington, D.C., office
with a view of the White House listening while the fund guys jousted with
the sharp-tongued Jeffrey Day, Aegis's chief financial officer, and a couple
of his retired UK military colleagues from the company's London headquarters. The point at issue was the valuation of the company. Aegis's
primary source of income, probably representing over 80 percent, was their
massive DOD Iraq contract worth over $100 million per annum. The
problem, of course, was that the ongoing drawdown of U.S. forces in Iraq

would inevitably mean a commensurate reduction in the contract value. The back-and-forth was not pleasant. Too bad, I thought, as I respected the company and could see a bright future working with the British security professionals employed by Aegis.

Finally I intervened to ask, "How about company operations in the oil fields?"

Jeffrey turned toward me across the table and responded, "Ah, Carter [pronouncing the 't' hard and clear in the English way], we see real opportunity there and are working especially hard to get with BP."

"Yes, we also see the future there for security operations," I said. "But we could achieve real synergy with your high-end protection capabilities and our construction skill set."

"We have to be careful, though, with how AISG is advertising itself," the finance man stated, as if he had rehearsed it. "You mention QRF [quick reaction force] under your security services. That is an offensive function and cannot be undertaken by contractors."

I responded, "We offered that service in Iraq when we ran the Iraqna cell phone security contract. It was in full accordance with Iraqi law."

I really hadn't thought about the question the way the Aegis management presented it. They had obviously encountered similar objections in the past, especially given their founder Tim Spicer's contractual involvement in offensive actions in support of the Sierra Leone government's battle against "Blood Diamonds" insurgents in the 1990s. In my mind, I could see our twelve-man, three-SUV QRF back in 2005 flying out the gate of Apache at night in response to calls from the villas we protected for Orascom International, the largest publicly traded corporation on the Cairo stock exchange and mother company for the Iraqna cell-phone network. Food for thought...after a competitive bidding process, the rapid nationwide expansion of cell phone coverage to nearly every home in Iraq (it had been banned under Saddam) represented a highly successful free market reform under Bremer's CPA. The participation of a prominent company from Egypt—the most populous Arab nation and a predominately Sunni one at that—offered a significant boost to the nascent post-Saddam, Shia-run Iraq (early 2004). This success might not have been sustainable if the dozens of Egyptian expatriates living in the Iraqi capital and necessary to operate the network had had to rely on QRF reinforcement (and evacuation of the wounded) from the just-recovering Iraqi emergency services or overstretched U.S. military, on a Baghdad battlefield of nightly attacks and multiple daily explosions.

Unfortunately, we couldn't come to terms for the Aegis acquisition; the fund guys controlling the money decided that right away.

The most fundamental issue with regard to contractor combatants remains unsettled *de jure*, but not *de facto*, in international law. Fast-moving events or "facts" on the ground have overtaken written law. There is some movement, however, to embed that reality in International Humanitarian Law (the new name for the Law of Land Warfare), which I applaud and support. In March 2012 the *Fordham University Law Journal* published a well-researched article titled, "Rethinking the Regulation of Private Military and Security Companies (PMSC) under International Humanitarian Law." The article calls for an amendment of the Geneva Conventions because they presume contractors on the battlefield to have civilian status, which provides greater protections, for example, from attack. It argues that "PMSCs hired to engage in activities that constitute direct participation in hostilities" are in a different category. "If PMSCs are contracted to perform specified activities constituting direct participation, defined below as 'contractor combatant activities,' they should be considered combatants."

These contractor combatant activities include:

> Participation in combat operations; Security in direct support of combat operations; Security of military infrastructure or checkpoints; Security of military personnel; Supply and maintenance of strategic weapon systems; Interrogation of detainees or prisoners; Military intelligence gathering; and Tactical

planning of operations.... Again, this list of activities relates to the actions for which PMSCs are contracted. PMSCs hired to perform civilian tasks (those which do not fall under the rubric of contractor combatant activities) may still find themselves directly participating in hostilities, but should not be considered to have been hired to perform contractor combatant activities.

The article recommends, therefore, that all civilians whose positions *contractually* require them to engage in the above listed activities on the battlefield must be classified as combatants by the Geneva Conventions defining International Humanitarian Law.[4]

Because contractors now have an established role in the American art of war as combatants and support elements for combat forces—playing a particularly critical role in counterinsurgency operations outside direct support for the U.S. military—we need to discuss oversight and accountability. As is typical with revolutionary developments, the response on the regulatory side has initially been *ad hoc*. The U. S. government does not generally institutionalize military experience very well. Clear proof of that inadequacy is the failure to capture lessons on COIN learned from the Vietnam War and impart them to succeeding generations of military leaders. Another example, less well known and explored but detailed extensively in *Southeast Asia: Building the Bases: The History of Construction in Southeast Asia* (a government-only publication that I read first when I was thirteen years old) has to do with the massive reconstruction program in South Vietnam. This program was operated by the Navy's Facilities Management Command, which effectively ran—after an initial year or so of struggles—a program management office that trained and employed over two hundred thousand Vietnamese on billions of dollars in projects undertaken by some of the same, or the forerunners of, massive U.S. construction companies involved in Iraq.[5] NavFac Management Command utilized highly experienced construction professionals from the Navy Seabees for performance and contract oversight.

I am not necessarily recommending the same setup for any future conflicts that require reconstruction activities. The key is having knowledgeable government employees or their trusted agents (including contractors) with a willingness to take physical risk in order to actually visit the work sites to ensure contract compliance. In 2008, the Army announced the establishment of the Field Engineering Support Teams (FEST) intended to bring contingency construction technical expertise to the maneuver level[6]—sort of Special Forces A-Teams for warzone construction funded by DOD. These eight-person teams—one team per Brigade Combat Team—mainly consist of uniformed soldiers but also include civilian experts with the mandate of going forward into hostile situations.

We never encountered the FEST units in Iraq, but finally did in early 2014 on the way out to the border near Waziristan at one of the last U.S. bases on this particular edge of the Afghan badlands, FOB Rushmore—so limited in space that you had to walk outside the wire to get to the helicopter landing zone. When we'd begun the build of the police HQ at Sar Hawza, the nearest American military presence was just a couple of miles below on the mountain. Because of the drawdown, the nearest—FOB Rushmore—now sat a long fifteen miles or so away. As a result, we could not count on timely QRF or immediately available refuge for our American site and Lebanese security managers. At the FOB Frank and I had a chance to talk with the FEST members, who seemed quite competent and committed but admitted, "We do not have all the engineering slots filled." They also thought they would be unable to travel out to our job site to inspect, which they wanted to do because "it was on our project list"—because that required an Infantry unit to transport and escort them in the Taliban-infested area, as the teams did not have their own security assets or vehicles. So, the FEST lieutenant said, "We probably won't get out that far."

The Pentagon's conduct of reconstruction in the early years of the Iraq War lacked effective actions in four crucial areas: integration, planning, execution, and oversight. And I would argue that the mission in Afghanistan continues to fail in all those areas. Considering the likelihood that the

United States will be involved in stability and reconstruction operations again in the near future, will we have to reinvent the wheel yet again? Currently on the floor of the U.S. Congress is a bill calling for the establishment of a United States Office of Contingency Operations (USOCO), which would integrate all USG reconstruction elements, especially the DOD bureaucracy, the uniformed services, the State Department, and USAID, along with the smaller missions of the Treasury and Justice Departments. This office could retain and inculcate lessons learned; develop a cadre of experts; and coordinate, plan, and prepare to oversee contingency reconstruction operations abroad in conjunction with Coalition forces and host nation governments. The estimated cost for USOCO tallies up to about $25 million per year, a bargain considering the costs of reconstruction in Iraq and Afghanistan, with the loss of billions in wasted taxpayer funds because of USG unpreparedness and mismanagement.

Part of the mandate for USOCO is to institutionalize the office of the Special Inspector General for Iraq Reconstruction (SIGIR) for future contingency operations. As I have said many times, the presence of SIGIR Stuart Bowen with his inspectors and auditors ensured that "all of us contractors were not tarred with the same brush as war profiteers." Bowen led an operation, from early 2004 until the agency shut itself down in October 2013 (a rarity in the history of the U.S. government), that has recovered or saved hundreds of millions of dollars in U.S. taxpayer funds and convicted over ninety Americans, mostly uniformed contracting personnel, for committing fraud in the Iraq reconstruction program.[7] SIGAR, SIGIR's Afghanistan counterpart, has in contrast achieved very little other than in recent years issuing "letters" calling attention to problems while taking little or no corrective action.

Another issue, which became international news with the Blackwater killings in Nusoor Square, is how to hold contractors accountable for criminal acts committed in the war zone. DOD contractors, who are doctrinally organic to the Total Force since the 2006 Quadrennial Review—the Pentagon's complete self-assessment every four years—

must be protected from arbitrary, corrupt, and politically motivated actions by the host nation legal system during wartime operations. After all, the host nation legal and political systems are—by the nature of a conflict situation—either in disarray or not mature enough to handle the complexities of prosecuting a foreigner with proper due process.

When the Iraqi parliament threatened to pass a law stripping Coalition contractors of their immunities from local prosecution and arrest, CBS News broadcast an interview with me on November 9, 2007.

> ANDRESS: There's no question it's a disaster if this got passed.
>
> CBS CORRESPONDENT DAVID MARTIN: Carter Andress is one of an estimated 8,500 private security contractors guarding diplomats, convoys and reconstruction sites for the U.S. He is not willing to let his employees be subject to arrest by an Iraqi police force he believes is riddled with corruption and infiltrated by enemy fighters.
>
> ANDRESS: How do we determine in that situation whether or not it's legitimate use of the rule of law or whether or not this is someone trying to kidnap one of us and take advantage of the situation?
>
> MARTIN: Despite troubles caused by out-of-control contractors American officials say they are indispensable to U.S. operations in Iraq. They're counting on the Iraqi parliament *not* to ratify the law. But Andress, who knows firsthand the public anger triggered by last September's infamous Blackwater shooting, is not so sure.
>
> ANDRESS: This may be the first law that parliament gets passed. Here's one they can all agree upon.
>
> MARTIN: If the parliament strikes back, the shooting, which left 17 Iraqis dead could end up killing off the entire network of private contractors on which the U.S. depends.[8]

The Iraqi parliament did not pass the law. The immunities granted by Bremer during the CPA ended on January 1, 2009, the effective date of the Status of Forces Agreement. Even then, although the Iraqi government had a "primary right of jurisdiction over United States Contractors" the SOFA implied a secondary right for U.S. forces to ensure that contractors received proper due process. Iraq, of course, had evolved into an entirely different place by the beginning of 2009, with combat operations—both Coalition and Iraqi—largely concluded and al-Qaeda and the Shia militias defeated. Consequently the rule of law had begun to prevail. For example, at American insistence Prime Minister Maliki had purged almost the entire leadership of the National Police, including the little brigadier general who had held the three AISG employees in late 2006. The "re-bluing" of the rest of the force with Coalition training on human rights and proper policing techniques professionalized and truly nationalized what had been a nest of Shia death squads. (We had built much of the base where that re-bluing took place: Camp Phoenix, which housed the Iraqi trainees and the Italian *Carabinieri*—paramilitary police—running the program.) To the credit of all sides involved, after the SOFA came into force and until the American military pulled out two years later, very few incidents occurred that caused the Iraqi authorities to arrest U.S. contractors or our non-Iraqi employees. That was quite a track record, given that thousands remained in country performing armed security operations on the highways and around the bases.

Nevertheless, just as U.S. soldiers commit crimes in the war zone, so too contractors have committed and will commit crimes. The mechanism for prosecution, which ensures that both the mission and the rights of the contractor are protected, is the Military Extraterritorial Jurisdiction Act. This federal law allows for the U.S. Department of Justice to exercise legal jurisdiction over DOD contractors who commit crimes abroad if they are felonies that would potentially warrant a sentence of a year or more in prison. All contractors doing honest and upright business in the war zone benefit from the rigorous and transparent enforcement of the rule of law—both because it eliminates the bad contractors (protecting the rest of the contractor community) and because it sets the right example for the people of the host nation, which at the end of the day *is* the mission.

The above discussion covers the *how* of contracting on the battlefield, not so much the *why*—other than touching on the fact that the U.S. military is not set up to handle many of the required current and future wartime tasks because of its size, structure, or training and experience. As a result of a deficit in one or more of those three areas, tasks the military is not suited to manage include large-scale construction, base operations and maintenance, logistics, food supply and preparation, specialized technical skills requiring decades of training and experience, static guard services, convoy security, and interpreters. The new role of contracting is a key to success in modern warfare. It represents a revolution in the American art of war that enabled us to defeat al-Qaeda in Iraq on a multi-dimensional battlefield that requires effectiveness in politics, economics, morality, and the exercise of force.

One subset of the reasons for contractors in the war zone has to do with the relevance of experience. U.S. Army Major Patricia Hinshaw, who wrote the review of *Contractor Combatants* in the *Army Lawyer*, criticized me for writing that many of us contractors were old enough to be the fathers of the soldiers deployed in Iraq and that age and experience had helped "season" us, a point that struck the reviewer as meaningless.[9] I probably could have put it better. Stan Cole, a fifty-three-year-old contractor fire chief, on the NATO military base on the north side of Kabul international airport, is the perfect example of what I meant.

Stan, who had been at war in Iraq or Afghanistan almost continuously for ten years, told me, "The difference between a military firefighter [and a civilian firefighter] is they may have answered less than a hundred calls a year on their base. Whereas, those of us out in the county and city [civilian] departments could easily see a thousand. You don't get many fires on military bases because of the safety discipline; not like in the civilian world where house and building fires are common. So we have tons of experience in real-life emergency situations."

We then got to talking about Iraq. Stan remembered how risky the early years at Camp Victory—home of the U.S. Iraq command—had been because of indirect fire (mortars and rockets). That's how I discovered that he'd most likely saved the life of Mark Culilap, the AISG Filipino employee struck by a rocket blast in mid-2004 while entering the Post Exchange at Victory. I had visited Mark in the U.S. Army–operated Ibn Sina combat trauma hospital in the Green Zone. He never woke up during my visits because his wounds had brought him so near to dying that doctors were keeping him in an induced coma to aid his recovery.

Stan continued, "I was the fire chief but when I felt that blast—I was that close—and saw him [Mark] go down, I instinctually reverted back to first responder and rushed to his side. As I recall, I had to apply a tourniquet to what was left of an arm. He had a rip down the side that had turned into a sucking chest wound. I looked over at a young Army medic who had appeared on the scene. He was shaking so bad that I had to grab his kit to apply the [special] bandage for the chest wound. Your guy was strong; he kept quiet during the entire time."

"You saved Mark's life. I'm sure, Stan. He was in a bad way even at the hospital when I saw him. Thank you very much. He got a big settlement from our insurance and is doing very well now in the Philippines." I then reached over and shook the man's hand.

*   *   *

What General Petraeus and many others have said about the Iraq and Afghan Wars will ring true in most future conflicts that the U.S. may find itself waging: there are only political solutions. Military action can only set the stage to allow the population inhabiting the battlefield to form or become part of representative government and enter the international community where rule of law prevails. Therefore, once again, we come to the crux of the issue: the people are the center of gravity, the source of victory or success in any situation where American forces must occupy a foreign land. The crucial question is whether resistance will emerge and metastasize into an anti-American insurgency. In Iraq, Afghanistan, South Vietnam, Somalia and Lebanon, the answer was *yes*. In Panama, Bosnia, Grenada, Kosovo, Haiti, Dominican Republic, Japan, West Germany, Kuwait, the Philippines (1944–46), and South Korea, no viable insurgency emerged, though in South Korea guerilla fighters did infiltrate from the North for years after the 1953 ceasefire. (That's quite a list since World War II, for those who choose to believe that the United States will not have ground-conflict operations again.)

There are manifold and complex reasons behind the development and sustainment of insurgencies unique to each of those countries that were in part or in total occupied by the American military. The one unifying factor, I think, is negative perceptions by the people, or by a significant population subgroup or groups, about their future political and economic position during and after the American occupation. There is one group of counterinsurgents that has proven itself able to provide the people with a positive vision and the practical skills to act on that vision: warzone DOD contractors. Development workers with USAID can and do provide long-term solutions and training. But they do not often work where the bullets fly, and it's difficult to lead by example (the only true form of leadership; otherwise it's management or teaching) on business skills when you're not part of a for-profit business. For broad-based wealth creation in a society, a regulated free market with space for entrepreneurial innovation has historically proven the most effective, long term. And that also is the American way—so we stay true to who we are, which, once again, makes it simpler to lead by example.

In quelling or preventing an insurgency, the military must provide security first, then rudimentary political assistance and limited contract oversight and management—potentially under fire. Beyond that, however, you get out in front of the skill sets for which the military trains or is prepared to undertake. Anything additional is *ad hoc*, with the results of unevenness and distraction from the core mission of providing security. The Commander's Emergency Response Program (CERP) manual published by DOD had the title *Money as a Weapon System* (MAAWS). The CERP program expended almost $4 billion in Iraq, which included paying the salaries of a hundred thousand members of the Sons of Iraq, the nationwide anti-al-Qaeda civil defense force that grew out of the Anbar Awakening. The vast majority of funds expended for reconstruction, however, consisted of "micro-grants" of just a few thousand dollars with only a "handful" exceeding one million dollars.

The final SIGIR report, *Learning from Iraq*, made the following assessment: "No Defense Department office has a comprehensive picture of what the program actually accomplished in Iraq. The best available CERP data provides a rough approximation of actual activities. This renders suspect commander narratives, academic studies, and other analyses that claim success based on that data."[10] At the least, the very nature of the unit rotation, whether the twelve or fifteen months for Army units or seven months for the Marines, made it difficult to sustain any and all CERP projects. AISG and other contractors operated on the ground 24/7 for years.

Reconstruction contractors, especially those focused on standing up the Iraqi security services, cut at least two ways for the COIN mission. We provided the security physical infrastructure that protected the population. We also employed hundreds of thousands of Iraqis—many local to the epicenters of conflict—providing them with income to feed their extended families, training them in technical trades to Western standards, and thereby preparing them for work after the conflict. More important, though, our work developed an entire network of entrepreneurs who supplied us with materials, equipment, and labor. By late 2008, our company vendor network included over a hundred Iraqi businesses, from Mom-and-Pop shops to companies doing tens of millions of dollars in sales annually. (One company that manufactured our project trailers, inside the MOI headquarters compound in Baghdad for security purposes, received so

much money from us—$3 to $4 million at a time during certain contracts—that I joked to the owner, a doctor turned entrepreneur, "AISG is
working for you, not the other way around!") Most of the businesses had
not existed before the establishment of AISG in March 2004. These business leaders, who had earned their money at great risk to themselves and
their families, along with the hundreds of millions of dollars we put into
the Iraqi economy, helped stimulate peace in Iraq by providing the vision
and the means for a prosperous future.

American civilians working hand in hand with Iraqis under exceed-
ingly dangerous circumstances in order to build, not destroy, set the way
forward. This shared risk and shared creation drained away the support
that al-Qaeda and the Shia militias had had among the Iraqi people. After
interviewing me, Camille Tuutti of ExecutiveBiz.com wrote on June 8,
2010:

> "You're a symbol of the occupation, of the military, all the
> angst, all the destruction—all the meaning of that, especially
> as a Department of Defense contractor," Carter Andress said.
> "But you're also a symbol of tremendous hope." Americans
> represented a new way out of what was truly a totalitarian,
> tyrannical dictatorship, where death, rape and mutilation were
> everywhere and ever-present underneath the surface. "If you
> were to say or do the wrong thing, or be in the wrong place—
> they lived in that kind of fear.... We as Americans represented
> the opportunity or potentially, a way out, or a better way of
> life."[11]

CHAPTER 16

AFTER-ACTION REVIEW

AL-QAEDA'S DEFEAT in the Iraq War appeared to end any claim the perpetrators of 9/11 had to be leading a popular Islam-wide movement. After the U.S. ran Osama bin Laden out of Afghanistan and destroyed al-Qaeda on the battlefields of Iraq, the Arab Spring erupted without a trace of jihadi influence even after the SEALs assassinated Osama bin Laden, making him a *shaheed* (martyr)—something that had, in the past, resonated so strongly in the Muslim world. This was the intellectual objective of the crucial war of ideas facing the post-9/11 American war strategy. No military effort alone could destroy the momentum of a rising jihadi Islam bent on annihilating Israel and the West as it had the Soviet Union in Afghanistan; the U.S. had to prove the Sunni Muslim extremists wrong on the battlefield and consequently in the minds of the Islamic world. That war of ideas was won in Iraq when Sunni Arabs from al Anbar Province and then all of Iraq rejected their co-religionists in AQI, supported the

Awakening, and sided with the American-allied, Shia-run democratic Government of Iraq.

Do not doubt that al-Qaeda in Iraq represented a pan-Arab phenomenon. Both the AQI leadership and the suicide bombers—suicide bombs were the primary weapons delivery system for the jihadis in their terror campaign to force America out of Iraq and overthrow the country's UN-recognized government—originated in Saudi Arabia, Jordan, Libya, Sudan, Yemen and every other Arab country. Syria served as a source and also the conduit and safe haven for these al-Qaeda operatives entering Iraq—from before the 2003 invasion, when their passports were stamped by Iraqi border control "for jihad,"[1] until today.

Further, one cannot question that al-Qaeda enjoyed tremendous popularity in the Arab and Islamic world in 2003.[2] Thousands of Muslims committed to killing themselves (and did) in the name of al-Qaeda in Iraq. Al-Qaeda's expulsion from Afghanistan at the end of 2001 put a dent in its appeal, but bin Laden's escape from the American war machine made us look even more the stumbling giant, expanding the "Sheikh's" recruiting. Success after success had followed the jihad: first its defeat of the Russians in Afghanistan (1989) and the Soviet Union's subsequent collapse (1991), then the attacks on the U.S. embassies in Kenya and Tanzania (1998) and the USS *Cole* (2000), and finally September 11, 2001. Should we just have waited for the next attack?

✶   ✶   ✶

The Iraq combat mission ended for the United States with the final and total withdrawal of American ground troops via Kuwaiti border crossings on December 18, 2011. Or at least it seemed to be over at that point—until the sudden advance of ISIS in June of 2014 and President Obama's decision to send three hundred American "military advisors" (shades of the early stages of the Vietnam War) into Iraq.[3] Meanwhile, the Iraq War's causes, achievements, and significance are still not thoroughly understood—and recent events only make it more important that they should be.

What brought about the post-9/11 decision by the George W. Bush administration to forcefully remove Iraq from the list of pariah states with predatory dictatorships? How did the Iraq War affect al-Qaeda as a threat to the U.S.? Did the war and the American-shepherded development of democracy in Iraq help precipitate the Arab Spring? These are the threshold questions to weigh in order to gauge the impact of the Iraq War at the strategic political, military, and economic levels—for the United States, and for the world.

Much of the impact of the U.S. decision to go to war in Iraq is already manifest. But the long-term implications for meeting the challenges of the postcolonial dictatorships and the resurgent radical Islam whose rise those dictatorships have facilitated are not fully known. Neither are the war's causes—the political, economic, and personal influences, and the strategic perceptions and choices whereby the Bush administration set out on the path to invade and transform Iraq after the terrorist attacks on New York and the Pentagon by Arab jihadis under the banner of al-Qaeda.

Iraq was a "war of choice" for George W. Bush. The Iraq War concluded unfinished business left over from the 1991 Gulf War for the U.S., made more urgent by 9/11, which brought home to Americans the escalating threatening chaos in the Middle East. The world's remaining superpower and the United Nations–authorized multinational coalition had pulled back at the very brink of destroying Saddam's power in February 1991 after forcing the Iraqi Army out of Kuwait. In 2003, Bush made the decision to field and sustain the force necessary to overwhelm the Saddam regime—to finish the job the United States had left incomplete in 1991.

The 1991 war against Iraq was over after a mere hundred hours of ground combat. The U.S. allowed the smashed remnants of the Iraqi Army, which had thoroughly pillaged Kuwait, to flee that oil-rich Gulf emirate. Some, however, got caught in a "turkey-shoot," so named by the Western media because U.S. Army Major General Barry McCaffrey's 24th Infantry

Division slaughtered retreating Iraqi soldiers under questionable circumstances, as it took place after President George H. W. Bush had already declared a ceasefire.[4] The greater number of the regime's surviving elite Republican Guard units escaped north to fight another day. As a result, the Iraqi Army quickly reasserted the dictatorship's iron grip on the country. Another twelve years of tyranny followed, and tens of thousands of (mainly Shia) Iraqis were massacred by their own UN-recognized government. In fact, the U.S. military's self-restraint before the gates of Baghdad had been bracketed by the Baathist totalitarian dictatorship's genocidal attacks on the Kurds (before the Gulf War) and on the Shia (afterwards).

Iraq and September 11, 2001, were intertwined to a complex degree. After 9/11, the Bush administration looked out at the array of foreign enemies publicly calling for the death of Americans and destruction of the United States. Al-Qaeda had been launching attacks from an amorphous darkness that seemed to be gathering in almost every corner of the Middle East, Asia, and, especially, Afghanistan. But until bin Laden struck the U.S. directly, the only state or non-state actor out there actually shooting at Americans with regularity was Iraq. On a daily basis the Iraqis targeted American aircraft enforcing the no-fly zones that had been placed over northern and southern Iraq to protect the Shias and Kurds from the genocidal practices of the minority Sunni Arab government of Saddam Hussein. Leading up to the invasion, there was clearly a strong drive—prior to, during, and after 9/11—within the U.S. civilian national security leadership to trace a connection between Iraq and al-Qaeda. As they made the decisions leading up to the war, American officials saw the unfinished war in Iraq as part of an ideological conflict in the heartland of the Arab world—the same conflict that had produced the nineteen jihadi hijackers who launched the most successful attack on the American homeland since Pearl Harbor.

There were manifold influences on the policymakers—starting with the president—who planned and executed what became an eight-year campaign costing the U.S. government up to a trillion dollars. The U.S.

military-industrial complex was driving to exercise and expand its power in the name of security post-9/11. American exceptionalists and human rights universalists were both striving to remake the world in the image of the West. And cold-hearted realists believed that there had to be enough jihadi blood in the sand to vitiate al-Qaeda's claim to a say in the Middle East and in Islam. What remains unclear about anti-al-Qaeda war deliberations in the Bush administration is whether there was a conscious strategy from the beginning to fight al-Qaeda in Iraq, or if the facts on the ground alone created the killing fields where twenty to thirty thousand al-Qaeda operators and supporters perished in Iraq between 2003 and 2011.

*   *   *

After the defeat of the Saddamist regime, the U.S. wasted nearly a year in getting the contracting process necessary for stabilization and reconstruction stood up. The U.S. military went into counterinsurgency mode only with great difficulty, having repressed the lessons of Vietnam in the trauma of America's first defeat. "We only do the Fulda Gap [in between East and West Germany] to stop the Soviets," the military planners and acquisition folks cried after the 1975 downfall of Saigon. The intellectual preparation for fighting a counterinsurgency campaign was not there for Army leaders, especially. Thus the armor-heavy Iraq invasion force was ill-suited for MOUT (military operations on urban terrain) and COIN. And even more important, the U.S. political leadership—including those in Congress who had voted for regime change in Iraq with large bipartisan majorities—failed to anticipate the potential for the war to turn into a years-long policing action. U.S. forces were simply not prepared for that possibility (which in retrospect seems so obvious) in planning, staffing, or equipment. There was no pre-invasion preparation for counterinsurgency forces to provide follow-on support to the heavily mechanized units structured for the long and dangerous four-hundred-mile dash from Kuwait to Baghdad. The invasion came a mere year and a half after 9/11, and almost immediately after the U.S. and Afghan allies gained control of Taliban Afghanistan, which within a couple of years would suffer from its own insurgency.

The average length of a full-blown modern counterinsurgency campaign has been well over a decade (for example, Malaya, El Salvador, the Moros, Polisario, Fatah, Algeria, Vietnam-Indochina), with victory uncertain, at best. The four-year turnaround from the American blitzkrieg that took Baghdad to the population-centric counterinsurgency approach of the Surge finally put the U.S. and our new Iraqi allies on the path to crushing the twin Iraqi insurgencies: al-Qaeda-led jihadis aligned with neo-Saddamists and the Iranian-influenced Sadrist Mahdi Army movement. As a result, al-Qaeda in Iraq was reduced to mounting episodic terrorism (until the withdrawal of substantive U.S. security support for Iraq, lack of American action in the Syrian civil war, and AQI's consequent resurrection as ISIS) and Moqtada al-Sadr, leader of the Mahdi Army, became a politician.

The two mutually exclusive currents within the insurgency reflected Iraqi history and the Shia-Sunni sectarian divide that began over 1300 years ago. Thus success for U.S. and Coalition forces in Iraq would require a political element because there had to be a certain level of reconciliation of the two sects. That this could only be assured through democratic means was fully acknowledged from the Bush administration's actions in late, post-invasion 2003 through the 2011 withdrawal of U.S. forces from Iraq. The implementation of the American plan to democratize Iraq during the war and its aftermath, however, is open to criticism. Iraq was caught between two forces that had been relentlessly hostile to one another for more than a millennium: on the one hand the aggressively proselytized Wahhabi Islam of the fundamentalist Sunnis, which spawned al-Qaeda, and the expansionist, radical Shiite theocracy of Iran, which was the prime backer of the Sadrist militias. There was also the ethnic divide between Persians and Arabs at the border with Iran, and an internal division between the

Iraqi Arabs and the Iraqi Kurds, an ethnically Iranian-Persian but religiously primarily Sunni people. These divisions were the key fracture points within and around Iraq that would make extremely difficult the execution of Bush's plan to transform the ancient land into a more democratic and globally connected country that would no longer threaten international security.

The U.S. and UK failed to obtain authorization from the UN Security Council for the use of force against Iraq (the motion was successfully resisted by NATO allies France and Germany) before the invasion, but afterwards, the Council, in an unanimous vote (14–0; Syria abstained) on May 22, 2003, mandated occupation powers over Iraq to the U.S. and the UK to act as sovereign for Iraq. The American-run occupation government, the Coalition Provisional Authority, which governed Iraq for thirteen months, does not fare well in *The Occupation of Iraq: Winning the War, Losing the Peace*, the seminal book by Iraq's former defense and finance minister Dr. Ali Allawi.[5] Security for everyone, Iraqis and Coalition personnel, only got worse between the CPA's inception and its speedy conclusion on June 28, 2004. (The rapid turnover of sovereignty to the Iraqis by the U.S. surprised the Arab press and the Arab world at large, which was closely watching this experiment, the first major intervention by America in the Middle East. Many had believed that this would be a long-term occupation, like Israel's occupation of the West Bank.) The CPA head, veteran U.S. diplomat L. Paul "Jerry" Bremer, in sole charge throughout the CPA's tenure, appointed as interim prime minister Iyad Allawi, a medical doctor and former CIA asset who had survived a Saddam-ordered axe attack during his thirty-year London exile. Then in 2005, after the demise of the CPA, Ibrahim al-Jaafari, with extensive support of the Shia religious establishment, successfully contested the first democratic parliamentary elections in Iraq's long history. Yet soon, because of his indecisive leadership, he proved not to the liking of either the Americans or his fellow Iraqis.

Nouri al Maliki emerged from obscurity to take Jaafari's place and was democratically elected prime minister in his own right in 2006, and then re-elected in 2010 by a nearly unanimous vote in parliament that included partisans of the former insurgent leader Moqtada al-Sadr. Maliki's State of Law coalition won a plurality in April 2014 in accordance with the 2005 Iraqi constitution that had been written and adopted under U.S. guidance. Maliki looked assured of a third term as prime minister until the jihadi invasion from Syria disrupted all political calculations. Since the U.S.-led invasion, the Shia majority has ascended to political dominance in alliance with a largely quiescent Kurdish nationalist front; together the Shia and the Kurds make up a super-majority of 80 percent of the country's population. The Sunni power base that had ruled Iraq practically since the time of the Prophet Mohammed was suddenly out of power because of their minority status. (In sharp contrast to Iraq, the greater Arab and Islamic world is, by far, majority Sunni.)

The 2003 invasion had been launched after an unplanned, opportunistic air strike authorized by President Bush, which failed to assassinate Saddam. The invading Americans advanced rapidly upon their primary objective: the "center of gravity," the seat of the dictatorship's government and one of the most-storied cities in Islam—Baghdad. One unexpected challenge arose along the way to the invasion launch when NATO member Turkey's recently elected moderate Islamic government would not allow U.S. forces to open a northern front by attacking across Turkey's southern border into Iraq. Thus the sole available route for the armored invasion force would be north out of the tiny Persian Gulf enclave of the Emirate of Kuwait, beholden to the U.S. for its liberation from Iraq in the Gulf War. Aside from the substantial aid of the United Kingdom, whose forces quickly subdued Basra—Iraq's second city, just over the border from the British imperial creation of Kuwait—the U.S. military for all practical purposes stood alone in the attack to seize the prize: Baghdad.

THE ROAD TO BAGHDAD

Baghdad shaped the Arab world and the greater Middle East in ways that would require too many Arabian nights to describe. At the onset of the Iraq War the thirty-year capital of the totalitarian regime of Saddam Hussein held myriad mysteries beyond the capabilities of the best intelligence agencies in the world. No one could see into Saddam's mind, nor keep his minions from doing their highly effective utmost to conceal all from the United Nations–mandated weapons inspectors. Only after the defection of Saddam's son-in-law in 1995—after four years of post–Gulf War, countrywide UN inspections—did the world even realize that Iraq still had an active bio-chemical weapons development program.

The coalition attack had two main objectives, of which by far the more important to this *coup de main* was capturing the capital, Baghdad. But Basra, along with nearby Umm Qasr, Iraq's main port, was temporally the first of the Coalition strategic objectives and the primary mission of the UK, supported by U.S. special-operations forces, air support, and logistics.

Army General Tommy Franks and his U.S. Central Command, responsible for the Middle East and Central Asia, developed a plan with two primary axes of advance, one to the east and the other to the west. The heavily armored U.S. Army 3rd Infantry Division formed the left fist shooting north, and the 1st Marine Division, of Guadalcanal fame, had the right hook. Operating at the mechanized corps level, for which they had rarely trained, the Marines faltered briefly before Nasiriyah on the Euphrates River two hundred miles south of Baghdad. As a consequence, the 1st Division commander, Major General James Mattis, relieved a regimental commander for a continued lack of aggressiveness at the follow-on battle for al Kut, according to the excellent description of the Marine advance in *Cobra II*, co-authored by retired USMC General Bernard Trainor.[6] Advancing in parallel to the Marines, the Army blitzkrieged at such a rate that just prior to the direct assault into the heart of the capital, they reached the staging objectives—codenamed Larry, Moe, and Curley—so quickly that they exposed supporting U.S. forces to counterattack and near-annihilation. The close-quarters firefight at Curley, where 3/15 Infantry's outnumbered troops battled foreign jihadis from Syria, might have been lost but for the clear-sightedness of the battalion's top enlisted man, Command Sergeant Major Bob Gallagher. He was one of a few American soldiers with urban combat experience; Gallagher had seen this show before when wounded as a Ranger platoon sergeant during the *Black Hawk Down* incident in Mogadishu, Somalia, in 1993.[7]

The drive north to the Iraqi capital, accomplished in nineteen days amid weak resistance by an airpower-devastated Iraqi military and the lightly armed but fanatical paramilitary *Fedayeen*, involved a remarkable logistics tour de force that the eminent British historian, John Keegan, described in the first quality history of the invasion—his prematurely titled *The Iraq War* (2004). The resupply effort, undertaken during a three-day sandstorm that shrouded all of central Iraq, refueled, rearmed, and refitted the more than ten thousand vehicles of the 3rd Division hundreds of miles from port and thousands of miles from the unit's home base near Savannah, Georgia. The Army then quickly seized Baghdad International Airport on the western edge of the city, in preparation for what many feared would be a reprise of Stalingrad—a meat grinder of an urban campaign fought house to house, with chemical and biological threats thrown in for extra measure.

Fortunately for the American ground forces, the Iraqi Army had by now melted away, with huge quantities of their abandoned tanks and vehicles left as smoldering ruins from precision U.S. airstrikes. Saddam never prepared the people of Baghdad for guerrilla conflict. His minister of information continued to claim the Iraqi Army was winning until he was practically run over by Marine tanks as he spewed disinformation before an incredulous international media camped out in Baghdad hotels. On April 9, 2003, the U.S. owned the ancient city, after the 3rd Infantry "thunder runs" across downtown and the Marines' seizure of east Baghdad off the march from Route 6 connecting al Kut to the capital. They surged onto Firdos Square, and the iconic toppling of the Saddam statue marked the end of the invasion of Iraq.

The final stage of that invasion had taken place over 350 miles north of the attacking force's line of departure out of Kuwait on the Persian Gulf.

Special operations forces and airborne units, reinforced by an airlifted company of M-1 tanks, landed in the north after some had flown nap-of-the-earth across hostile Syria.[8] Alongside Kurdish *Peshmerga* ("those who face death"), these American troops created the semblance of the northern front earlier denied by Turkey. With the Kurds operating in lockstep with U.S. Army Special Forces, the Coalition occupied Iraq's third largest city, Mosul, without serious resistance from the majority Sunni population.

The American advance, undertaken with just two augmented divisions—with follow-on support from two light Infantry divisions, the 101st Airborne (Air Assault) and 82nd Airborne—altogether totaling not more than one hundred thousand troops, was an exceptionally economic use of force against an overmatched foe whose military nevertheless numbered over four hundred thousand soldiers equipped with thousands of armored vehicles and heavy artillery. Speed enabled surprise—the principle most critical to victory in maneuver warfare, according to the founding theorist of the armor attack, pre–World War II British General J. F. C. Fuller.[9] And surprise was decisive in a conflict where coalition forces brought explosive yet precise force to bear on the *schwerpunkt*—the decisive point—at each stage in the campaign to conquer Iraq. After the rapid seizure of Baghdad, Basra, and Saddam's hometown of Tikrit—where the feared last stand of the dictator's tribally based adherents failed to materialize—the U.S., with the UK in the south, now possessed Iraq.

THE OCCUPATION

The problems arose when the mission of U.S. forces changed from attack to occupation. In hindsight, the Bush administration's original plan looks indefensibly naive: a quick handover to an exile leadership that would assume the reins of an extant and functional bureaucracy with American troops drawn down to thirty thousand by August 2003, less than five months after the seizure of Baghdad.[10] It is not yet clear when or how the plan changed from a quick exit to an extended occupation, but

the assumption of the role of commander-in-chief of Central Command
by General John Abizaid, an Arab American with extensive experience in
the Middle East, sparked a reassessment. When Abizaid stated in mid-
2003—in direct contravention of the line from U.S. Defense Secretary
Donald Rumsfeld—that an insurgency had sprung up in Iraq, the Bush
administration decided there was no leaving Iraq quickly, except to chaos
of potentially genocidal proportions.

It was not until January of 2007, after three-plus years of nightly gun
battles and explosions, that Baghdad began to grow quiet. That was six
months before the arrival of the full complement of U.S. Surge troops,
whose presence would cement the victory over AQI. Their promised arrival
had already helped turn the tide. A Kurdish brigade from Kirkuk had road-
marched down to the capital as a part of a quid pro quo from the Iraqis for
an additional forty thousand American troops, negotiated by President
Bush. The president actively participated in war strategy, holding regular
video-conferences with the Iraqi prime minister. Maliki had no other
available forces, yet he had committed the Iraqi government, and so here
were Kurdish forces from Kirkuk, which Saddam had ethnically cleansed
(in a population transfer of Arabs for Kurds), but which was still the
Jerusalem of the Kurdish people. Saddam supporters, who had only
recently controlled the capital city and its wealthy neighborhoods, could
not help but fear retaliation for past genocide. Once the Peshmerga began
to patrol downtown Baghdad, the city ceased to be a combat zone—with
the exceptions of Sadr City, home turf to Moqtada Sadr, and the limited
Sunni areas such as Adhamiya and the Abu Hanifa mosque, Dora around
the main city power-plant, and the Abu Ghraib area to the immediate west
on the road to Fallujah and Ramadi on the Euphrates River. Those two
cities became the locations of the greatest battles of the counterinsurgency
against al-Qaeda and the neo-Saddamists. The battles in al Anbar province
can be compared with Hue in the Vietnam War's Tet Offensive for urban
intensity. Innovative use of aggressively positioned snipers and signals
intelligence–driven raids made urban warfare dangerous for the insurgents.

The top sniper in American history, Navy SEAL Chris Kyle, scored a record 160 confirmed kills in the fights for Fallujah and Ramadi.[11]

At the battles for Fallujah (April and November–December 2004) and Ramadi (July–December 2006), the U.S. military destroyed the most critical insurgent safe havens—both located less than sixty miles west of Baghdad. After warning the city's people to flee the self-declared jihadi emirate, Marine and Army troops took a wrecking-ball approach in depopulated Fallujah. The result? Decapitated mosques and a tank round or infantry-blasted holes in practically every house. The key campaign in Ramadi, the capital of al Anbar province, by contrast, was one of precision and the coordinated use of force. Following the COIN mantra of living with the people, Army Colonel Sean MacFarland's command built small neighborhood combat outposts citywide. Step by step, in a classic "ink-blot" pattern, security spread throughout Ramadi, forcing AQI out of a city it had once controlled near-absolutely. The Bedouin tribes of western Iraq now turned on al-Qaeda as the terrorist group became more extreme—and vulnerable—as it amassed a growing catalogue of defeats. During the final throes of the battle for Ramadi, the *Sahwa* (Awakening) rose up in what had been the ultimate safe haven in Iraq for the radical jihadis: the austere Sunni desert cities and villages. The tribes revolted against the primarily foreign suicide-bombers and leadership of al-Qaeda in Iraq after the extremists killed several sheikhs who had resisted them, forced marriages on Anbari women, and committed other atrocities characteristic of their Taliban-style totalitarianism. The decision of the Sunnis in Anbar to deny the insurgents safe haven signaled the beginning of the end for the al-Qaeda-led insurgency in Iraq.

But at the end of 2006, the situation still looked grim for the Coalition and the Iraqi government. Defeat was in the air. Ever since al-Qaeda's February 2006 bombing of the Askari Mosque in Samarra, one of the holiest sites in Shia Islam, the country had teetered on the brink of civil war. The U.S. military was the only obstacle to utter chaos and potential genocide. Sunni suicide bombers and Shia death squads continued to slaughter thousands of civilians every month in Baghdad, the key terrain for the Iraq War. In that year U.S. troop fatalities averaged seventy per month, with an additional 330 wounded,[12] with no end in sight. Prime Minister Maliki's government was barely functioning; it appeared to be merely an extension of the sectarian Shia political parties.

Democrats, campaigning on an anti–Iraq War platform, won control of both houses of the U.S. Congress in the November 2006 election. The slightest of edges remained in the U.S. Senate for the Republicans to block war-defunding efforts by the new majority that was bent on withdrawing American troops from Iraq as quickly as possible. The frequent "end of the tunnel" prognostications coming out of the Pentagon as real progress in Iraq seemed to be elusive not only generated bad memories of the Vietnam War but reinforced claims of deception by the Republican administration after investigators reported they had not found the weapons of mass destruction they expected to find in Iraq—a principal *casus belli*. Bush's credibility on the war had begun to slip away. The American people were suffering from fatigue after four years of war with no clear conclusion in sight; their exhaustion with the war had probably been accelerated by the pre-war rhetoric of officials in the Republican administration who forecast a relatively easy pacification of Iraq and quick extraction of U.S. forces after the invasion. Army General George Casey, Iraq commander from 2004 to 2007, advised the president repeatedly that the U.S. needed to continue to draw down American forces and turn the battle over to the Iraqi security services, ready or not. From June to October of 2006 two consecutive campaigns—"Together Forward" I & II—that had been launched to clear the insurgents out of Baghdad and intended to show new Iraqi military effectiveness had failed.

But in 2007 almost forty thousand additional U.S. Surge troops entered the fray, pushing up total American forces on the ground to 170,000 by July, with the vast majority going to Baghdad. Bush, against the advice of his commanders, the Pentagon civilian leadership, Congress, the polls and almost every other point of political pressure, had pulled the trigger on the Surge. He had also found his commander. General David Petraeus had worked hard to inculcate the necessity of population-centric protective measures and to establish that counterinsurgency (COIN) offered the way to victory in Iraq. He had already put COIN doctrine into practice on small scale immediately post-invasion in Mosul where his work with the local people included stimulating trade with nearby Syria.[13] Petraeus had stood up the training program for the Iraqi security services, but he now believed that program had not yet finished the job. The U.S. needed to provide further time and space for the Iraqis to develop their own internal defense. Americans would pay for those two precious commodities with more of their blood, treasure, sweat, and tears. But no other path presented itself, other than to cut and run. And unlike the loss in Vietnam, this defeat would most likely follow us home, considering 9/11. The U.S. had to destroy the insurgency that had been created by our invasion before we could leave Iraq. As former U.S. Secretary of State Colin Powell had said, "We broke it; we own it." Now we had to repair it.

Beyond stepping up combat operations (both conventional and Spec Ops), training the Iraqi security services, and moving U.S. troops off the giant FOBs (where the old strategy had concentrated them) and out in among the people to provide local protection, the new strategy demanded integration and action alongside the Sunni Awakening that had begun just before the Surge. The U.S. military finally and fully embraced the Sahwa, expanding it into the Sons of Iraq with a membership of more than a hundred thousand (mostly Sunnis) taking the local fight to al-Qaeda by late 2007.[14]

Although the media-savvy Petraeus didn't discuss it much with the press, the American military was picking up the pace of combat operations. Joint Special Operations Command under General Stanley McChrystal conducted tens of raids per night in Baghdad initiated by signals intelligence, especially cellphones (captured phones' "recent calls" lists would often lead to follow-on raids the same night). These operations increased in effectiveness with a growing collaboration between Spec Ops and conventional forces established on the ground. U.S. Army units built dozens of fortified bases throughout Baghdad, expanded the use of blast-walls for neighborhood security, and collected intelligence from the now-protected population exhausted with jihadi extremism. Inexorably, members of the capital branch of AQI got chewed up, with fewer and fewer places to hide.

In the summer of 2007, with all Surge forces in place, the Coalition finally had enough troops to attack AQI insurgent areas in all directions around Baghdad, in Operation Phantom Strike. Petraeus called this his "Anaconda" strategy—after Winfield Scott's Civil War plan to squeeze the Confederacy from all sides. As Colonel Peter Mansoor, the Iraq commander's executive officer, explains, "The momentum of these operations took its toll on al-Qaeda, as the organization began to lose leaders faster than it could find qualified replacements. In Iraq, there would be no enemy surprise akin to the Tet Offensive during the Vietnam War."[15]

THE GOVERNMENT OF IRAQ STEPS UP

With the Surge's deadly impact on al-Qaeda in Baghdad becoming more and more apparent, the challenge that remained was how to defeat the Iranian-allied militias. Prime Minister Maliki had resisted going after the Jaish al Mahdi (JAM), the armed wing of the Sadrists and by far the most powerful of the anti-U.S. Shia militias, because members of their political party, "the Office of the Martyr Sadr," belonged to his government. In addition, Maliki understandably did not see the Shia extremists as existential threats to the Iraqi government in the way he did the Sunni insurgents. Nevertheless, the continual indirect fire (mortars and rockets, primarily supplied by Iran) launched from Sadr City finally had taken their toll on the Iraqi leader and GOI officials located in the Green Zone.

In late August 2007, gun battles between JAM and Iraqi security forces in the Shia holy city of Karbala resulted in over fifty deaths and the wounding of two hundred more attendees of a religious festival celebrating the birth of the Mahdi.[16] The lawlessness represented by the Mahdi Army had to stop. The time had come for the final reckoning in the intra-Shia conflict between Maliki, the leader of the Iraqi government, and Moqtada Sadr, insurgent warlord. The prime minister had declared operation *Fard al Qanoon* (Enforcing the Law) in February 2007 to extend Iraqi government control over the entire city. Now he would follow through by letting U.S. forces enter Sadr City.

Initially American troops entered the Shia slum in east Baghdad to build a wall that blocked off the southwestern part of Sadr City, which had been serving as a sweet spot for launching artillery projectiles into the Green Zone. Then in early 2008 the U.S. Army went in for a bloody fight and finally cleared the urban sprawl of the Mahdi Army militants after over two months of continuous combat. Stryker units—centered on an eight-wheeled armored car mounting a .50 caliber machinegun remotely aimed with night vision sights, which could move quickly and quietly through urban congestion—led the way, sweeping the militia off the streets while the infantry dismounted from the vehicles and fought house to house.

The Iranians continued to stir the pot even as the al-Qaeda in Iraq threat diminished in 2007. The Quds (Jerusalem) paramilitary force, whose commander reported directly to the Supreme Leader of Iran, Ayatollah Khamenei, were in charge of Iranian state policy in Iraq—and Tehran's ambassador to Baghdad.[17] These specially trained operatives infiltrated into Iraq under several guises, including as pilgrims to the great Shia shrines of Karbala and Najaf. After U.S. Spec Ops captured several Quds commandos, including a member of Lebanese Hezbollah, Iran backed off paramilitary operations but continued to supply explosively formed penetrators (EFP) that shot a molten slug of metal able to destroy any American armored vehicle. Iran-supplied Shia "Special Groups" (splinter militias that had ostensibly spun off JAM after Moqtada Sadr declared a truce in April 2008) received the anti-armor mines, with EFPs becoming the number one killer of U.S. troops, especially around Baghdad.

Down south, the Sadrists launched rockets into the last UK army base at Basra airport, some reportedly from nearby Iran. Iranian Revolutionary Guards kidnapped fifteen British sailors off the Iraqi side of the Shatt al Arab waterway, displaying the Brits on Tehran TV before releasing them after several days. Because of massive anti-war sentiment in Great Britain, Prime Minister Tony Blair, Bush's partner in the invasion and Occupation, could not keep his political position in Parliament and conduct active combat operations in south Iraq. By early 2008, Moqtada Sadr's partisans had extended a harsh form of sharia law throughout Basra; they paid absolutely no attention to edicts from the seat of national government to the north, Baghdad.

At this point, Maliki made the single most important decision that ensured his position as a truly national figure, not just a Shia sectarian. With al-Qaeda and the neo-Saddamists on the wrong side of the power curve—and dying out as a result—Maliki decided to go after the Shia Sadrists in Basra under his own personal command of Iraqi forces in March 2008. With the British out of the fight at Basra airport, the U.S. military had to step in when the Iraqi forces began to fall apart in their first large-scale combat operation on their own—putting Maliki's life at risk. No matter, Baghdad regained control of Basra, with the JAM finally broken. The prime minister's personal courage and his willingness to take on his fellow Shiites boded well for a future non-sectarian Iraq.

After Maliki's military victories against JAM, Moqtada Sadr called a ceasefire to save what was left of his force, which had once been strong enough to battle U.S. troops to a standstill at the Imam Ali mosque in Najaf and nearly shut down Baghdad in April 2004. Sadr then became a full-time politician and fled to Qom, Iran, where he unconvincingly claimed to be studying the Islamic jurisprudence necessary to be recognized as *marj al taqlid* (worthy of emulation)—a title that his father had achieved prior to his execution by Saddam.

Presently the Sadrists continue to cooperate with Maliki's State of Law coalition, but Moqtada has called for Maliki to step down as a candidate for prime minister.[18] Sadr's militia, formerly inactive, has now joined the fight against ISIS.[19] Reconciliation and compromise out of necessity is the lifeblood of democracy. This is what we have seen—ugly and dirty but largely without inter-party violence—in the Iraqi parliament since political independence from the CPA. Now in caretaker mode as the result of the April elections, the ruling alliance in Baghdad, led by the Shiite al Maliki and anchored by a Shia electoral majority, includes secular and religious Sunnis from Baghdad, Anbar, and Mosul, along with the self-ruling Kurds.

Prime Minister Maliki's efforts to assert national authority, even at the expense of his co-sectarian Shia, paid off in the January 2009 provincial elections when his State of Law coalition took a plurality in nine of seventeen provincial legislatures. (Unsettled Kirkuk did not have elections.) Maliki's risky embrace of the Awakening in 2007—at the time, who knew if the Sunni nationalists, with many former AQI supporters among them, would turn against him or not?—garnered political dividends when the Sahwa political party supporting the Baghdad government won control over the al Anbar council. The ever-reliable Kurds of the twin parties the Kurdish Democratic Party (KDP) and Patriotic Union of Kurdistan (PUK), who had allied with all iterations of the U.S.-supported Iraqi government from the beginning, maintained their grip on power in the three provinces of the autonomous Kurdish Regional Government (KRG). Alone in Iraq, Maliki now had a power base that extended throughout the country from the local level to the national parliament.

Then came the next test for the nascent democracy. Could Maliki be re-elected fairly? In 2010, Iraq had UN-certified democratic parliamentary elections. U.S. combat forces, per the SOFA, remained outside the cities during the vote. The first Iraqi-protected *intehab* (election) went off with hardly a hitch. AQI, reduced to waging a terrorism campaign, weakly tried—and failed—to deter voting through several minor explosions scattered around the capital. The approximately 90 percent drop in violence since the end of 2006 had engendered a sense of optimism among the Iraqi people.

When the votes were counted after the March 2010 election, the Sunni-dominated *Iraqiyya* party of Iyad Allawi, the former interim prime minister under the CPA, had won a plurality of one over Maliki's ruling State of Law coalition, but neither party had the necessary votes to form a government. After eight months, Maliki cobbled together a majority across sectarian and ethnic lines (according to Christopher Hill, then the U.S. ambassador to Iraq, *Iraqiyya* could not obtain another single vote during the entire time). The process, undertaken while the prime minister continued to run a counter-terrorism campaign against AQI remnants and Iranian-supported militants, was at the time the longest delay between a parliamentary election and forming a government in world history. (Strangely, Belgium—a staunch NATO ally—surpassed Iraq's record the next year.) On December 27, 2010, the Council of Representatives near-unanimously approved the new Maliki government.

On January 1, 2009, after Sadr City was pacified and the Iraqi government was solidly in control of the capital at large, the U.S. military handed over to Iraqi security forces the gates and blast walls dividing the Green Zone from the rest of Baghdad. This, in both a practical and a symbolic way, ended the Iraq War. Now that the Iraqi security services could take over the fight from the Coalition, the glide path to U.S. withdrawal had begun—just under six years from the date Coalition forces crossed the line of departure from Kuwait, kicking off the invasion of Iraq, which would reshape the Arab world. From this point forward, the American-allied Iraqi government took control over the strategic direction of the country. At the end of 2008, UN resolutions had ceased to mandate to the U.S. a position in Iraqi political and military affairs under international law; from that point on a contract between sovereign nations—the Status of Forces Agreement—governed American forces in the country. A few terrorists remained active, and some malign interference from outside Iraq's borders continued, but the tide had turned. The war begun to oust a bloody dictator had been won, and the new democracy in Iraq had the extremists, both inside and outside its borders, on the run.

WAR STRATEGY

The strategic success of the Iraq War is measured by this question: did the war significantly contribute to the defeat of the post-9/11 al-Qaeda terrorist threat to the United States? Many would say no, the effort was misplaced, counterproductive. Or the cost in U.S. lives and treasure was too great a price to pay for what was achieved. "Iraq was a brazen attack," asserts Clandestine Service officer Henry "Hank" Crumpton, who led the post-9/11 CIA ground strike against al-Qaeda in Afghanistan, in his 2012 memoir *The Art of Intelligence.* Among a multitude of harsh critics in the media, academia, and Congress and at the CIA (but not so evident among staff at the Bush White House or the Pentagon), Crumpton castigated the Iraq invasion as a distraction from the main effort against bin Laden's organization in Afghanistan and Pakistan. Crump does, however, agree with most strategic thinkers immediately after 9/11 on the principle that to defeat al-Qaeda "we must attack the political-social-economic conditions the enemy exploits."[20] And that was the very reason that Bush took the war beyond Afghanistan—and even beyond Pakistan (the weak U.S. ally that harbored an isolated bin Laden for almost a decade). The U.S. strategy was to take on the geographically and ideologically dominant Arab center of the jihadi terrorism that had killed almost three thousand Americans in the September 11, 2001, surprise attack. The publicly stated U.S. policy goal of transforming the Middle East from an authoritarian hotbed of religious extremism into the final major region of the world to embrace democracy required a sweeping long-term strategy. The second stage of this strategy—after the conquest of Taliban Afghanistan's safe haven for the jihadis—would start on the road to Baghdad. Given all the unknowns and the multiple variables involved in this bold line of attack, the Iraq invasion clearly was a high-risk decision by the United States.

Thousands of foreign jihadis under the aegis of al-Qaeda fought the Americans in Iraq. Before the invasion, Saddam had invited foreign extremists to join in the "mother of all battles" against America; as we have seen, "jihad" was stamped on their passports as their reason for entry into Baathist Iraq. Upon the occupation and the CPA, thousands more infiltrated the borders, primarily from Syria, where Damascus harbored the senior surviving uncaptured member of the Saddam government, the redheaded army general Izzat al Douri. Foreign al-Qaeda-connected elements already in Iraq before the invasion included jihadi leader Abu Musab al Zarqawi, who like bin Laden had escaped as the U.S. rout of Taliban Afghanistan became inevitable in late 2001. The Jordanian Islamic extremist and bin Laden fellow traveler was chief of the *Tawhid wa Jihad* (One God and Holy War), a Gulf Arab-funded Sunni insurgency that after the fall of Baghdad changed its name to a more media-friendly "al-Qaeda in Iraq." Zarqawi openly swore *bayaat* (allegiance) to Osama bin Laden in 2004.

The Pentagon evidently realized the potential of a vast killing field in Iraq to draw in the perpetrators of 9/11 (whether or not that consequence of the war had been contemplated before the invasion). The Fort Meade, Maryland–based National Security Agency gathered and processed signals intelligence from cellphone calls, which proved to be the Achilles heel of the Sunni insurgency. In order to not lose this window into the communications of the talkative guerrillas, the U.S. generally allowed cell towers in Fallujah and other Anbari locations to remain functional—though they were sometimes destroyed in battle as unintended collateral damage. In June 2008, a U.S. Air Force F-16 dropped a bomb that killed Zarqawi near Baquba, northeast of Baghdad, after the AQI leader filmed himself in the desert taunting the Americans. The assassination left no one of note to take his place in the al-Qaeda in Iraq leadership. According to documents found on the Iraq battlefield and with bin Laden's body in Abbottabad, Pakistan, the founder of al-Qaeda had unsuccessfully pleaded for his Iraqi affiliate to cease massacring fellow Muslims with suicide bombers. Apparently the organization of the jihadi "sheikh" was so decimated that he communicated with his allies—including the Iraqi resistance—through a sole messenger. This trusted longtime courier, Abu Ahmed al Kuwaiti, ended up leading U.S. intelligence to his boss's hideaway, where American special operations forces killed him in May 2011. In his irrelevance, Osama had mulled over changing the name of al-Qaeda because in the war of ideas the organization was irredeemably tainted now with failure and nihilistic extremism. The Iraq War had dried up the swamp whence al-Qaeda sprung.

The twin objectives of the post-Saddam Iraq War strategy were to destroy al-Qaeda's legitimacy in the Islamic world on the battlefield and to win the war by winning the populace—at least, to win enough of the people for the democratic electoral process to have legitimacy—which would serve as a catalytic example for the authoritarian remainder of *al ummah*, the international Muslim community. The key to this second objective was holding onto the majority Iraqi Shia since the Kurds, a 20 percent minority in the national population, were with the U.S. from the beginning.

The Shia or *Shiat Ali* (partisans of the Imam Ali) hark back to the great schism in Islam that occurred in the seventh century CE. The founding fathers of Islam, the *Al Rashidun*, the rightly guided deputies of the Prophet Mohammed (the first four leaders, or caliphs, of Islam after the Prophet's death in 632 CE) ended their era in Iraq. The fourth and last of the *Rashidun* was Ali, cousin and son-in-law of Mohammed, who was assassinated in Kufa, Iraq. Ali's death forced the great schism in Islam. The Shia broke away from the Sunni on the importance of the deputies being of the Prophet's bloodline. After the martyrdom of the Prophet's grandson Hussein in central Iraq, the Shia continued to demand caliphs from Mohammed's family only, and the Sunni went the other way. A significant majority of the Islamic world followed the Sunni path; the Wahhabi of Saudi Arabia and many holy men of jihad, such as those of al-Qaeda, are Sunni. Sunnis are not the majority in Iraq, though, where the Arab Shia became the majority, three times greater in population than each of the next two ethno-religious groups: the Sunni Arabs and Kurds.

More than twelve centuries after the Shia-Sunni split, a Shia rebellion forced the end of colonial Britain's control of Iraq in 1932, the greatest setback for the global empire in the interwar period. London left behind something very much like what the Ottoman Turks had solidified in the sixteenth century and lost to the UK at the end of WWI: a minority Sunni government ruling over a majority Shia population. In keeping with history, the Shia teed up a martyr to foil the U.S. efforts in Iraq: Moqtada al Sadr. Al-Sadr (meaning *from the chest*) was the unaccomplished son of the last great Shia martyr, who had been executed by Saddam in 1999.

In April 2004, CPA Administrator Bremer shut down Sadr's newspaper, *al Hawza*, after it published one of Moqtada's sermons calling for "Death to the Americans!" Practically from the beginning of his tenure as head of the CPA, Bremer had been calling for the arrest of Moqtada, under an Iraqi magistrate's order, for his partisans' killing of a Shia cleric, Abdul Majid al-Khoei, who was working with the Coalition in Najaf during the invasion. The CPA, however, possessed no arrest-capable force and in any case wanted the action taken by Iraqi police. But only the Coalition combat troops could provide the supporting force required to enforce the Iraqi judge's order on the increasingly popular Shia firebrand.[21] The first post-invasion Iraq commander, Army Lieutenant General Ric Sanchez, did not act on the arrest warrant originally issued in mid-2003. Unfortunately, Sadr could have been effectively silenced only by being made a martyr. The unbroken chain of Shia martyrs from the Early Middle Ages would then have continued. The United States dodged a bullet with Moqtada, who continued to bedevil the U.S. in Iraq but never rose to the existential threat he could have presented to American war aims.

Keeping Shia as well as Kurdish support entailed the wholesale rebuilding of the Iraqi government and army. The first post-dictatorship Iraq president, Jalal Talibani, a seventy-year-old Kurdish warrior-politician, stated that otherwise the new governing leadership would constantly fear a coup from the barracks—a well-practiced Baathist specialty. Talibani, and more importantly Maliki, demanded of the army absolute loyalty to the newly democratic political order; elected leaders would be in charge of state-controlled violence, which Saddam had used formerly to massacre tens of thousands of Shia and Kurds. Starting from scratch, the Iraqi Army grew from zero after Bremer's 2003 order disbanding the Saddamist army to over 250,000 trained soldiers in 2008.

There are still fracture points between the Kurds and Baghdad, principally over oil exports and Kirkuk. Until the recent stunning success of ISIS, the politicians haggled over money and budgetary issues, rather than engaging in ancient Persian-Arab blood feuds, but renewed war gave the Kurds both reason and opportunity to seize polyglot Kirkuk, home to some of Iraq's ever-diminishing Christian minority. The KRG (autonomous Kurdish region), with its capital at Irbil, Iraq's fourth-largest city, has achieved a level of security. Turkey is heavily involved in the KRG through businesses operating in the autonomous Kurdish economy, but Turkish forces also conduct pinprick attacks across the border into the Iraqi Kurdish region against the PKK—a resistance group fighting for Kurdish rights in Turkey using what the U.S. and others call terrorist tactics. Syria's Kurdish population, upended by the Arab Spring and subsequent civil war in Syria, looks for possible union with greater Iraqi Kurdistan and their brethren in southeastern Turkey and northwestern Iran. The Kurds are one of the largest ethnic groups in the world with no population-majority UN-recognized state. Nevertheless, by the standards of their history, the Kurds are now relatively secure within the autonomy of their mountain fastness squashed between Turkey, Iran, Syria, and Iraq proper. Consequently, the Iraqi Kurds remain the most loyal American allies in the Middle East outside Israel.

During the twelve-year period between the Gulf War and the Iraq War, Israelis lived in fear of chemical and biological weapons raining down on them in Scud missiles launched by Saddam, as had happened with conventional warheads in 1991. Most Israeli families kept gas masks and had a sealed room within their homes in preparation for this terrible and constant threat controlled by a genocidal anti-Semitic maniac.[22] Freeing

Israel of this existential fear was a principal reason for the invasion and disarming of Iraq, both from a moral perspective and from the perspective of America's national interest.

STRATEGIC GOALS AND LEGAL ASPECTS OF THE IRAQ WAR

We have reviewed the history of the successful battles for Iraq. The remaining question is, did victory in Iraq achieve America's strategic goals? After the surprisingly rapid conquest of the Taliban in Afghanistan by U.S. and local forces, the Bush national security team decided to stay on offense (rather than hide within a TSA-protected homeland) through the invasion and democratic transformation of Iraq. There were some old—and ongoing—problems to be solved in Saddamist Iraq. The three strategic goals contemplated in the U.S. Iraq War deliberations were: (1) destroy Saddam and his regime, thereby ending a source of regional and global terror and instability; (2) establish a UN-accepted Iraqi democracy—in line with what the United States had done in Germany, Japan, South Korea, and Panama—as an example to the rest of the Arab and greater Islamic world; (3) create existential problems for al-Qaeda, making it difficult for the terrorist organization to continue to operate and recruit in its Arabian Peninsula homeland. With two men—Dick Cheney and Donald Rumsfeld—in his war cabinet having served as Secretary of Defense in previous administrations, the president could call upon a wealth of knowledge and experience within his inner circle in the fraught work of war-forecasting.

No illegitimate attack could possibly beget a legitimate occupation. But after Iraq violated over fifteen UN resolutions from the invasion of Kuwait in 1990 until the 2003 end of the Baathist dictatorship, post-invasion UN Security Council deliberations were *pro forma*. The Security Council voted unanimously to establish and, later, to extend sovereign control of the U.S. over Iraq in trust for its people just liberated from the tyrannical rule of Saddam Hussein.

Saddam Hussein's Iraq had given the international community good reason to authorize the U.S. occupation. For over ten years before the invasion, Saddam's elite air-defense troops had plotted ambushes on U.S. and UK (and from 1991 to 1998 French) aircraft enforcing no-fly zones, with Iraqi anti-aircraft forces shooting at American and British combat jets almost daily. Primarily because of superior U.S. technology, the Iraqis never actually shot down a Coalition aircraft during the interwar period. More than twenty airmen and other U.S. personnel, however, lost their lives patrolling the kinetic hostility above Iraq in a friendly fire incident when a U.S. jet fighter destroyed a fully loaded American helicopter.

During the Clinton administration, the CIA got briefly run out of the American-airpower-protected, southwestern KRG (the area under the Kurdish Regional Government) by Saddam-directed tank-heavy army units that inflicted hundreds of casualties on the U.S.-allied Kurds. Mark on a map the regional terrorism incidents engendered by Sunni radicalism in Somalia, Chechnya, Lebanon, Egypt, Pakistan, Afghanistan, and Israel from 1991 through 2001 along with the al-Qaeda attacks on the USS *Cole* in Yemen and the American embassies in East Africa, and you'll find the Arab heartland at dead center of those attacks. The nerve center of jihadi Islam was not in Afghanistan—as even now it is not in Pakistan. These peripheries were only hiding places and staging grounds.

The Sunni Abbasid caliphate, the greatest Arab empire in history, spanning the globe from Italy to Central Asia, had as its capital Baghdad— now in majority-Shia Iraq. Osama bin Laden proclaimed his jihad to defeat the West and its minions in the Islamic world in order to reclaim the lands of the Abbasid Empire.

But the Iraq War exposed the utter moral nihilism of al-Qaeda, which had already slaughtered unsuspecting men, women and children just going about their everyday lives on 9/11. This moral nihilism became a fatal flaw for the terrorist organization when it turned the Anbari Sunnis against AQI and into the open arms of the U.S. military and then into an alliance with the Shia government in Baghdad. The result of all the senseless killing in Iraq was an erosion of Muslim support worldwide that turned even Osama bin Laden himself against his own; as we have seen, he actually pleaded with Abu Musab al Zarqawi, the leader of the al-Qaeda franchise in Iraq that was now the group's main embodiment, to change his *takfiri* ways (killing "apostate" Muslims). The massacre of thousands of Shia Muslim women and children in Iraq by *intehareen* (suicide bombers) had damaged the "good" name of al-Qaeda.

The Arab Spring emerged almost simultaneously with the establishment of the second democratically elected Maliki government in December 2010. Initially, democratic and human rights–driven popular movements dominated the revolutions throughout the Middle East. With social media such as Twitter and Facebook playing a large role, and Egyptian protest posters displaying U.S.-deposed Saddam on the gallows in Cairo's Tahrir Square, the American and Iraqi influence in these revolutions was, even if indirect, readily apparent. Nowhere in the origins of the Arab Spring could you find al-Qaeda and Osama bin Laden.

✶   ✶   ✶

The recent history of the Islamic World reflects the difficulty of foreign military operations by a democracy—as first documented by Thucydides, who recounted the debilitating Athenian debates over the empire during the Peloponnesian War in the fifth century BCE. He showed how the competitive nature of party politics in a democracy tends to undermine the unity required to conduct war abroad—a principle that was demonstrated once again in the course of America's war in Iraq.

As a result, a vacuum has opened, into which the forces unleashed by the Iraq War have rushed—with the consequences still unfolding. Authoritarian Arab regimes—military dictatorships and oil-rich Gulf monarchies—had effectively suppressed the forces that are now engulfing much of the Middle East. There are three political and cultural movements at work. First, sparked by the self-immolation of a street vendor, youthful movements agitating for secular democracy (and against authoritarian regimes) sprung up in Tunisia, quickly followed by Egypt, Libya, Yemen, and, finally, Syria. Second, the Shia-Sunni schism has caused violence, first in Bahrain and then in the Syrian civil war. Then, there are the tribal differences—the most ancient fault lines of all—now roiling Libya and Yemen. All three of these different causes of conflict are playing a role in Iraq as a result of the 2003 invasion. In greater or lesser degrees, each was a cause of the bloody insurgency. It is difficult to overestimate the American role in quelling these forces and helping the Iraqi people channel these potentially destructive elements into politics—as we can see from the consequences of America's premature disengagement.

The Arab Spring—originally a positive development—now appears to have devolved, with a swing backward into war and tyranny. The difference between now and the recent past—even before the 2003 invasion—is that for the first time in more than two decades, America is not really in the mix.

Conceivably, the results of our withdrawal could ultimately be good, if the Arab peoples win their bloody struggle with themselves and achieve the democracy that they saw us help establish in Iraq. (When I hear someone comment that the Arabs just can't "do" democracy, I always wonder if there may be a touch of racism in the remark. What makes the Arabs any different from the Latin Americans, East Europeans, Africans, Indians, Taiwanese, Indonesians, and South Koreans—or the rest of the world, for that matter, that, with a few exceptions, has embraced democracy? Are the Arabs not covered by the UN *Universal Declaration of Human Rights*, which says, "The will of the people shall be the basis of the authority of government; this will shall be expressed in periodic and genuine elections which shall be by universal and equal suffrage and shall be held by secret vote or by equivalent free voting procedures.")

There are encouraging developments. Yemen has stabilized despite an ongoing sectarian-tribal war, and al-Qaeda is on the defensive there; the high-water mark of the terrorists' success was when they temporarily seized a couple of towns in 2012. And Egypt, the most populous Arab country, has turned away from the popularly elected Muslim Brotherhood (an Islamic political movement that was a historical antecedent to the much more radical al-Qaeda) and back to the army in a move that, hopefully, will return them to a Turkish-style path to democracy. How long that will take is anybody's guess, but the people of Egypt have overthrown two governments in a row in less than two years. So President Abdel-Fattah al-Sisi shouldn't get too comfortable in his position; he may well find himself out of power if he doesn't deliver—especially economically. Uncharismatic Ayman Zawahiri, an Egyptian medical doctor who is now the leader of al-Qaeda and hiding somewhere in Pakistan, has no real standing in the country of his birth, nor does his organization.

But our complete withdrawal from Iraq did, at the very least, not make the Arabs' struggle for democracy any easier. In Syria there are now over 150,000 dead; the revolution against Assad's dictatorship could have benefited from more U.S. support, especially in the early stages when pro-democracy, secular forces were leading the movement against the Baathist regime. We did not need to put U.S. troops on the ground, just to help with air power and financial support. Many of us reconstruction contractors, honed to a sharp edge in Iraq and Afghanistan, continue to stand ready to enter the Syrian conflict.

And now al-Qaeda in Iraq, under a new name—ISIS, or the Islamic State of Iraq and Syria (or the Levant), or now simply the Islamic State—has reappeared in Iraq, regenerated from safe havens across the border in lawless areas of Syria now deep in civil war. Iraqis who fought with U.S. forces—and who were my brothers in arms, in my role as a contractor combatant—are now facing barbaric terrorists who delight in lining up prisoners and shooting them en masse, Nazi-style.

On September 11, 2001, the same Sunni terrorist movement struck New York, Virginia, and Pennsylvania, with devastating effect. The United States took al-Qaeda on in Afghanistan, and then in Iraq. We destroyed AQI on the battlefield. We succeeded in establishing the first truly democratic Arab state. And it seemed that America had won the hearts and minds of the Arabs for freedom and democracy (when, in the Sunni Awakening, even Iraq's disaffected former ruling sect rejected al-Qaeda)— and cast yet another totalitarian movement into the dustbin of history. But now the Arab peoples' mighty struggle for freedom and against al-Qaeda's terror has entered a more dangerous phase. America's friends and allies in Iraq need our support to defeat their enemies, who are also our enemies. We will all benefit if they succeed.

ACKNOWLEDGMENTS

FIRST OF ALL, I WANT TO THANK my outstanding co-author, Malcolm McConnell. This journey would have been a more fraught one without his guiding wisdom. Then I want to express my deepest gratitude for my Brothers at AISG for all your courage and support: Kiffer, Tony, Mark, Frank, Abu Hind, Brahim, Samir, Sher Mohammed, Rony, Firas, Carlos, Dennis. And to my generous mentors: Judd Gould, Bob Kelley, Tom Overby, and Marvin Stirman, who have so helped me along the way. My father, Miller, paved the road I've traveled and will travel, and made it as smooth and straight as only a Seabee can. Mel Berger, you got it done—much thanks. Outstanding work by our superb editor, Elizabeth Kantor of Regnery, in truly capturing the dynamic events informing this book. Graham Wiggins—you're the real deal for hanging with us. My greatest appreciation and love, of course, is for my wife, Tanya, and my children, Callie and Henry. They've lived this war and this book for over ten years.

Any mistakes herein are my own.

Lake Como, Italy

August 6, 2014

NOTES

FOREWORD

1. For clarity, we do not transliterate the final "S" in ISIS as "Sham," but translate it as "Syria." From an Islamic historical perspective *al Sham* denotes greater Syria that included all of what is now Syria, Israel, Lebanon, the Palestininan territories, and Jordan (also collectively called the "Levant").

2. Patrick Cockburn, "Mosul: Who is the Isis Jihadi leader Abu Bakr al-Bagh-dadi," *The Independent*, June 10, 2014, http://www.independent.co.uk/news/world/middle-east/mosul-emergency-who-is-abu-bakr-albaghdadi-9523070.html.

3. Rebecca Kaplan, "Will ISIS plan a 9/11-style terror plot against the U.S.?" CBS News, June 16, 2014, http://www.cbsnews.com/news/will-isis-plan-a-911-style-terror-plot-against-the-u-s/.

4. Richard Spencer, "Iraq Crisis: ISIS jihadis execute dozens of captives: The shocking pictures show ISIS herding purported deserters and members of Shia groups together in Tikrit before being shot," *Telegraph*, June 15, 2014, http://

www.telegraph.co.uk/news/worldnews/middleeast/iraq/10901866/Iraq-crisis-ISIS-jihadists-execute-dozens-of-captives.html.

5.   "Senator: No Arms to Iraq unless Congress gets info," Associated Press, July 24, 2014, http://www.washingtonpost.com/politics/congress/senator-no-arms-to-iraq-unless-congress-gets-info/2014/07/24/9ca79976-1344-11e4-ac56-773e54a65906_story.html.

6.   Adam Entous, Julian E. Barnes and Siobhan Gorman, "Secret US plan to aid Iraq," *Wall Street Journal*, June 21, 2014, http://online.wsj.com/articles/secret-u-s-plan-to-aid-iraq-1403308039?mod=mktw.

7.   Liz Sly, "Iran claims victory with Assad's anticipated win in Syrian election," *Washington Post*, June 2, 2014, http://www.washingtonpost.com/world/middle_east/iran-claims-victory-with-assads-anticipated-win-in-syrian-election/2014/06/02/314f43a3-164a-4817-94bb-3b4483fa9dc6_story.html.

CHAPTER ONE: THE BEGINNING OF THE END FOR AL-QAEDA IN IRAQ

1.   As told to Carter Andress by Dave Scantling, a founding executive of the Pentagon's Business Transformation Agency who became Assistant Deputy Under Secretary of Defense for Expeditionary Business Systems. Dave was present during the April 2006 video conference, which he set up with the help of U.S. Army Brigadier General Lee Donne Olvey (ret.) and John Olvey, the author's then-business partner.

2.   U.S. Army Corps of Engineers Gulf Region Division (International Zone, Baghdad, Iraq) Logistics Movement Monitoring Center: "Monitored Convoys" Monthly Results, January 1, 2007–October 31, 2008.

3.   Kira Walker, "Iraq, Turkey and Syria: 'The Opportunity to Use Water as Something That Unites Us,'" Rudaw.net, March 3, 2014, http://rudaw.net/english/kurdistan/09032014.

4.   William Doyle, *A Soldier's Dream: Captain Travis Patriquin and the Awakening of Iraq* (New York: Penguin Books, 2011), 143–44.

5.   Peter R. Mansoor, *Surge: My Journey with General David Petraeus and the Remaking of the Iraq War* (New Haven: Yale University Press, 2013), 171.

6.   Marion Farouk-Sluglett and Peter Sluglett, *Iraq Since 1958* (London: I.B. Tauris Publishers, 2003), 49–50.

7.   Michael R. Gordon and Bernard E. Trainor, *Endgame: The Inside Story of the Struggle for Iraq, from George W. Bush to Barack Obama* (New York: Pantheon Books, 2012), 223–28.

8.   Campbell Robertson, "New U.S. Embassy Dedicated in Baghdad as Bombs Explode Elsewhere," *New York Times*, January 5, 2009, http://www.nytimes.com/2009/01/06/world/middleeast/06embassy.html.

CHAPTER TWO: THE AWAKENING JOINS THE IRAQI SECURITY SERVICES

1.   MNF-I Charts accompanying General David Petraeus Congressional testimony 8–9 April 2008, 4, http://www.defense.gov/pdf/Testimony_Handout_Packet.pdf.

2.   Chris Kyle and Scott McEwen, *American Sniper: The Autobiography of the Most Lethal Sniper in U.S. Military History* (New York: HarperCollins, 2012), 141.

CHAPTER THREE: THE ULTIMATE COUNTERINSURGENTS

1.   Carl von Clausewitz, *On War* (Princeton: Princeton University Press, 1984), 485–87.

2.   Email exchange between Ambassador L. Paul Bremer and the authors.

3.   B. H. Liddell Hart, *The Classic Book on Military Strategy* (New York: The Penguin Group, 1991), xx.

4.   E. M. Walters, "Surfaces and Gaps Primer," SmallWarsJournal.com, http://smallwarsjournal.com/documents/Surfaces_Gaps_Primer.pdf.

5.   John Keegan and Andrew Wheatcroft, *Zones of Conflict: An Atlas of Future Wars* (New York: Simon and Schuster, 1986).

6.   Stuart W. Bowen Jr., *Hard Lessons: The Iraq Reconstruction Experience* (Washington, DC: U.S. Government Printing Office, 2009), 104–14.

7.   Bowen, *Hard Lessons*, 279.

8.   *Learning from Iraq: A Final Report from the Special Inspector General for Iraq Reconstruction* (March 2013), 58–59.

9.   Bowen, *Hard Lessons*, 288.

10.   Mohammed M. Hafez, *Suicide Bombers in Iraq: The Strategy and Ideology of Martyrdom* (Washington, DC: United States Institute of Peace Press, 2007), 251–56.

11. Peter R. Mansoor, *Surge: My Journey with General David Petraeus and the Remaking of the Iraq War* (New Haven: Yale University Press, 2013), 121.

CHAPTER FOUR: BACK TO FALLUJAH: CONTRACTORS TAKE THE LEAD

1. Peter R. Mansoor, *Surge: My Journey with General David Petraeus and the Remaking of the Iraq War* (New Haven: Yale University Press, 2013), 55, 303.

2. Jim Michaels, "19,000 insurgents killed in Iraq since '03," *USA Today*, September 26, 2007, http://usatoday30.usatoday.com/news/world/iraq/2007-09-26-insurgents_N.htm.

3. William Doyle, *A Soldier's Dream: Of Captain Travis Patriquin and the Awakening of Iraq* (New York: Penguin Books, 2011), 105–16.

4. General Stanley McChrystal, *My Share of the Task* (New York: The Penguin Group, 2013), 174.

5. Adeed Dawisha, *Iraq: A Political History from Independence to Occupation* (Princeton: Princeton University Press, 2009), 247.

6. Kanan Makiya, *Republic of Fear: The Politics of Modern Iraq* (Berkley: University of California Press, 1989), 70–72.

7. McChrystal, *My Share of the Task*, 222–23.

8. *The U.S. Army and Marine Corps Counterinsurgency Field Manual* (Chicago: The University of Chicago Press, 2007), 285.

CHAPTER FIVE: THE SURGE

1. Bob Woodward, *The War Within: A Secret White House History 2006–2008* (New York: Simon & Schuster, 2008), 255.

2. Woodward, *The War Within* (New York: Simon & Schuster, 2008), 345.

3. Robert M. Gates, *Duty: Memoirs of a Secretary at War* (New York: Alfred A. Knopf, 2014), 38.

4. Chris Kyle and Scott McEwen, *American Sniper: The Autobiography of the Most Lethal Sniper in U.S. Military History* (New York: HarperCollings, 2012), 122–23.

5. Mark Urban, *Task Force Black: The Explosive True Story of the Secret Special Forces War in Iraq* (New York: St. Martin's Press, 2010), 174.

6.   Pratap Chatterjee, *Halliburton's Army: How a Well-Connected Texas Oil Company Revolutionized the Way America* Makes War (New York: Perseus Books Group, 2009), 214.

7.   Stuart A. Herrington, *Silence Was a Weapon: The Vietnam War in the Villages* (Novato: Presidio Press, 1982), 224.

8.   Peter Sluglett, *Britain in Iraq: Contriving King and Country* (London: I.B. Tauris, 2007), 231.

9.   John Althouse, "Army chief: Force to occupy Iraq massive," *USA Today*, February 25, 2003, http://usatoday30.usatoday.com/news/world/iraq/2003-02-25-iraq-us_x.htm.

10.   General David H. Petraeus, *Report to Congress on the Situation in Iraq* (September 10–11, 2007), 5, http://www.defense.gov/pubs/pdfs/petraeus-testimony20070910.pdf.

11.   Carter Andress, "This Isn't Civil War," *Wall Street Journal*, August 28, 2007, http://online.wsj.com/news/articles/SB118826659303110584.

12.   William Safire, "Suspension of Disbelief" *New York Times*, October 7, 2007, http://www.nytimes.com/2007/10/07/magazine/07wwln-safire-t.html?_r=0.

13.   Clark Hoyt, "Betraying Its Own Interests," *New York Times*, September 23, 2007, http://www.nytimes.com/2007/09/23/opinion/23pubed.html.

14.   *U.S. Department of Defense Quadrennial Defense Review* (2006), 4, http://www.defense.gov/qdr/report/report20060203.pdf.

15.   "Defense Contractors (Part One)" CBS News, October 9, 2007, http://www.cbsnews.com/videos/defense-contractors-part-one/.

16.   Ralph Peters, "Hired Guns," *Washington Post*, December 21, 2008, http://www.washingtonpost.com/wp-dyn/content/article/2008/12/18/AR2008121803316.html.

17.   John J. McGrath, *The Other End of the Spear: Tooth-to-Tail Ratio* (Fort Leavenworth, KS: Combat Studies Institute Press, 2007), 52, http://www.cgsc.edu/carl/download/csipubs/mcgrath_op23.pdf.

18.   Joseph Schumpeter, *Capitalism, Socialism, and Democracy* (New York: Harper Row, 1975), 135–38.

CHAPTER SIX: BLACKWATER

1. Pratap Chatterjee, *Halliburton's Army: How a Well-Connected Texas Oil Company Revolutionized the Way America Makes War* (New York: Perseus Books Group, 2009), 214.

2. David Ivanovich, "Contractor deaths up 17 percent in Iraq in 2007," *Houston Chronicle*, February 10, 2008, http://www.chron.com/news/nation-world/article/Contractor-deaths-up-17-percent-in-Iraq-in-2007-1561776.php.

3. "Blackwater booted from Iraq?" CNN Transcript, September 17, 2007, http://edition.cnn.com/TRANSCRIPTS/0709/17/ywt.01.html.

4. "Blackwater," CBS News, September 17, 2007.

5. CNN Transcript, September 18, 2007, http://edition.cnnw.com/TRANSCRIPTS/0709/18/cnr.05.html.

6. Arwa Damon and Joe Sterling, "Contractor: Losing Immunities would hurt Iraq mission." CNN, July 31, 2008, http://edition.cnn.com/2008/WORLD/meast/07/31/iraq.contractors/index.html.

CHAPTER SEVEN: THE TIPPING POINT

1. Carter Andress, "The Connection: View from the Red Zone," National Review Online, September 11, 2007, http://www.nationalreview.com/articles/222070/connection/carter-andress.

2. Victor Davis Hanson, *The Savior Generals* (New York: Bloomsbury Press, 2013), 244.

3. David Andelman, "The Spy of Saigon," *Forbes*, December 11, 2007, http://www.forbes.com/2007/12/11/spy-saigon-vietnam-books-cx_daa_1211perfectspy.html.

4. David Cloud and Greg Jaffe, *The Fourth Star: Four Generals and the Epic Struggle for the Future of the United States Army* (New York: Crown Publishers, 2009), 60.

5. Thomas E. Ricks, *Fiasco: The American Military Adventure in Iraq* (New York: The Penguin Press, 2006), 232–33.

6. Edward Luce, "Was Blair Bush's Poodle?", *Financial Times*, May 10, 2007, http://www.ft.com/cms/s/0/1b706386-fe22-11db-bdc7-000b5df10621.html#axzz2w8oXEAw0.

7. Carter Andress, "The Tipping Point: View from the Red Zone," National Review Online, October 4, 2007, http://www.nationalreview.com/articles/222385/tipping-point/carter-andress.

8. Enes Dulami, Cal Perry, Kianne Sadeq, and Mohammed Tawfeeq, "Iraq mourns stampede victims," CNN, September 1, 2005, http://edition.cnn.com/2005/WORLD/meast/09/01/iraq.main/.

9. Harry Summers Jr., *On Strategy: A Critical Analysis of the Vietnam War* (New York: Dell Publishing Co., Inc., 1982), 165–66.

10. Aaron Y. Zelin, "Abu Bakr al-Baghdadi: Islamic State's driving force," BBC, July 31, 2014, http://www.bbc.com/news/world-middle-east-28560449.

11. Jay Tolson, "The Long Reach of the Caliphates," *US News & World Report*, January 2, 2008, http://www.usnews.com/news/world/articles/2008/01/02/caliph-wanted.

CHAPTER EIGHT: SADDAM'S YELLOWCAKE

1. Carter Andress, *Contractor Combatants: Tales of an Imbedded Capitalist* (Nashville: Thomas Nelson, 2007), 44–46.

2. Jim Frederick, *Black Hearts: One Platoon's Descent into Madness in Iraq's Triangle of Death* (New York: Harmony Books, 2010), 264–68

3. Frederick, *Black Hearts,* 302–4.

4. *15th Infantry Regiment Unit History,* http://www.15thinfantry.org/.

5. Dan Reiter, "Preventive Attacks Against Nuclear Programs and the 'Success' at Osiraq," *Nonproliferation Review* 12, no. 2 (July 2005): 357, http://www.diplomatie.gouv.fr/fr/IMG/pdf/Osirak.pdf.

6. USMC Lieutenant General John Sattler told me at a 2011 lunch in Annapolis, Maryland that one of the last things he made sure to accomplish before he retired as the U.S. Joint Chiefs of Staff Director of Strategic Plans and Policy (J-5) in August 2008 was to remove the yellowcake from Iraq.

CHAPTER NINE: THE RAID

1. Peter R. Mansoor, *Surge: My Journey with General David Petraeus and the Remaking of the Iraq War* (New Haven: Yale University Press, 2013), 149, 167.

2. M. C. Jaspersen, "Iran, Syria Accused of Counterfeiting US Dollars," USIA, July 1, 1992, https://www.fas.org/news/iran/1992/920701-233652.htm.

3. "Inside Guantanamo," *60 Minutes*, November 2, 2013, http://www.cbsnews.com/news/inside-guantanamo/.

4. Konrad Ludwig, *Stryker: The Siege of Sadr City* (California: Roland-Kjos, LLC, 2011), 291.

5. Thomas E. Ricks, *Fiasco: The American Military Adventure in Iraq* (New York: The Penguin Press, 2006), 335–59.

CHAPTER TEN: "DEATH TO AL-QAEDA!"

1. Peter R. Mansoor, *Surge: My Journey with General David Petraeus and the Remaking of the Iraq War* (New Haven: Yale University Press, 2013), 233–43.

2. Tim Shipman, "Basra pullout was a defeat for Britain in Iraq, generals say," *Daily Mail*, September 29, 2010, http://www.dailymail.co.uk/news/article-1316061/Basra-pullout-defeat-Britain-Iraq-say-generals.html.

3. Christopher Catherwood, *Churchill's Folly: How Winston Churchill Created Modern Iraq* (New York: Carroll & Graf Publishers, 2004), 186–87.

4. Stuart W. Bowen Jr., *Hard Lessons: The Iraq Reconstruction Experience* (Washington, DC: U.S. Government Printing Office, 2009), 309.

5. "The Bradley Fighting Vehicle," University of Maryland A. James Clark School of Engineering Study, http://www.eng.umd.edu/~austin/enes489p/lecture-resources/BradleyFightingVehicle-Scenario.pdf.

6. Carl von Clausewitz, *On War* (Princeton: Princeton University Press, 1984), 119–21.

7. Robert Baer, "Perpetuating the al-Qaeda-Iraq Myth," *Time*, June 2, 2008, http://content.time.com/time/world/article/0,8599,1811318,00.html.

8. Carter Andress, "Death to al-Qaeda! The View from the Red Zone," National Review Online, June 24, 2008, http://www.nationalreview.com/articles/224843/death-al-qaeda/carter-andress#.

9. "Al Qaida finished in Iraq, author claims," UPI, June 24, 2008, http://www. upi.com/Business_News/Energy-Resources/2008/06/24/Al-Qaida-finished-in-Iraq-author-claims/UPI-92191214335650/.

10. Jim Garamone, "Threat of Terrorist IEDs Growing, Expanding, General Says," Defense.gov, September 21, 2012, http://www.defense.gov/news/newsarticle. aspx?id=117975

11. Robert M. Gates, *Duty: Memoirs of a Secretary at War* (New York: Alfred A. Knopf, 2014), 124.

12. Hanna Batatu, *The Old Social Classes and the Revolutionary Movements of Iraq* (London: Saqi Books, 2004), 1220.

13. Iraq Sets New Quotas for Female Civil Servants," Radio Free Europe/Radio Liberty, January 5, 2012; available online at: http://www.rferl.org/content/ iraq_sets_new_quotas_for_women_at_ministries/24443069.html.

14. "US Passes Control of Green Zone," CBS News, January 1, 2009, http://www. cbsnews.com/news/us-passes-control-of-green-zone-to-iraq/.

CHAPTER ELEVEN: THE OILFIELDS

1. Stephen Biddle, Michael E. O'Hanlon, and Kenneth M. Pollack, "The Evolution of Iraq Strategy," The Brookings Institution (December 2008), 31, http://www. brookings.edu/~/media/research/files/papers/2008/12/iraq%20biddle/12_ iraq_biddle.pdf.

2. "Iraq," U.S. Energy Information Administration, May 30, 2013, http://www. eia.gov/countries/country-data.cfm?fips=iz.

3. Jill Dougherty and Jomana Karadsheh, "Iraqi lawmakers reach deal on non-US troops," CNN, December 21, 2008, http://edition.cnn.com/2008/WORLD/ meast/12/21/iraq.british.troops/index.html.

4. "LOGCAP III Task Order continues support in Iraq," Army.mil, May 5, 2010, http://www.army.mil/article/38607/LOGCAP_III_Task_Order_continues_ support_in_Iraq/.

5. William R. Polk, *Understanding Iraq* (New York: HarperCollins, 2005), 125–26.

6. Steve Coll, *Private Empire ExxonMobil and American Power* (New York: The Penguin Press, 2012), 573–75.

7. Coll, *Private Empire ExxonMobil and American Power*, 394–98.

CHAPTER TWELVE: THE LAST OF THE OCCUPIERS

1. Robert M. Gates, *Duty: Memoirs of a Secretary at War* (New York: Alfred A. Knopf, 2014), 169–70.

2. "Obama sets date to end Iraq combat mission," NBC News, February 27, 2009, http://www.nbcnews.com/id/29371588/ns/world_news-mideast_n_africa/t/obama-sets-date-end-iraq-combat-mission/.

3. "Iraq Coalition Casualty Count," icasualties.org, http://icasualties.org/Iraq/Index.aspx.

4. Vali Nasr, *The Dispensable Nation: American Foreign Policy in Retreat* (New York: Doubleday, 2013), 150.

5. Michael R. Gordon and Bernard E. Trainor, *Endgame: The Inside Story of the Struggle for Iraq, from George W. Bush to Barack Obama* (New York: Pantheon Books, 2012), 670.

6. Leon Panetta, "Secretary Panetta Speaking to Service Members in Naples, Italy," Defense.gov, October 7, 2011, http://www.defense.gov/transcripts/transcript.aspx?transcriptid=4900

7. "Obama, Romney on strategy in Iraq," Presidential Debate Video, *Wall Street Journal*, October 22, 2012, http://live.wsj.com/video/obama-romney-on-strategy-in-iraq/A59F5311-8EB3-4021-95AC-473767667713.html#!A59F5311-8EB3-4021-95AC-473767667713.

8. "Iraqi general says planned US troop pull-out 'too soon,'" BBC, August 12, 2010, http://www.bbc.co.uk/news/world-middle-east-10947918.

9. Michael Gisick, "Looming U.S. exit to complicate Iraqi training," *Stars & Stripes* (January 2, 2010), http://www.stripes.com/news/looming-u-s-exit-to-complicate-iraqi-training-1.97706.

10. "U.S.-Iraq Status of Forces Agreement," Department of State, November 17, 2008, http://www.state.gov/documents/organization/122074.pdf.

11. Mark Urban, *Task Force Black: The Explosive True Story of the Secret Special Forces War in Iraq* (New York: St. Martin's Press, 2010), 82–83.

12.   *Learning from Iraq: A Final Report from the Special Inspector General for Iraq Reconstruction*, (March 2013), 109.

13.   Walter Pincus, "Top Diplomat defends size, cost of State Dept. presence in Iraq," *Washington Post*, February 1, 2011, http://www.washingtonpost.com/wp-dyn/content/article/2011/02/01/AR2011020106523.html

14.   Patrick Osgood, "Country Focus: Iraq's New Dawn," *Arabian Oil & Gas*, August 15, 2011 (this is an abbreviated version of the magazine article in *Middle East Oil & Gas*, August 2011), http://www.arabianoilandgas.com/article-9339-country-focus-iraqs-new-dawn/2/.

15.   Tom Bergin and Ahmed Rasheed, "Exxon signs Kurd deals; Baghdad issues warning," *Reuters*, November 11, 2011, http://www.reuters.com/article/2011/11/11/exxon-kurdistan-idUSL5E7MB0YP20111111.

16.   Neil Hume, "IEA says supply surge led by Iraq will ease oil tensions," *Financial Times*, March 14, 2014, http://www.ft.com/intl/cms/s/0/6496d312-ab5c-1e3-aad9-0014 4fe ab7de.html#axzz2w8oXEAw0.

17.   Ben Lando, "Iraq Oil Exports Drop," *Iraq Oil Report*, July 9, 2014, http://www.iraqoilreport.com/oil/production-exports/iraq-oil-exports-drop-june-12655/.

CHAPTER THIRTEEN: THE ARAB SPRING

1.   Vali Nasr, *The Dispensable Nation: American Foreign Policy in Retreat* (New York: Doubleday, 2013), 153.

2.   Peter R. Mansoor, *Surge: My Journey with General David Petraeus and the Remaking of the Iraq War* (New Haven: Yale University Press, 2013), 8–12.

3.   Mansoor, *Surge*, 150.

4.   "Mass Graves 'hold 300,000 Iraqis'" BBC, November 8, 2003, http://news.bbc.co.uk/2/hi/middle_east/3253783.stm.

5.   Jim Michaels "19,000 insurgents killed in Iraq since '03," *USA Today*, September 26, 2007, http://usatoday30.usatoday.com/news/world/iraq/2007-09-26-insurgents_N.htm.

6.   Dallas Boyd, Lewis A. Dunn, Aaron Arnold, Michael Ullrich, James Scouras, and Jonathan Fox, "Why Have We Not Been Attacked Again? Competing and Complementary Hypotheses for Homeland Attack Frequency," Defense Threat

Reduction Agency's Advanced Systems and Concepts Office and Science Applications International Corporation Report (June 2008): 21, https://www.hsdl.org/?view&did=487979.

7. Matthew Michael Carnahan, *World War Z: An Oral History of the Zombie War*, Plan B Entertainment, 2013.

8. Carter Andress, *Contractor Combatants: Tales of an Imbedded Capitalist*, (Nashville: Thomas Nelson, 2007), 301–2.

9. Gilles Kepel, *Jihad: The Trail of Political Islam* (Cambridge: The Belknap Press, 2003), 271–74.

10. Mansoor, *Surge,* 121–22. Author Carter Andress's wife, Tanya, who has two PhDs in theoretical mathematics—the first focused on Chaos Theory—helped him greatly with this section.

11. William S. Angerman, "Coming Full Circle with Boyd's OODA Loop Ideas" Thesis, Department of the Air Force Air University, March 2004; available online at: www.dtic.mil/cgi-bin/GetTRDoc?AD=ADA425228.

12. Thomas E. Ricks, *The Gamble: General David Petraeus and the American Military Adventure in Iraq, 2006–2008* (New York: The Penguin Press, 2009), 60.

13. Jim Michaels, *A Chance in Hell: The Men Who Triumphed Over Iraq's Deadliest City and Turned the Tide of War* (New York: St. Martin's Press, 2010).

14. "Bin Laden eyed name change for al-Qaeda to repair image," *USA Today,* June 24, 2011; available online at: http://usatoday30.usatoday.com/news/world/2011-06-24-Osama-bin-Laden-Al-qaeda_n.htm.

15. Ashraf Khalil, *Liberation Square: Inside the Egyptian Revolution and the Rebirth of a Nation* (New York: St. Martin's Press, 2011), 47.

16. Ernesto Londono and Leila Fadel, "For joyous throngs, history never materializes," *Washington Post,* February 11, 2011; available online at: http://www.washingtonpost.com/wp-dyn/content/article/2011/02/10/AR2011021007581.html.

17. Robert M. Gates, *Duty: Memoirs of a Secretary at War* (New York: Alfred A. Knopf, 2014), 503.

CHAPTER FOURTEEN: AFGHANISTAN: HOW NOT TO DO IT

1. *Learning From Iraq: A Final Report from the Special Inspector General for Iraq Reconstruction*, (March 2013), 59.

2. Special Inspector General Afghanistan Reconstruction, "Quarterly Report to the U.S. Congress," July 30, 2012, 3, http://www.sigar.mil/pdf/quarterlyreports/2012-07-30qr.pdf.

3. Kevin Sieff, "After billions in U.S. investment, Afghan roads are falling apart," *Washington Post*, January 30, 2014, http://www.washingtonpost.com/world/asia_pacific/after-billions-in-us-investment-afghan-roads-are-falling-apart/2014/01/30/9bd07764-7986-11e3-b1c5-739e63e9c9a7_story.html.

4. Garry Trudeau, "Doonesbury Flashbacks," *Washington Post*, June 10, 2010.

5. Richard Spencer "Karzai family, villas in Dubai, fears over Afghan aid," *Telegraph*, September 10, 2010, http://www.telegraph.co.uk/news/worldnews/middleeast/dubai/7994754/The-Karzai-empire-villas-in-Dubai-and-fears-over-Afghan-aid.html.

6. Lisa Novak, "Task Force re-inspecting US facilities in Iraq for faulty wiring," *Stars and Stripes*, November 1, 2009, http://www.stripes.com/news/task-force-re-inspecting-u-s-facilities-in-iraq-for-faulty-wiring-1.96075.

7. "Military construction delayed in Afghanistan by push to award contracts to Afghan firms," Associated Press, May 2, 2010, http://www.foxnews.com/world/2010/05/02/military-construction-delayed-afghanistan-push-award-contracts-afghan-firms/.

8. Joshua Partlow, "Taliban fighters driven back, killed in attack on U.S. base," *Washington Post*, November 11, 2011, http://www.washingtonpost.com/world/middle_east/us-base-in-eastern-afghanistan-attacked/2011/11/09/gIQAPBas4M_story.html.

9. Donald F. Busky, *Communism in History and Theory: Asia, Africa, and the Americas* (Westport, CT: Praeger Publishers, 2002), 39–41.

10. Gerald D. Swick, "'The Battle for Marjah' HBO Documentary—Marines in Afghanistan," February 24, 2011, http://www.historynet.com/the-battle-for-marjah-hbo-documentary-marines-in-afghanistan.htm.

11. Robert M. Gates, *Duty: Memoirs of a Secretary at War* (New York: Alfred A. Knopf, 2014), 358.

12. Gates, *Duty*, 371.

13. Alastair Jamieson, "Suicide blast, gunfire rock Green Village compound in Kabul; at least 2 Afghans dead," NBC News, October 19, 2013, http://www.nbcnews.com/news/world/suicide-blast-gunfire-rock-green-village-compound-kabul-least-2-v21024553.

14. Nathan Hodge, "Afghans Jail U.S. Man in Business Dispute," *Wall Street Journal*, April 5, 2013, http://online.wsj.com/news/articles/SB10001424127887324100904578404812387092002?KEYWORDS=afghanistan+hodge+american+jail&mg=reno64-wsj.

CHAPTER FIFTEEN: CONTRACTORS AT WAR

1. "Contractors' Support of U.S. Operations in Iraq," U.S. Congressional Budget Office, (August 2008), 11–12, http://www.cbo.gov/sites/default/files/cbofiles/ftpdocs/96xx/doc9688/08-12-iraqcontractors.pdf.

2. "Contractor Combatant," Wiktionary, http://en.wiktionary.org/wiki/contractor_combatant.

3. Patricia K. Hinshaw, "Book Review: 'Contractor Combatants: Tales of an Imbedded Capitalist,'" *The Army Lawyer* (January 2009), 64, https://www.jagcnet.army.mil/DOCLIBS/ARMYLAWYER.NSF/c82df279f9445da185256e5b005244ee/78230447d725d215852575610060903e/$FILE/Article%205%20-%20By%20MAJ%20Patricia%20K.%20Hinshaw.pdf.

4. Joseph C. Hansen, "Rethinking the Regulation of Private Military and Security Companies Under International Humanitarian Law," *Fordham International Law Journal* (March 2012), 723–28, http://papers.ssrn.com/sol3/papers.cfm?abstract_id=1895546.

5. Richard Tregaskis, *Southeast Asia: Building the Bases* (Washington, DC: U.S. Government Printing Office, 1975), 265.

6. Michael A. Alexander, "U.S. Army Corps of Engineers Support of Combatant Commands," U.S. Army War College Strategy Research Project (March 25, 2008), 8, www.dtic.mil/docs/citations/ADA479072.

7.   "Final Listing of Audit and Other Reports Issued by SIGIR on Reconstruction Spending in Iraq: A Notice by the Special Inspector General For Iraq Reconstruction," *Federal Register,* September 24, 2013, https://www.federalregister.gov/articles/2013/09/24/2013-22971/final-listing-of-audit-and-other-reports-issued-by-sigir-on-reconstruction-spending-in-iraq.

8.   David Martin, "New Law May Spell End to Iraq Contractors," CBS News, November 9, 2007, http://www.cbsnews.com/news/new-law-may-spell-end-to-iraq-contractors/.

9.   Patricia K. Hinshaw, "Book Review: 'Contractor Combatants: Tales of an Imbedded Capitalist,'" *The Army Lawyer,* January 2009, 66, https://www.jagcnet.army.mil/DOCLIBS/ARMYLAWYER.NSF/c82df279f9445da185256e5b005244ee/78230447d725d215852575610060903e/$FILE/Article%205%20-%20By%20MAJ%20Patricia%20K.%20Hinshaw.pdf.

10. *Learning From Iraq: A Final Report from the Special Inspector General for Iraq Reconstruction* (March 2013), 66.

11. Camille Tuutti, "Carter Andress: We as Americans represented the opportunity in Iraq," executivebiz.com, June 8, 2010, http://blog.executivebiz.com/2010/06/carter-andress-we-as-americans-represented-the-opportunity-in-iraq/10197/.

CHAPTER SIXTEEN: AFTER-ACTION REVIEW

1.   Michael R. Gordon and Bernard E. Trainor, *Cobra II: The Inside Story of the Invasion and Occupation of Iraq* (New York: Pantheon Books, 2006), 366.

2.   "Osama bin Laden Largely Discredited Among Muslim Publics in Recent Years, al Qaeda Too," *Pew Research Global Attitudes Project,* May 2, 2011, http://www.pewglobal.org/2011/05/02/osama-bin-laden-largely-discredited-among-muslim-publics-in-recent-years/.

3.   Arlette Saenz and Jonathan Karl, "Obama to Send Up To 300 U.S. Military Advisers To Iraq," ABC News, June 19, 2014, http://abcnews.go.com/Politics/obama-send-300-us-military-advisers-iraq/story?id=24212956.

4.   Georgie Anne Geyer, "Seymour Hersh's Gulf War Misconceptions," *Chicago Tribune,* May 19, 2000, http://articles.chicagotribune.com/2000-05-19/news/0005190093_1_iraqis-gulf-war-24th-division.

5.   Ali A. Allawi, *The Occupation of Iraq: Winning the War, Losing the Peace* (New Haven: Yale University Press, 2007), 260–05, 316.

6.   Michael R. Gordon and Bernard E. Trainor, *Endgame: The Inside Story of the Struggle for Iraq, from George W. Bush to Barack Obama* (New York: Pantheon Books, 2012), 367–69.

7.   Gordon and Trainor, *Endgame*, 398–400.

8.   Frank Antenori and Hans Halberstadt, *Roughneck Nine-One: The Extraordinary Story of a Special Forces A-Team at War* (New York: St. Martin's Press, 2006), 89.

9.   Matthew L. Smith, "'J.F.C. Fuller: His Methods, Insights and Vision,' Strategic Research Project," U.S. Army War College (April 1, 1999), 12, http://handle. dtic.mil/100.2/ADA363919.

10. Thomas E. Ricks, *Fiasco: The American Military Adventure in Iraq* (New York: The Penguin Press, 2006), 97.

11. Chris Kyle and Scott McEwen, *American Sniper: The Autobiography of the Most Lethal Sniper in U.S. Military History* (New York: HarperCollins, 2012), 5.

12. "Iraq Coalition Casualty Count," icasualties.org, http://icasualties.org/Iraq/ Index.aspx.

13. Stephen J. Glain, "US officials fume at trade by Iraq, Syria," *Boston Globe*, October 23, 2003, http://www.boston.com/news/nation/washington/ articles/2003/10/23/us_officials_fume_at_trade_by_iraq_syria/?page=full.

14. Peter R. Mansoor, *Surge: My Journey with General David Petraeus and the Remaking of the Iraq War* (New Haven: Yale University Press, 2013), xiv.

15. Mansoor, *Surge*, 173.

16. Mansoor, *Surge*, 174.

17. Mansoor, *Surge*, 168.

18. Raheem Salman, Ned Parker and Maggie Fick, "Shi'ite cleric Sadr wants Maliki's bloc to choose new Iraq PM candidate," Reuters, July 6, 2014, http:// www.trust.org/item/20140706110933-bp5yf/?source=fiOtherNews3.

19. Janine di Giovanni, "The View from Baghdad as It Braces for ISIS Onslaught," *Newsweek*, June 23, 2014, http://www.newsweek.com/view-baghdad-it-braces- isis-onslaught-255902.

20. Henry A. Crumpton, *The Art of Intelligence: Lessons from a Life in the CIA's Clandestine Service* (New York: The Penguin Press, 2012), 8, 177.

21. "Interview L. Paul Bremer III," PBS *Front Line*, April 17, 2007, http://www.pbs. org/wgbh/pages/frontline/gangsofiraq/interviews/bremer.html.

22. From 1998–1999, author Carter Andress's father, Miller Andress, worked in Israel as construction manager for Ben Gurion airport. In his house in Herzliya, he kept a sealed room and gas masks for himself and his wife Jenny as protection from Saddam's chemical-biological threat.

BIBLIOGRAPHY

Abdullah, Thabit A. J. *A Short History of Iraq.* New York: Pearson, 2011.

Aboul-Enein, Cdr. Youssef H. *Iraq in Turmoil: Historical Perspectives of Dr. Ali Al-Wardi, From the Ottoman Empire to King Feisal.* Annapolis: Naval Institute Press, 2012.

Abrams, David. *Fobbit.* New York: Black Cat, 2012.

Abu-Rabi, Ibrahim M. *Contemporary Arab Thought.* London: Pluto Press, 2004.

Ajami, Fouad. *The Foreigner's Gift: The Americans, the Arabs, and the Iraqis in Iraq.* New York: Free Press, 2006.

Al-Ali, Zaid. *The Struggle for Iraq's Future: How Corruption, Incompetence and Sectarianism Have Undermined Democracy.* New Haven: Yale University Press, 2014.

Allawi, Ali A. *The Occupation of Iraq: Winning the War, Losing the Peace.* New Haven: Yale University Press, 2007.

Alsamari, Lewis. *Out of Iraq: The Terrifying True Story of One Man's Escape from the Harshest Regime of the Modern Era.* London: Bantam Press, 2007.

Andress, Carter. *Contractor Combatants: Tales of an Imbedded Capitalist.* Nashville: Thomas Nelson, 2007.

Andrew, Christopher, and Vasili Mitrokhin. *The World Was Going Our Way*.
    Cambridge: Perseus Books Group, 2005.
Anonymous. *Imperial Hubris*. Washington, DC: Brassey's, Inc., 2004.
Antenori, Frank, and Hans Halberstadt. *Roughneck Nine-One: The Extraordinary
    Story of a Special Forces A-Team at War*. New York: St. Martin's Press, 2006.
Armstrong, Stephen. *War PLC: The Rise of the New Corporate Mercenary*. London:
    Faber and Faber, 2008.
Arnold, James R. *Jungle of Snakes: A Century of Counterinsurgency Warfare from
    the Philippines to Iraq*. New York: Bloomsbury Press, 2009.
Atkinson, Rick. *Crusade: The Untold Story of the Persian Gulf War*. New York:
    Houghton Mifflin Co., 1993.
Atwan, Abdel Bari. *The Secret History of al Qaeda*. Berkeley: University of
    California Press, 2008.
Aussaresses, General Paul. *The Battle of the Casbah: Terrorism and
    Counterterrorism in Algeria 1955–1957*. New York: Enigma Books, 2002.
Baker, James A., and Lee H. Hamilton. *The Iraq Study Group Report*. New York:
    Random House, 2006.
Barfield, Thomas. *Afghanistan: A Cultural and Political History*. Princeton:
    Princeton University Press, 2010.
Batatu, Hanna. *The Old Social Classes and the Revolutionary Movements of Iraq*.
    London: Saqi Books, 2004.
Baxter, William P. *Soviet Airland Battle Tactics*. Novato, CA: Presidio Press, 1986.
Bellavia, David, with John Bruning. *House to House: An Epic Urban Warfare*.
    London: Simon & Schuster, 2007.
Bergen, Peter L. *The Longest War*. New York: Simon & Schuster, 2011.
———. *Man Hunt: The Ten Year Hunt for Osama bin Laden from 9/11 to
    Abottabad*. New York: Random House, 2012.
Blaber, Pete. *The Mission, the Men and Me: Lessons from a Former Delta Force
    Commander*. New York: Berkley Publishing Group, 2008.
Blair, Tony. *A Journey: My Political Life*. New York: Alfred A. Knopf, 2010.
Bodansky, Yossef. *The Secret History of the Iraq War*. New York: HarperCollins,
    2004.
Bogdanos, Matthew, with William Patrick. *Thieves of Baghdad*. New York:
    Bloomsbury Publishing, 2005.
Borovik, Artyom. *The Hidden War: A Russian Journalist's Account of the Soviet War
    in Afghanistan*. New York: Atlantic Monthly Press, 1990.

Bowden, Mark. *Black Hawk Down.* New York: Penguin Group, 2000.

———. *Guests of the Ayatollah: The First Battle in America's War with Militant Islam.* New York: Atlantic Monthly Press, 2006.

Bowen, Stuart W. *Hard Lessons: The Iraq Reconstruction Experience.* Washington, DC: U.S. Government Printing Office, 2009.

Bradley, Rusty. *Lions of Kandahar.* New York: Bantam Books, 2011.

Bremer, L. Paul, III., with Malcolm McConnell. *My Year in Iraq.* New York: Simon & Schuster, 2006.

Brinkley, Paul. *War Front to Store Front: Americans Rebuilding Trust and Hope in Nations Under Fire.* New York: Wiley, 2014.

Brownson, Carleton L. *Xenophon: Anabasis.* Cambridge: Harvard University Press, 2001.

Bruning, John R. *The Devil's Sandbox: With the 2nd Battalion, 162nd Infantry at War in Iraq.* St. Paul: Zenith Press, 2006.

Brzezinski, Zbigniew. *Strategic Vision: America and the Crisis of Global Power.* New York: Perseus Books Group, 2012.

Burgoyne, Michael L., and Albert J. Marckwardt. *The Defense of Jisr al-Doreaa.* Chicago: University of Chicago Press, 2009.

Burleigh, Michael. *Blood and Rage: A Cultural History of Terrorism.* London: HarperPress, 2008.

Bush, George W. *Decision Points.* New York: Crown Publishers, 2010.

Carafano, James Jay. *Private Sector, Public Wars: Contractors in Combat—Afghanistan, Iraq, and Future Conflicts.* Westport, CT: Praeger Security International, 2008.

Carter, Jimmy. *Palestine Peace Not Apartheid.* New York: Simon & Schuster, 2006.

———. *We Can Have Peace in the Holy Land: A Plan That Will Work.* New York: Simon & Schuster, 2009.

Carter, Terry, and Lara Dunston. *Dubai.* Melbourne: Lonely Planet Publications, 2006.

Catherwood, Christopher. *Churchill's Folly: How Winston Churchill Created Modern Iraq.* New York: Carroll & Graf Publishers, 2004.

Cawthorne, Nigel. *Confirmed Kill: Heroic Sniper Stories from the Jungles of Vietnam to the Mountains of Afghanistan.* Berkeley: Ulysses Press, 2012.

Chandrasekaran, Rajiv. *Imperial Life in the Emerald City.* London: Bloomsbury Publishing, 2007.

Chatterjee, Pratap. *Halliburton's Army: How a Well-Connected Texas Oil Company*

Revolutionized the Way America Makes War. New York: Perseus Books Group, 2009.

Chehab, Zaki. *Inside the Resistance: The Iraqi Insurgency and the Future of the Middle East*. New York: Avalon Publishing Group, 2005.

———. *Iraq Ablaze*. New York: I. B. Tauris Publishers, 2006.

Chehabi, H. E. *Distant Relations: Iran and Lebanon in the Last 500 Years*. London: I. B. Tauris Publishers, 2006.

Cheney, Dick, with Liz Cheney. *In My Life*. New York: Simon & Schuster, 2011.

Clammer, Paul. *Afghanistan*. Oakland: Lonely Planet Publications, 2007.

Clausewitz, Carl von. *On War*. Princeton: Princeton University Press, 1984.

Cleveland, William L. *A History of the Modern Middle East*. Boulder: Perseus Books Group, 2004.

Cloud, David, and Greg Jaffe. *The Fourth Star: Four Generals and the Epic Struggle for the Future of the United States Army*. New York: Crown Publishers, 2009.

Coll, Steve. *Ghost Wars: The Secret History of the CIA, Afghanistan, and Bin Laden, from the Soviet Invasion to September 10, 2001*. New York: Penguin Press, 2004.

———. *Private Empire ExxonMobil and American Power*. New York: Penguin Press, 2012.

Conroy, Jason, with Ron Martz. *Heavy Metal: A Tank Company's Battle to Baghdad*. Dulles: Potomac Books, 2005.

Cooley, John K. *An Alliance Against Babylon*. London: Pluto Press, 2005.

Cooper, Andrew Scott. *The Oil Kings*. New York: Simon & Schuster, 2011.

Coughlin, Con. *Saddam: King of Terror*. New York: HarperCollins Publishers, 2002.

Crile, George. *Charlie Wilson's War*. New York: Grove Press, 2003.

Crist, David. *The Twilight War: The Secret History of America's Thirty-Year Conflict with Iran*. New York: Penguin Press, 2012.

Crumpton, Henry A. *The Art of Intelligence: Lessons from a Life in the CIA's Clandestine Service*. New York: Penguin Press, 2012.

Dabrowska, Karen. *Iraq: The Bradt Travel Guide*. Bucks: Bradt Travel Guide, 2002.

Darke, Diana. *Discovery Guide to Jordan and the Holy Land*. London: Immel Publishing, 1993.

Dawisha, Adeed. *Iraq: A Political History from Independence to Occupation*. Princeton: Princeton University Press, 2009.

———. *The Second Arab Awakening: Revolution, Democracy and the Islamist Challenge from Tunis to Damascus*. New York: W. W. Norton, 2013.

DeLong, Lt. Gen. Michael. *A General Speaks Out*. St. Paul: MBI Publishing
     Company, 2004.
DiMarco, Louis A. *Concrete Hell: Urban Warfare from Stalingrad to Iraq*. New
     York: Osprey Publishing, 2012.
Dinackus, Thomas D. *Order of Battle: Allied Ground Forces of Operation Desert
     Storm*. Central Point, OR: Hellgate Press, 2000.
Dobson, Christopher, and Ronald Payne. *Counterattack: The West's Battle Against
     the Terrorists*. New York: Facts On File, 1982.
Donald, Mark L. *Battle Ready: Memoir of a SEAL Warrior Medic*. New York: St.
     Martin's Press, 2013.
Dostan, Hama. *Saddam Land*. London: Janus Publishing Company, 2007.
Doyle, William. *A Soldier's Dream: Captain Travis Patriquin and the Awakening of
     Iraq*. New York: Penguin Books, 2011.
Durant, Michael J. *In the Company of Heroes*. New York: G.P. Putnam's Sons, 2003.
Earle, Robert. *Nights in the Pink Motel: An American Strategist's Pursuit of Peace in
     Iraq*. Annapolis: Naval Institute Press, 2008.
Edwards, Maj. John E. *Combat Service Support Guide*. Mechanicsburg, PA:
     Stackpole Books, 2004.
El Fadl, Khaled Abou. *The Great Theft: Wrestling Islam from the Extremists*. New
     York: HarperCollins, 2005.
Engbrecht, Shawn. *America's Covert Warriors*. Dulles: Potomac Books, 2011.
Etherington, Mark. *Revolt on the Tigris: The Al-Sadr Uprising and the Governing of
     Iraq*. Ithaca, NY: Cornell University Press, 2005.
Everyday Life in Bible Times. National Geographic Society, 1967.
Fainaru, Steve. *Big Boy Rules: America's Mercenaries Fighting in Iraq*. Philadelphia:
     Perseus Books Group, 2008.
Fallows, James. *Blind Into Baghdad: America's War in Iraq*. New York: Random
     House, 2006.
Faroqhi, Suraiya. *Subjects of the Sultan: Culture and Daily Life in the Ottoman
     Empire*. London: I. B. Tauris, 2005.
Farouk-Sluglett, Marion, and Peter Sluglett. *Iraq Since 1958*. London: I.B. Tauris
     Publishers, 2003.
Farwell, Byron. *Armies of the Raj: From the Mutiny to Independence, 1858–1947*.
     New York: W.W. Norton & Company, 1989.
———. *Queen Victoria's Little Wars*. New York: W.W. Norton & Company, 1972.
Fattah, Moataz Abdel. *Democratic Values in the Muslim World*. Cairo: American

University in Cairo Press, 2006.

Filkins, Dexter. *The Forever War*. New York: Random House, 2009.

Fisher, Sidney Nettleton. *The Middle East: A History*. New York: Alfred A. Knopf, 1979.

Franks, Tommy, with Malcolm McConnell. *American Soldier*. New York: HarperCollins, 2004.

Frantz, Douglas, and Catherine Collins. *The Nuclear Jihadist*. New York: Hachette Book Group USA, 2007.

Frederick, Jim. *Black Hearts: One Platoon's Descent into Madness in Iraq's Triangle of Death*. New York: Harmony Books, 2010.

Friedman, Thomas L. *From Beirut to Jerusalem*. New York: Farrar, Straus, and Giroux, 1989.

Fuller, J. F. C. *The Foundation of the Science of War*. London: Books Express, 2012.

Gabriel, Richard A. *Operation Peace for Galilee*. New York: Hill and Wang, 1985.

Gaiduk, Ilya V. *The Soviet Union and the Vietnam War*. Chicago: Ivan R. Dee, 1996.

Galula, David. *Counterinsurgency Warfare: Theory and Practice*. New York: Frederick A. Praeger Publishers, 2005.

Gardner, Lloyd C., and Marilyn B. Young. *Iraq and the Lessons of Vietnam*. New York: New Press, 2008.

Gates, Robert M. *Duty: Memoirs of a Secretary at War*. New York: Alfred A. Knopf, 2014.

Gelvin, James L. *The Arab Uprisings*. New York: Oxford University Press, 2012.

Geraghty, Tony. *Soldiers of Fortune: A History of the Mercenary in Modern Warfare*. New York: Pegasus Books, 2009.

Gerges, Fawaz A. *Journey of the Jihadist*. Orlando: Harcourt, 2006.

Gettleman, Marvin E., and Stuart Schaar. *The Middle East and Islamic World Reader*. New York: Grove Press, 2003.

Gompert, David C., Terrance K. Kelly, Brooke Stearns Lawson, Michelle Parker, and Kimberly Colloton. *Reconstruction Under Fire: Unifying Civil and Military Counterinsurgency*. Santa Monica: Rand Corporation, 2009.

Gordon, Michael R., and Bernard E. Trainor. *Cobra II: The Inside Story of the Invasion and Occupation of Iraq*. New York: Pantheon Books, 2006.

Grau, Lester W. *The Bear Went Over the Mountain*. Washington, D.C.: Books Express Publishing, 2010.

Gulf Oil in the Aftermath of the Iraq War Strategies and Policies. Abu Dhabi: Emirates Center for Strategic Studies and Research, 2005.

Haass, Richard N. *War of Necessity, War of Choice: A Memoir of Two Iraq Wars.* New York: Simon & Schuster, 2009.

Hafez, Mohammed M. *Suicide Bombers in Iraq: The Strategy and Ideology of Martyrdom.* Washington, DC: United States Institute of Peace Press, 2007.

Hamid, Mohsin. *The Reluctant Fundamentalist.* Orlando: Harcourt, 2007.

Hamza, Khidhir, with Jeff Stein. *Saddam's Bombmaker.* New York: Scribner, 2000.

Hanson, Victor Davis. *The Savior Generals.* New York: Bloomsbury Press, 2013.

Hashim, Ahmed S. *Insurgency and Counter-Insurgency in Iraq.* Ithaca, NY: Cornell University Press, 2006.

Herrington, Stuart A. *Silence Was A Weapon: The Vietnam War in the Villages.* Novato, CA: Presidio Press, 1982.

Herzog, Chaim. *The Arab-Israeli Wars.* New York: Random House, 1982.

Hiro, Dilip. *Inside Central Asia.* New York: Outlook Duckworth, Peter Mayer Publishers, 2009.

Hobsbawm, Eric. *Globalisation, Democracy and Terrorism.* London: Little, Brown Book Group, 2007.

Hodge, Nathan. *Armed Humanitarians: The Rise of the Nation Builders.* New York: Bloomsbury, 2011.

Holden, David, and Richard Johns. *The House of Saud: The Rise and Rule of the Most Powerful Dynasty in the Arab World.* New York: Holt, Rinehart and Winston, 1981.

Hopkirk, Peter. *The Great Game.* New York: Kodansha America, 1994.

Horne, Alistair. *A Savage War of Peace: Algeria 1954–1962.* Middlesex: Penguin Books, 1977.

Hosseini, Khaled. *The Kite Runner.* New York: Berkley Publishing Group, 2003.

Hourani, Albert. *A History of the Arab Peoples.* New York: MJF Books, 1991.

Howard, Roger. *The Oil Hunters.* New York: Continuum Books, 2008.

Hussain, Zahid. *Frontline Pakistan: The Struggle with Militant Islam.* London: I. B. Tauris, 2007.

Images of Iraq. The Task Force for Business and Stability Operations, 2009.

Inati, Shams C. *Iraq.* New York: Humanity Books, 2003.

Isby, David. *Afghanistan.* New York: Pegasus Books, LLC, 2010.

Jabar, Faleh A., and Hosham Dawod. *Tribes and Power: Nationalism and Ethnicity in the Middle East.* London: SAQI, 2003.

Jackson, General Sir Mike. *Soldier: The Autobiography.* London: Bantam Press, 2007.

Jalali, Ali Ahmad, and Lester W. Grau. *Afghan Guerrilla Warfare*. Minneapolis: MBI Publishing Company, 2001.

Jamail, Dahr. *Beyond the Green Zone: Dispatches from an Unembedded Journalist in Occupied Iraq*. Chicago: Haymarket Books, 2007.

Jones, Seth G. *In the Graveyard of Empires: America's War in Afghanistan*. New York: W.W. Norton & Company, 2010.

Junger, Sebastian. *War*. New York: Hachette Book Group, 2010.

Kahlili, Reza. *A Time to Betray: The Astonishing Double Life of a CIA Agent inside the Revolutionary Guards of Iran*. New York: Simon & Schuster, 2010.

Karsh, Efraim. *The Iran-Iraq War 1980–1988*. New York: Osprey Publishing, 2002.

Keegan, John. *The Iraq War*. New York: Alfred A. Knopf, 2004.

Keegan, John, and Andrew Wheatcroft, *Zones of Conflict: An Atlas of Future Wars*. New York: Simon and Schuster, 1986.

Kelly, J. B. *Arabia, the Gulf and the West*. New York: Basic Books, 1980.

Kenderian, Shant. *1001 Nights in Iraq*. New York: Atria Books, 2007.

Kepel, Gilles. *Jihad: The Trail of Political Islam*. Cambridge, MA: Belknap Press, 2003.

Khalidi, Rashid. *Resurrecting Empire*. Boston: Beacon Press, 2005.

Khalil, Ashraf. *Liberation Square: Inside the Egyptian Revolution and the Rebirth of a Nation*. New York: St. Martin's Press, 2011.

Kilcullen, David. *The Accidental Guerrilla: Fighting Small Wars in the Midst of a Big One*. Oxford: Oxford University Press, 2009.

King, R. Alan. *Twice Armed: An American Soldier's Battle for Hearts and Minds in Iraq*. St. Paul: MBI Publishing Company, 2006.

Kouyoumdjian, Zaven. *Lebanon: Shot Twice*. Chamas Printing & Publishing, 2003.

Krakauer, Jon. *Where Men Win Glory: The Odyssey of Pat Tillman*. New York: Anchor Books, 2010.

Kung, Hans. *Islam: Past, Present, & Future*. Cairo: American University in Cairo Press, 2007.

Kyle, Chris, and Scott McEwen. *American Sniper: The Autobiography of the Most Lethal Sniper in U.S. Military History*. New York: HarperCollins, 2012.

Lacey, Jim. *Take Down: The 3rd Infantry Division's Twenty-One Day Assault on Baghdad*. Annapolis: Naval Institute Press, 2007.

Lawrence, T. E. *Seven Pillars of Wisdom*. New York: Penguin Books, 1926.

Learning From Iraq: A Final Report from the Special Inspector General for Iraq Reconstruction. March 2013.

Ledwidge, Frank. *Losing Small Wars: British Military Failure in Iraq and Afghanistan*. New Haven: Yale University Press, 2011.

Leverett, Flynt. *Inheriting Syria: Bashar's Trial by Fire*. Washington, DC: Brookings Institution Press, 2005.

Lewis, Bernard. *The Middle East: A Brief History of the Last 2,000 Years*. New York: Scribner, 1995.

Liddell Hart, B. H. *The Classic Book on Military Strategy*. New York: Penguin Group, 1991.

Louis, Wm. Roger. *Ends of British Imperialism: The Scramble for Empire, Suez and Decolonization*. London: I. B. Tauris, 2006.

Lowry, Richard S. *New Dawn: The Battles for Fallujah*. New York: Savas Beatie, 2010.

Ludwig, Konrad. *Stryker: The Siege of Sadr City*. California: Roland-Kjos, 2011.

Luttrell, Marcus, with Patrick Robinson. *Lone Survivor*. New York: Little, Brown and Company, 2007.

Maalouf, Amin. *The Crusades through Arab Eyes*. London: SAQI, 2006.

Mackintosh-Smith, Tim. *The Travels of Ibn Battutah*. London: Picador, 2002.

Makiya, Kanan. *Republic of Fear: The Politics of Modern Iraq*. Berkeley: University of California Press, 1989.

Maley, William. *The Afghanistan Wars*. London: Palgrave Macmillan, 2009.

Malm, Andreas, and Shora Esmailian. *Iran on the Brink*. London: Pluto Press, 2007.

Mansoor, Peter R. *Baghdad at Sunrise*. New Haven: Yale University Press, 2008.

———. *Surge: My Journey with General David Petraeus and the Remaking of the Iraq War*. New Haven: Yale University Press, 2013.

Mao Tse-tung. *On Guerrilla Warfare*. New York: Classic House Books, 2009.

Mayhew, Bradley, Greg Bloom, John Noble, and Dean Starnes. *Central Asia*. Oakland: Lonely Planet Publications, 2007.

McChrystal, General Stanley. *My Share of the Task*. New York: Penguin Group, 2013.

Michaels, Jim. *A Chance in Hell: The Men Who Triumphed Over Iraq's Deadliest City and Turned the Tide of War*. New York: St. Martin's Press, 2010.

Miller, John, and Aaron Kenedi. *Inside Iraq*. New York: Marlowe & Company, 2002.

Miller, T. Christian. *Blood Money: Wasted Billions, Lost Lives, and Corporate Greed in Iraq*. New York: Little, Brown and Company, 2006.

Mockaitis, Thomas R. *The Iraq War*. Santa Barbara: Greenwood, 2012.

Moore, Robin. *Task Force Dagger: The Hunt for Bin Laden*. New York: Random House, 2003.

Moorhouse, Geoffrey. *On the Other Side: A Journey through Soviet Central Asia*. New York: Henry Holt and Company, 1990.

Moss, Kenneth B. *Undeclared War and the Future of U.S. Foreign Policy*. Washington, D.C.: Woodrow Wilson Center Press, 2008.

Moyar, Mark. *A Question of Command*. New Haven: Yale University Press, 2009.

Munier, Gilles. *Iraq: An Illustrated History and Guide*. Northampton: Interlink Books, 2004.

Munro, Alan. *Arab Storm: Politics and Diplomacy behind the Gulf Wars*. London: I. B. Tauris, 2006.

Nagl, John A. *Learning to Eat Soup with a Knife: Counterinsurgency Lessons from Malaya and Vietnam*. Chicago: University of Chicago Press, 2005.

Nakash, Yitzhak. *The Shi'is of Iraq*. Princeton: Princeton University Press, 2003.

Nasiri, Omar. *Inside the Jihad*. New York: Perseus Books Group, 2006.

Nasr, Munir. *Lebanon*. Lebanon: Arab Printing Press.

Nasr, Vali. *The Dispensable Nation: American Foreign Policy in Retreat*. New York: Doubleday, 2013.

———. *The Shia Revival*. New York: W. W. Norton & Company, 2006.

Neville, Leigh. *Special Operations Forces in Afghanistan*. New York: Osprey Publishing, 2008.

———. *Special Operations Forces in Iraq*. New York: Osprey Publishing, 2008.

The Oil and Gas Year: Kurdistan Region of Iraq 2009. Seine: Rupert Smith, 2009.

Omrani, Bijan, and Matthew Leeming. *Afghanistan: A Companion and Guide*. New York: Odyssey Books & Guides, 2007.

Oren, Michael B. *Power, Faith, and Fantasy: America in the Middle East: 1776 to the Present*. New York: W.W. Norton & Company, 2007.

Owen, Mark, with Kevin Maurer. *No Easy Day: The Autobiography of a Navy Seal: The Firsthand Account of the Mission that Killed Osama Bin Laden*. New York: Penguin Group, 2012.

Packer, George. *The Assassins' Gate: America in Iraq*. New York: Farrar, Straus, and Giroux, 2005.

Pantano, Ilario, and Malcolm McConnell. *Warlord*. New York: Threshold Editions, 2006.

Pelton, Robert Young. *Three Worlds Gone Mad: Dangerous Journeys through the*

War Zones of Africa, Asia, and the South Pacific. Guildford: Lyons Press, 2003.

Phares, Walid. *The War of Ideas: Jihadism against Democracy.* New York: Palgrave Macmillan, 2007.

Pillar, Paul R. *Intelligence and U.S. Foreign Policy: Iraq, 9/11, and Misguided Reform.* New York: Columbia University Press, 2011.

Polk, William R. *Understanding Iraq.* New York: HarperCollins, 2005.

Pollack, Kenneth M. *The Persian Puzzle: The Conflict between Iran and America.* New York: Random House, 2004.

Poole, H. John. *Tactics of the Crescent Moon.* Emerald Isle: Posterity Press, 2004.

Prados, John. *Safe for Democracy: The Secret Wars of the CIA.* Chicago: Ivan R. Dee, 2006.

Pritchard, Tim. *Ambush Alley: The Most Extraordinary Battle of the Iraq War.* New York: Random House, 2007.

The Qur'an. The. A new translation by Abdell Haleem. New York: Oxford University Press, 2004.

Randal, Jonathan C. *Going All The Way: Christian Warlords, Israeli Adventurers, and the War in Lebanon.* New York: Random House, 1983.

Rashid, Ahmed. *Descent into Chaos: The U.S. and the Disaster in Pakistan, Afghanistan, and Central Asia.* New York: Penguin Books, 2009.

———. *Taliban.* New Haven: Yale University Press, 2001.

Report on Human Rights Practices: Country of Iraq. Lexington: U.S. Department of State, 2013.

Ricks, Thomas E. *Fiasco: The American Military Adventure in Iraq.* New York: Penguin Press, 2006.

———. *The Gamble: General David Petraeus and the American Military Adventure in Iraq, 2006-2008.* New York: Penguin Press, 2009.

Ridgeon, Lloyd. *Religion and Politics in Modern Iran.* New York: I. B. Tauris & Co, 2005.

Ritter, Scott. *Endgame: Solving the Iraq Crisis.* New York: Simon & Schuster, 1999.

Rodriguez, Jr., Jose A. *Hard Measures: How Aggressive CIA Actions After 9/11 Saved American Lives.* New York: Simon & Schuster, 2012.

Rogers, Paul. *Iraq and the War on Terror: Twelve Months of Insurgency 2004/2005.* London: I. B. Tauris, 2006.

Romano, David. *The Kurdish Nationalist Movement: Opportunity, Mobilization and Identity.* Cambridge: Cambridge University Press, 2006.

Rosen, Nir. *In the Belly of the Green Bird: The Triumph of the Martyrs in Iraq.* New

York: Simon & Schuster, 2006.

Roux, Georges. *Ancient Iraq*. London: Penguin Books, 1992.

Rumsfeld, Donald. *Known and Unknown: A Memoir*. New York: Penguin Group, 2011.

Said, Edward W. *Orientalism*. New York: Random House, 1979.

Sampson, Anthony. *The Seven Sisters: Great Oil Companies and the World They Made*. New York: Bantam Books, 1983.

Sassaman, Lt. Col. Nathan with Joe Layden. *Warrior King: The Triumph and Betrayal of an American Commander in Iraq*. New York: St. Martin's Press, 2008.

Scahill, Jeremy. *Blackwater: The Rise of the World's Most Powerful Mercenary Army*. New York: Nation Books, 2008.

Scales, Robert H., Jr., *Certain Victory: The U.S. Army in the Gulf War*. Washington, DC: Potomac Books, 2006.

Scheuer, Michael. *Osama Bin Laden*. Oxford: Oxford University Press, 2011.

Schmidt, John R. *The Unraveling: Pakistan in the Age of Jihad*. New York: Farrar, Straus, and Giroux, 2011.

Schroen, Gary C. *First In: An Insider's Account of How the CIA Spearheaded the War on Terror in Afghanistan*. New York: Presidio Press, 2006.

Schumacher, Colonel Gerald. *A Bloody Business: America's War Zone Contractors and the Occupation of Iraq*. St. Paul: Zenith Press, 2006.

Schumpeter, Joseph A. *Capitalism, Socialism and Democracy*. New York: Harper & Row, 1942.

September 11: A Testimony. Reuters. Prentice-Hall, 2002.

Shadid, Anthony. *Night Draws Near: Iraq's People in the Shadow of America's War*. New York: Henry Holt and Company, 2005.

Shaffer, Lt. Col. Anthony. *Operation Dark Heart: Spycraft and Special Ops on the Frontlines of Afghanistan—and the Path to Victory*. New York: Thomas Dunne Books, 2010.

Simons, Suzanne. *Master of War: Blackwater USA's Erik Prince and the Business of War*. New York: HarperCollins, 2009.

Singer, P. W. *Corporate Warriors: The Rise of the Privatized Military Industry*. New York: Cornell University Press, 2003.

Sluglett, Peter. *Britain in Iraq: Contriving King and Country*. London: I. B. Tauris, 2007.

Smith, Michael. *Killer Elite: The Inside Story of America's Most Secret Special Operations Team*. New York: St. Martin's Press, 2007.

Sorley, Lewis. *A Better War: The Unexamined Victories and Final Tragedy of America's Last Years in Vietnam.* New York: Harcourt Brace & Co., 1999.

Stanton, Doug. *Horse Soldiers: The Extraordinary Story of a Band of US Soldiers Who Rode to Victory in Afghanistan.* New York: Simon & Schuster, 2009.

Summers, Jr., Harry G. *On Strategy: A Critical Analysis of the Vietnam War.* New York: Dell Publishing Co., 1982.

Tanner, Stephen. *Afghanistan: A Military History from Alexander the Great to the War against the Taliban.* Philadelphia: Da Capo Press, 2002.

Teller, Matthew. *The Rough Guide to Jordan.* New York: Rough Guides, 2006.

Tenet, George. *At the Center of the Storm: My Years at the CIA.* New York: HarperCollins, 2007.

Tomsen, Peter. *The Wars of Afghanistan.* New York: Perseus Books, 2011.

Traboulsi, Fawwaz. *A History of Modern Lebanon.* London: Pluto Press, 2007.

Tregaskis, Richard. *Southeast Asia: Building the Bases.* Washington, DC: U.S. Government Printing Office, 1975.

Tucker, Ernest. *The Middle East in Modern World History.* Boston: Pearson, 2013.

Tucker, Mike. *Among Warriors in Iraq.* Guilford: Lyons Press, 2005.

Ucko, David. H. *The New Counterinsurgency Era.* Washington, DC: Georgetown University Press, 2009.

Urban, Mark. *Task Force Black: The Explosive True Story of the Secret Special Forces War in Iraq.* New York: St. Martin's Press, 2010.

The U.S. Army and Marine Corps Counterinsurgency Field Manual. Chicago: University of Chicago Press, 2007.

Van Buren, Peter. *We Meant Well: How I Helped Lose the Battle for the Hearts and Minds of the Iraqi People.* New York: Metropolitan Books, 2011.

West, Bing. *No True Glory: A Frontline Account of the Battle for Fallujah.* New York: Bantam Dell, 2005.

———. *The Strongest Tribe: War, Politics, and the Endgame in Iraq.* New York: Random House, 2008.

Wheatcroft, Andrew. *Infidels.* New York: Random House, 2003.

Williamson Jr., Samuel R. *The Politics of Grand Strategy.* London: Ashfield Press, 1990.

Winnefeld, James A., and Dana J. Johnson. *Joint Air Operations: Pursuit of Unity in Command and Control, 1942–1991.* Santa Monica: Rand Books, 1993.

Wittes, Benjamin. *Law and the Long War.* New York: Penguin Press, 2008.

Woods, Kevin M. *The Iraqi Perspectives Report.* Annapolis: Naval Institute Press, 2006.

Woodward, Bob. *Bush at War*. New York: Simon & Schuster, 2002.

————. *The Commanders*. New York: Simon & Schuster, 1991.

————. *Obama's Wars*. New York: Simon & Schuster, 2010.

————. *Plan of Attack: The Definitive Account of the Decision to Invade Iraq*. New York: Simon & Schuster, 2004.

————. *State of Denial: Bush at War, Part III*. New York: Simon & Schuster, 2006.

————. *The War Within: A Secret White House History 2006–2008*. New York: Simon & Schuster, 2008.

Wright, Col. Darron L. *Iraq Full Circle: From Shock and Awe to the Last Combat Patrol in Baghdad and Beyond*. Long Island City: Osprey Publishing, 2012.

Wright, Evan. *Generation Kill: Devil Dogs, Iceman, Captain America and the New Face of American War*. New York: Berkley Publishing Group, 2008.

Wright, Lawrence. *The Looming Tower: Al-Qaeda and the Road to 9/11*. New York: Alfred A. Knopf, 2009.

Yergin, Daniel. *The Quest: Energy, Security, and the Remaking of the Modern World*. New York: Penguin Press, 2011.

Yon, Michael. *Moment of Truth in Iraq*. Richard Vigilante Books, 2008.

Zakariyya, Fouad. *Myth and Reality in the Contemporary Islamist Movement*. London: Pluto Press, 2005.

Zalloum, Abdulhay Yahya. *Oil Crusades: America through Arab Eyes*. London: Pluto Press, 2007.

Zayani, Mohamed. *The Al Jazeera Phenomenon*. London: Pluto Press, 2005.

Zedalis, Rex J. *The Legal Dimensions of Oil and Gas in Iraq*. New York: Cambridge University Press, 2009.

Zubaida, Sami. *Law and Power in the Islamic World*. New York: I. B. Tauris & Co., 2005.

INDEX

M

Rice, Condoleeza, 204, 206
  2005 pro-democracy speech in Cairo, 204, 206
Ring Road, the, 216
Rock (AISG deputy security director), 116–20, 122, 135, 137, 144–45, 147, 152–54, 218–19, 229
Rolling Stone, 214
Romania, 176
Rome, Romans, 217
Romney, Mitt, 179
"Roof of the World," the, 220
"Route Recon," 170, 187
Royal Air Force, the, 142
Royal Navy, the, 166
Rubh al Khalli. See "Empty Quarter, the"
Rumsfeld, Donald, 176, 196, 266, 280
Russia, Russian, xvi, 3, 30, 97, 169, 176, 192, 219, 227, 256
Ryder, Rob, 100–1, 162

S

Sadler, Brent, 89
Sadr City, 4, 11, 23, 32, 36–37, 56, 60, 70–71, 95, 124, 127, 132, 139, 140–41, 146, 152, 156, 196, 266, 270–71, 274
Sadrist(s), xv, 67, 98–100, 110, 113, 127–29, 141, 163, 166, 176, 179, 196–97, 260, 270–72
Safavid Empire, 202

Sahib, Abbas Fadhil, 180
Sahwa, the, 20, 27, 33, 50–52, 66, 115, 141, 200, 202, 267, 269, 273. *See also* Awakening, the
Sahwaat al-Iraq (the Iraq Awakening). *See* Sahwa, the
Saigon, 72, 95, 227, 230, 259
  "Saigon exit," 95
Salaamat al Iraq, 86
Salafi Islam, 45
Sallyport, 74
Salman Pak, 121
Samarra, Iraq, 15, 64, 71, 116, 118, 120, 267
Samawa, 99, 101–2, 162
Samsung Engineering, 166, 192
Sanchez, Ric, 278
Sandhurst, 101
Sar Hawza, 225, 227–29, 233–34, 237, 246
Sarobi, Afghanistan, 219
satellite phones, 22, 116
Saudi Arabia, xi, 33, 41, 61, 99, 107, 155, 162, 167, 180, 256, 277
Savannah, Georgia, 264
Savior Generals, The (Hanson), 95
sayyid, 218
Scania tractor trailors, 38, 124
Schumpeter, Joseph, 77
schwerpunkt, 33, 265. *See also* center of gravity
Science Applications International Corporation (SAIC), 132, 198

Y

Z